# THE FIRE OF
# DELAYED
# ANSWERS

### are you
### waiting
### for your
### prayers
### to be
### answered?

## BOB SORGE

Seventh Printing — 2004

Other books by Bob Sorge:
◆*ENVY: THE ENEMY WITHIN*
◆*LOYALTY*
◆*FOLLOWING THE RIVER: A VISION FOR CORPORATE WORSHIP*
◆*THE FIRE OF GOD'S LOVE*
◆*IN HIS FACE: A prophetic call to renewed focus*
◆*EXPLORING WORSHIP: A practical guide to praise and worship*
◆*Exploring Worship WORKBOOK & DISCUSSION GUIDE*
◆*GLORY: When Heaven Invades Earth*
◆*SECRETS OF THE SECRET PLACE*
◆*DEALING WITH THE REJECTION AND PRAISE OF MAN*
◆*PAIN, PERPLEXITY AND PROMOTION: A prophetic interpretation of the book of Job*

THE FIRE OF DELAYED ANSWERS
Copyright © 1996 by Bob Sorge
Published by Oasis House
P.O. Box 127
Greenwood, Missouri 64034-0127

Printed in the United States of America
Library of Congress Catalog Card Number: 96-92243
International Standard Book Number: 0-9621185-3-2

This book is dedicated to my wonderful parents, Arvin and Irma Sorge, whose awesome testimony is mentioned briefly in Chapter Fourteen. Their example during their own delayed answers has helped to establish my steps as I've pressed into the purposes and ways of God. And their prayers have sustained me. The fruit of their godly lives is going out to the ends of the earth.

# Contents

## Part 2: Quietness And Confidence (Isaiah 30:15)

# Introduction

I'm glad you're picking this book up because its message is straight from my heart. This book is intensely personal. It is the product of a very impassioned search into the heart and ways of God. A season of physical pain and disability has caused me to press into God with all my heart and soul, and the truths herein are a reflection of that search.

God will always remain beyond our complete comprehension, but He has invited us to explore and uncover His ways — the ways in which He has chosen to relate to man. God's ways are always self-consistent, but they are beyond our ability to analyze definitively. God will not be put in a box. But He does want us to grow in our knowledge of Him.

As I have pressed into a fuller understanding of God's ways, there is one aspect of God's ways that has captured my attention, and it is the central theme of this book. Let me condense it into what might be considered a "thesis statement" or "summary statement" for all that follows:

**Sometimes God delays the answers to our prayers in order to produce a greater maturity and fruitfulness in us.**

The word "sometimes" is an important qualifier in that statement because God doesn't always delay His answers. Many times He sends immediate relief. But I am observing that many saints in this present hour are facing great challenges because their prayers appear to be unanswered, and they don't understand God's purposes in the season of delay. They look at the unchanged circumstances, decide that God must be saying "no" to their prayers, and as a consequence make some very unfortunate decisions.

Dear reader, let me implore you: If you are ever to mature into greater dimensions of fruitfulness in the kingdom of God, then you must commit yourself to understanding how God uses delay to refine His chosen ones.

The refining process is never comfortable. God's fire is always hot. David Ruis has written a great song that says, "There's a fire burnin', falling from the sky, awesome tongues of fire consuming you and I...Oh, sweet fire, come and burn over me." It's a beautiful thing when we invoke this refining fire in our lives, but it's also a very serious thing. If you're willing to embrace His fire, then prepare yourself for some pain. Christ calls us to the cross because we'll never become like Him apart from pain.

God's first priority in our lives is to make us fruitful — it is not first and foremost to make us comfortable. God doesn't enjoy leading us through painful circumstances, and He really does love to bless us. But what they say in athletics is also true spiritually: "No pain, no gain." The chronicles of the Israeli nation testify that in times of comparative comfort and blessing, the hearts of the people of Israel wandered into idolatry. Distress was necessary to turn their hearts back to God.

In a similar way, we don't typically choose the strenuous path of maturity apart from the incentive of pain. Oh yes, we sincerely long to mature in Christ. But when times are smooth, our pursuit of God loses its edge of diligence, and often we're not even aware that it's happening. In His infinite grace, God personalizes some troubles with our name on them, in order to help us toward His design for our lives.

The Bible is chock full of passages in which God has promised to answer our prayers. I emphatically maintain that God desires to answer our prayers that are in accordance with His will. When we claim a Bible promise that is quickened to our hearts by the Holy Spirit, we are praying according to His will. And He will answer us. It's just that He sometimes delays the answer for very purposeful reasons. The focus of this book is to explore the reasons **why** He sometimes delays His answers.

Maybe you think it's carnal to ask why. But many of the Psalms ask the why question with no apparent reproof from the Lord. When God begins to reveal His purposes to our searching hearts, and we begin to understand His ways, it helps to keep us from crawling off the altar. We find grace to persevere in tribulation because we understand that the present pain will produce a future harvest (see Hebrews 12:10).

I don't expect this book to be "fun reading." But I do trust that it will be comforting, particularly to those who are experiencing the fire of heretofore unanswered prayers. What is the nature of your own ongoing trial?

Financial pressure?
A difficult relationship?
Physical affliction or infirmity?
Sickness or disease?
Family turmoil?
Unexpressed ministry giftings?
Unattained goals?
Grief over the death of a loved one?
Emotional upheaval?
Unfulfilled desires?
Great personal loss?

The list goes on, but if you find yourself in the category of waiting on God for unanswered prayers, then I trust that you will gain fresh fuel for the journey as you join me in exploring the ways of God.

Bob Sorge
April, 1996

# Part One

# The
# Furnace
# of
# Affliction

CHAPTER 1

# REFINER'S FIRE

*"For the LORD your God is a consuming fire, a jealous God"* (Deuteronomy 4:24).

## God Is A Fire

God is extremely intense. The intensity of His personhood is described in Hebrews 12:29, "Our God is a consuming fire." Nothing sinful can survive the fire of God's immediate presence. Fire issues forth from God's mouth when He speaks (Isaiah 30:27). The word which proceeds from His mouth is itself a living flame which burns until it completely fulfills the intent for which God sent it (Jeremiah 23:29; Isaiah 55:11). Psalm 29:7 tells us that God's voice divided the tongues of fire that rested upon the early believers when the Holy Spirit first fell in the upper room (see Acts 2:1-4).

God is a holy fire, and He burns away impurities from our lives so that we might stand completely purified in His presence. Several scriptural passages describe God as a refiner of our hearts, much like a blacksmith refines gold or silver in a furnace. Some examples are:

- For You, O God, have tested us; You have refined us as silver is refined (Psalm 66:10).
- Behold, I have refined you, but not as silver; I have tested you in the furnace of affliction (Isaiah 48:10).
- I will bring the one-third through the fire, will refine them as silver is refined, and test them as gold is tested. They will call on My name, and I will answer them. I will say, "This is My people"; and each one will say, "The LORD is my God" (Zechariah 13:9).
- But who can endure the day of His coming? And who can stand when He appears? For He is like a refiner's fire and like

launderer's soap. He will sit as a refiner and a purifier of silver; He will purify the sons of Levi, and purge them as gold and silver, that they may offer to the LORD an offering in righteousness (Malachi 3:2-3).

> **The imagery of Jeremiah 23:29 is that of God taking us up in His tongs, sticking us into His fiery furnace, waiting till we're red-hot, pulling us out, setting us down on His anvil, and then hammering us into shape.**

## God Is A Refiner

The imagery of Jeremiah 23:29 is that of God taking us up in His tongs, sticking us into His fiery furnace, waiting till we're red-hot, pulling us out, setting us down on His anvil, and then hammering us into shape. Such a vivid metaphor carries graphic implications for us that include pain, loss of control, intense pressure, and violent change. Welcome, dear son of Levi, to God's refining fire!

God had called Jeremiah to serve as an assayer of His people: "I have set you as an assayer and a fortress among My people, that you may know and test their way" (Jeremiah 6:27). As an assayer, Jeremiah became a symbol of Christ, who is the true Assayer of men's hearts. An assayer is someone who tests metals or ore for its components and judges the value or worth of a metal based upon its purity of composition. Jesus has eyes of fire (Revelation 1:14) that pierce through every strata of our being, discerning the true condition of our hearts.

Jesus is both a Refiner and an Assayer. We see Jesus functioning as Assayer when He confronted the Pharisees. He weighed and judged their hearts and then dealt with them accordingly. Jesus still does the same thing with us today. He examines our hearts, evaluates our true spiritual condition, and then brings His fire to effect a greater purity and usefulness.

## God's Purifying Fire

God's fire resides among His people: "Whose fire is in Zion and whose furnace is in Jerusalem" (Isaiah 31:9). Because His affections are there, God's fire abides in Zion. God is intensely passionate over Zion (His Church), so He has placed His fiery residence in the midst of His chosen ones. Which means if you live in Zion, you will get away with nothing. God's fire will burn in your life. This is the "occupational hazard" (and the joy) of living in Zion — God's fire will not leave you alone. O blessed fire, which accomplishes three glorious things among God's people: 1) it forces the hypocrite to a decision (Isaiah 33:14); 2) it purges the sincere from sin (Isaiah 6:6-7); 3) and it enflames the heart with fresh passions for the Son of God (Acts 2:3-4). The Lord will never remove this fire from Zion. We live in a furnace of holy fire.

When hypocrites and the half-hearted can dwell in our midst without being convicted or made uncomfortable, then something's wrong. God intends for His fire to so envelope the local church that hypocrites will not be able to stay, and the devout will not be able to remain unchanged.

When the heat is first turned up in our lives, initially we feel like the Lord has abandoned us. But as we persevere in faithfulness, we'll begin to see more and more how close Jesus has been to us all along. Like the three Hebrew men in Nebuchadnezzar's blazing furnace, we'll discover that when we're in the fire Jesus is present with us.

Many of us have cried out with great sincerity, "O Lord, please come to me!" The Lord loves to answer that prayer, but He knows we don't always realize what we're asking. The Scripture testifies, "A fire goes before Him" (Ps. 97:3). When Jesus visits us, His face is always preceded by His fire. He knows we won't be prepared for His face until we've been purified by His fire. So if you're feeling the fire of God in your life, cheer up; it means that God is coming to you. This is the fire that precedes Him. He is drawing you closer to Himself, and His glory is starting to consume you. The fire is His assurance that you are being drawn into a place of greater intimacy and knowledge of God!

> **So if you're feeling the fire of God in your life, cheer up; it means that God is coming to you. This is the fire that precedes Him.**

## Buying Gold

There are two ways we receive from God. Some things are **given** to us, and some things are **bought**. Thank God for the things that are just outright given to us! He gives us eternal life; He gives us His Holy Spirit; He gives us peace and joy, etc. So many things in the Kingdom of God are free gifts, poured graciously from God's benevolent heart upon His children.

> **There are two ways we receive from God. Some things are given to us, and some things are bought.**

There are certain things in the Kingdom, however, that are not given; they must be bought. Jesus talks about this in Revelation 3:18 when He says, "I counsel you to buy from Me gold refined in the fire, that you may be rich."

First of all, what is this gold that is refined in the fire? The answer is two-fold:

1) <u>This gold is a purified faith.</u> "That the genuineness of your
   faith, being much more precious than gold that perishes, though
   it is tested by fire, may be found to praise, honor, and glory at
   the revelation of Jesus Christ" (1 Peter 1:7). When we survive
   the fire, we come out on the other side with a much stronger
   faith.

2) <u>This gold is refined character.</u> "But He knows the way that I
   take; when He has tested me, I shall come forth as gold" (Job
   23:10). In a word, this gold is **Christlikeness**. When fiery
   trials have effectively made us more like Jesus, then we have
   indeed gained true riches.

Notice that this gold is bought. We do not earn or deserve it, but we
do pay a price for it. What is the price we pay to buy such valuable
spiritual treasure? It is purchased at the cost of great personal pain.
This gold is bought in the fire and is attained <u>only as we persevere</u>
and endure <u>through the fiery trials that</u> God sends us. God's purpose in allowing difficulties,
tribulations, calamity, infirmity, persecutions, and hardship to
come our way is that we might take advantage of the opportunity and buy gold. When the crisis ex-
plodes, God wants us to fix our focus on Him, find Him in the adversity,
and discover the Spirit's pathway to renewed victory.

> God's purpose in allowing dif-
> ficulties, tribulations, calam-
> ity, infirmity, persecutions,
> and hardship to come our way
> is that we might take advan-
> tage of the opportunity and
> buy gold.

## God's Initiative

We can't choose to buy this gold any time we want. We don't wake
up in the morning and decide, "I'm ready to buy gold today. Yeah, that's
what I'm going to do. I'm going to grow in Christlikeness today!" Your
best efforts will be to no avail.

God is the one who must give us the opportunity to have our faith
tested. It is all of His initiative. In fact, we don't even tell Him when
we're ready to buy gold. He alone knows when we're ready. You would
do well not to go looking for trials, difficulties, calamity, or pressure. In
fact, when Jesus taught us to pray, "Lead us not into temptation," He was
cautioning us against asking God for these kinds of pressures. We tend
to think more highly of ourselves than we ought and don't properly ap-
preciate how devastating calamity can be. We're really not as strong as
we sometimes feel. God knows how much you can bear, and He will
allow "the perfect crisis" to hit your life at the perfect time, in order to

do His perfect work in you.

So we do nothing to initiate the buying of this gold. All we can do is respond properly when God gives us the opportunity. "As many as I love, I rebuke and chasten" (Revelation 3:19). We need not fear or dread the calamity; if it comes, it is customized in advance by our loving heavenly Father just for us. We can embrace it with expectancy, knowing that our perseverance will produce true riches.

When the time of testing comes, and the fire is turned up in your life, you have a choice: You can give up ("Forget it, I can't deal with this"), or you can go for the gold ("I'm going to press into the Lord now more than ever").

> **When the time of testing comes, and the fire is turned up in your life, you have a choice: You can give up, or you can go for the gold.**

## The Value Of Buying

We naturally cherish and appreciate something far more if we've had to pay a price for it. Take for example the instance of two teenagers who each got a car. One teen was given a car by his parents; the other purchased his car with his own hard-earned money. Which one will appreciate his car more? You're right — the one who bought a car with his own money.

In the same way, when you buy gold in the fire of personal pain and calamity, it's extremely precious in your eyes. That deepened character came to you at a great price. You won't sell it, you won't squander it, you won't lose it, you won't neglect it, you won't forget it, you won't trade it, and you won't give it away. When you buy gold in the fire, it's yours!

When God turns up the heat in our lives, sometimes we find ourselves asking, "But God, why does it have to be so hot?" The

> **The Lord gently says, "The price tag of what you've asked for is very high."**

Lord has a gentle answer that He wants to whisper to your heart: "The price tag of what you've asked for is very high." Yes, the fire is hot, but the final product (Christlikeness) is worth it!

## Is Infirmity From God?

Sometimes the Lord allows the fires of infirmity to touch us so that we can buy gold that's been purified in the fire. Someone might raise the argument, "Infirmity can't be from God, because He has given us specific promises in His word that He would deliver us from all affliction." I will deal with this question at some length later, but let me summarize my understanding of this issue here, before we go any further.

The biblical witness is very clear: God desires to deliver His chosen ones from all affliction. The most notable verse here is Psalm 34:19, "Many are the afflictions of the righteous, but the LORD delivers him out of them all." This Scripture is a marvelous testimonial to the ways of God.

Yes, God delivers us from all affliction, but sometimes He **delays** His provision in order to try us by fire. The delay itself is a fire ordained by God to produce a deep work in our hearts. God has a design for our deliverance, but He also has a purpose for the fiery delay. Make no mistake, delayed answers are a fire. When you're in crisis and have His promise of deliverance, but there's no change in sight, the

> **Make no mistake, delayed answers are a fire.**

heat can become very hot indeed! His purpose in the delay is to strengthen our faith, kindle our love to new depths of passion and maturity, and impart the heart and character of Christ to us — all in order to make us a more useful vessel.


## Why Infirmity And Affliction?

Again someone might ask, "Why would God send infirmity and affliction to His people? He can use persecutions and tribulations to purify our hearts, why does He have to use sickness and affliction?"

I don't claim to have the complete answer to that question, but let me share what I see from my limited perspective. The end-times church is often referred to as the "Laodicean church" because it is characterized by the qualities of the Laodicean church in Revelation 3:14-22. The cities of Laodicea and Corinth in Bible times had this in common: They were both given to "religious toleration." The saints in those cities were not harassed and persecuted, but they faced a challenge of a different nature. Because of the multicultural toleration of their communities, the believers were tempted with materialism, hedonism (pleasure-seeking), and the apathy that comes from relative comfort and security. Interestingly, these are the chief besetting sins of the church today. It's clear that we're living in the last of the last days.

When the fires of persecution have given way to a pseudo-toleration of Christianity, what should God do? Should He just allow that church to mutate and to degenerate into a lukewarm, milquetoast, insipid, self-centered, powerless form of religion? No, He's too jealous for that to happen.

So what does God do? (To understand this, we must be convinced that His ways are higher than ours.) **In His mercy,** He allows other fires to put the heat on our lives: financial distress; physical distress (sickness, infirmity); family distress. Without the heat, so often our love grows cold. You say, "Those things can't be from God because He has given us specific promises in His word that He would deliver us from those things." He does deliver us, but He uses the delay period (while we're waiting for the deliverance) as a purifying fire in our lives.

Our lukewarmness has our faith in such a sickly condition that when these fires arise, we don't have the faith to quench them. God's intention is that when these fires blaze against us, that they challenge and provoke our faith. God has a design for our deliverance, but in the process, the fire of these distresses will have been used of God to renew and restore our faith to a refined purity and to incite our love to new depths of fervency and maturity.

So see this clearly: The fiery distress you face is the mercy of God to you.

> **The fiery distress you face is the mercy of God to you.**

## Salted With Fire

Mark 9:47, And if your eye causes you to sin, pluck it out. It is better for you to enter the kingdom of God with one eye, rather than having two eyes, to be cast into hell fire — 48 where "Their worm does not die, and the fire is not quenched." 49 For everyone will be seasoned with fire, and every sacrifice will be seasoned with salt. 50 Salt is good, but if the salt loses its flavor, how will you season it? Have salt in yourselves, and have peace with one another.

Gehenna was a place outside Jerusalem where King Josiah, in his godly reforms, destroyed the altars of idolatry. It became a place where refuse was burned. It was the city's incinerator. The purpose of Gehenna was the purification of the life of the city. In time, Gehenna came to be the name for the fire of hell. Gehenna (hell) is set ablaze by the holiness of God. Fire destroys the perishable and perfects that which is imperishable.

Jesus said, "everyone will be seasoned [literally, salted] with fire." In other words, the fire of God is going to touch every human being. The only question concerning being salted with fire seems to be when — when will we be seasoned with fire? Either we will know God's purifying fire in this life, or we will suffer the eternal flame of His holy wrath. I hear Jesus saying, "Unless this holy fire burns within you now, bringing you to true purity and peace, then you will have no escape from the fire of Gehenna which consumes forever." Be encouraged, dear reader, that the fire is your friend. We can embrace Christ's fire gratefully, knowing that it leads to the salvation of our souls.

## Aflame For Jesus

The psalmist declares that God makes "His ministers a flame of fire" (Psalm 104:4). The Hebrew word for "ministers" ("sharat") means: Someone who waits on, who serves, who ministers, who attends. Although this verse in its context is describing angels, it can also be applied to us. We have come into God's house as His attendants, those who serve Him and wait upon Him. I love the promise of this verse: Those who come before Him to serve Him and touch His heart are made into a flame of fire. The fire represents God's holiness and passionate love. Think of it — you're destined to be an eternal flame and to shine as brightly as a star!

We become the light of the world when our passion for Jesus burns as a flame before others. As His holiness and love burns in our hearts, we will not be able to hide the witness that will shine from our lives.

God's fiery dealings in my life are radically changing my heart motivations. I always used to express the vision of my heart with statements such as, "I want to touch more people in our city for Christ," or, "I want to equip more leaders for the work of the ministry." But then God's fire started to burn through my life. Now, I find the vision of my heart changing, and it's becoming more like, "I want to develop a greater love and fervency for Jesus." "I want to get to know Jesus more intimately." I'm discovering that God really does want the first commandment (to love God) to be first in my life, and the second commandment (to love others) to be second. When the two become inverted, nothing works right. When our passion for God becomes the foremost fire in our lives, then the impacting of others' lives becomes the inevitable outflow of that dynamic relationship with God.

> **When our passion for God becomes the foremost fire in our lives, then the impacting of others' lives becomes the inevitable outflow of that dynamic relationship with God.**

## The Last Days' Fire

Carefully read the words God spoke to Daniel, as He gave Daniel insight into the very last of the last days: "Many shall be purified, made white, and refined, but the wicked shall do wickedly; and none of the wicked shall understand, but the wise shall understand" (Daniel 12:10). God was telling Daniel that the very last days would be known as a time when God would be purifying and refining His saints. The wicked will not understand this fire, so they'll run from it (and in the end be destroyed by it). But the righteous will understand what this fire is all about. They will embrace the fire, and rather than finding it destructive they will discover it to be constructive in their lives.

This truth is emphasized again in the letter to the Laodicean church (Revelation 3:14-22). The last days' church will be filled with people whose love has become lukewarm (Revelation 3:16). But at the same time, there will be those who will buy gold refined in the fire (Revelation 3:18), and their love for Christ will become a flaming torch. God is going to turn up the heat on His last days' church, because if He doesn't, His saints will succumb to apathy, greed, lukewarmness, materialism, and the self-indulgent spirit of the entertainment industry. Be ready for it in this hour, dear saint. God is going to send or permit calamity to come against His children, and He's going to delay the answers to our cries for relief in order that He might perfect us into the image of Christ. In time He will answer our prayers, but in the meantime our love will have been purified and strengthened, and we will have become incredibly sensitized to the tactics of the beast to pull us into areas of compromise.

Finally, here's yet one more passage that points to this last day's fire:

> Malachi 3:1, "Behold, I send My messenger, and he will prepare the way before Me. And the Lord, whom you seek, will suddenly come to His temple, even the Messenger of the covenant, in whom you delight. Behold, He is coming," says the LORD of hosts. 2 "But who can endure the day of His coming? And who can stand when He appears? For He is like a refiner's fire and like launderer's soap. 3 He will sit as a refiner and a purifier of silver; He will purify the sons of Levi, and purge them as gold and silver, that they may offer to the LORD an offering in righteousness."

This passage describes the nature of Christ's ministry in His first coming, but it also points to the nature of His ministry as His second coming approaches. Even as the Lord prepared the way for His first coming with the fiery ministry of John the Baptist, the Lord will also prepare the way for His second coming by sending His "refiner's fire." There is a fire going forth before Him, and it is preparing us for His long-awaited return.

"He will purify the sons of Levi, and purge them as gold and silver." This is a reference to all believers, for we are all called to offer spiritual sacrifices before God (Romans 12:1). But I see it applying in particular to those that accept God's call to leadership in the body of Christ. God is going to turn up the heat on His pastors and leaders. The end result will be wonderful, however, for a company of leaders will arise in the last days who will offer to the Lord "an offering in righteousness." Instead of loving their labors, they will love their Lord. Instead of gaining fulfillment in their ministries, they will find fulfillment in offering themselves without guile to God in adoration.

> **God is going to turn up the heat on His pastors and leaders. The end result will be wonderful, however, for a company of leaders will arise in the last days who will offer to the Lord "an offering in righteousness."**

These servants will be the gold vessels of 2 Timothy 2:21, "a vessel for honor, sanctified and useful for the Master, prepared for every good work."

# THE PERSEVERANCE OF JOB

*"You have heard of the perseverance of Job"* (James 5:11).

The Book of Job was the first book of the Bible ever put on paper. As such, it's fascinating to consider what was the first message that the Holy Spirit wanted to establish with quill and ink. It's no accident that the Holy Spirit specifically intended for the first written scriptural witness to God's ways to be precisely this: the fire of delayed answers.

The Book of Job may well be the most misunderstood book of the entire Bible. The reason being scholars try to interpret the book without having themselves experienced a Job-like trauma. I found that, after going through the depths of my own personal crisis, my understanding of Job's life was totally changed.

A personal friend, Jeannie Schantz, jotted me the following note in the summer of 1995: "Those who have only read but have not lived the book of Job cannot imagine the stress on a struggling human heart which, held powerless by His power, is still required to trust the love it cannot see and to pray for the friends who have not been friends at all."

For theologians, to understand the Book of Job is a project; for those in the fire, it is a book of great comfort and consolation.

## Holy Man & Prophet

The cornerstone to understanding the book of Job is found in the opening verse: You must not compromise the integrity of Job's life. Job was a holy man of God. "There was a man in the land of Uz, whose name was Job; and that man was blameless and upright, and one who feared God and shunned evil" (Job 1:1). When interpreters try to suggest that Job's calamity hit him because he was doing this thing wrong, or doing that thing wrong, then be assured they have no idea what the book is about. The book rotates on this central thought: Grievous ca-

> **The book rotates on this central thought: Grievous calamity devastated a blameless and holy man who had done absolutely nothing to deserve or incur the disaster.**

lamity devastated a blameless and holy man who had done absolutely nothing to deserve or incur the disaster.

The New Testament takes it a step further and calls Job a prophet. "My brethren, take the prophets, who spoke in the name of the Lord, as an example of suffering and patience. Indeed we count them blessed who endure. You have heard of the perseverance of Job and seen the end intended by the Lord — that the Lord is very compassionate and merciful" (James 5:10-11). James tells us to look to the prophets for encouragement when facing suffering, and then he gives a specific example of a prophet we should consider — Job. Job was a prophet of God, a man of great spiritual stature. The Bible consistently testifies to Job's holiness before God.

Keep in mind that Job wasn't writing a book of the Bible. He was journaling his honest, gut-wrenching wrestlings with God. He's not tip-toeing through the tulips in his discourses, trying to say it nicely, nor is he trying to keep from offending God. You're getting him in the privacy of his inner thoughts, and in that transparency we see a man who survived a horrific ordeal but never relinquished his fundamental faith in and trust in God.

The thing that's stunningly amazing is that Job survived his ordeal without the aid of written Scripture, without the support of godly friends, and without anyone who could speak the prophetic word of the Lord to him. He describes his aloneness with haunting metaphors — "I am a brother of jackals, and a companion of ostriches" (Job 30:29). All he had was his own personal connection with God, and even that was seemingly cut off (Job 23:8-9). The fact that Job came through with his faith intact is a testimony both to the grace of God on his life and to the eminent stature of his spirituality. Job needs to be honored as the giant of faith that he was.

When Job maintains his integrity throughout the book, he is not being arrogant or self-vindicating. He is being straight-out honest. He affirms over and over that this calamity did not come because of sin in his life. And he's right. The book begins to open to us when we realize that God purposely allowed horrible disaster to afflict a man who had done nothing but serve God faithfully.

## Job's Three Friends

It is a little difficult to know what to do with the discourses of Job's friends. On the one hand, God said they had not spoken of Him what was right, as Job had (Job 42:8). On the other hand, Paul quotes Eliphaz's statement of Job 5:13, "He catches the wise in their own craftiness," which is obviously the Holy Spirit's endorsement on Eliphaz's theology (see 1 Corinthians 3:19). So we're left to wondering — did Eliphaz speak what was right — or did he not?

The fact is, Eliphaz and his friends spoke godly truth. They laid forth many biblical principles that are supported throughout the rest of Scripture. The problem was they had the right words for the wrong situation. Job retorted to them, "How forceful are right words! But what does your arguing prove?" (6:25). They spoke what would have been right in most

> **The problem was they had the right words for the wrong situation.**

situations, but God was doing something exceptional in Job, and they didn't have room in their hearts for God to work beyond their understanding.

If Job's calamity had been because of sin in his life, they would have been right. But Job's calamity had an entirely different cause and purpose, and as a result their counsel was wrong. Even so, their words can have application to our lives today, so we ought not to throw out their discourses as totally invalid for spiritual instruction.

Job ends his discourses (chapter 31) with one final cry: "This hasn't happened to me because of any sin in my life!" Although his friends have done nothing but accuse him, he gathers himself to utter one last refutation of his personal holiness before God. Here's his testimony:

*v.1, he's kept himself from lust
*v.5, he has maintained honesty and avoided lies
*v.9, he's kept himself from adultery
*v.13, he has treated his servants with fairness and dignity
*v.16, he has honored the poor with alms, food, and clothing
*v.24, he has kept himself from avarice and greed (idolatry)
*v.26, he has kept himself from the worship of false gods
*v.29, he did not rejoice when evil befell his enemies
*v.31, he has lodged the sojourner
*v.33, he kept himself from secret sins
*v.38, he has honored his land, and paid his laborers fairly

So Job ceases speaking by reinforcing for the last time his contention that he has walked blamelessly before God. He is saying, "God's ways are more complex than you fellows think. God has not afflicted me because He is displeased with me but because He has chosen to refine me and bring me higher. You guys don't understand the complexity of God's ways." Turns out Job was right.

## Stop And Listen

Job's three friends insisted that there must be sin in Job's life because they had no conception of a God who would afflict someone who was walking in total obedience and faith. They completely mis-diagnosed Job's crisis. "If you'll just repent," they told Job, "then God will heal and restore you."

How can we be sure that we today don't become like Job's friends and totally misread what God is doing in someone's life? We must follow Jesus' example, who said, "As I hear I judge" (John 5:30). Jesus was saying, "I look at a situation, but then I stop to listen to the Father. What is He saying about this person? When He gives me His perspective on the situation, then I can speak to it and judge it correctly." Job's friends erred because they judged by what they saw rather than by what they heard.

> **Job's friends erred because they judged by what they saw rather than by what they heard.**

One day a sister in the Lord, whom I've never met, called me to tell me how much my first book, Exploring Worship, had blessed and impacted her life. When I told her about my physical infirmity, she immediately went into a tirade against the devil, and prayed a royal rebuke against the enemy. I really appreciated her sincerity, but it illustrated to me how readily we launch into praying about things concerning which we know absolutely nothing. Her prayer seemed so far removed from what I believe God was doing in spiritual realms at that time. When we pray for someone, we would do better to stop first and ask the Lord how we can pray according to His heart.

The Lord has also changed my perspective on counseling people. After they come to me and pour out their hearts, I find myself stopping and saying to them, "Let's pray silently and wait upon the Lord to see if He'll speak anything to us." Then we wait upon the Lord until He gives us some direction. I desire greatly to bring the mind of the Lord to needy situations now rather than simply pooling from the reservoir of my own experiential wisdom.

> **Sometimes the greatest adversity comes to those God loves most.**

I want to warn you against making a quick judgment about somebody just because great adversity hits his or her life. It's tempting to immediately assume, "I wonder what she did wrong." Eliphaz made the mistake of saying to Job, "Well, if this were happening to me, I would do such and such" (see 5:8). He was arrogant enough to think that he would know how to handle such calamity properly. Sometimes the greatest adversity comes to those God loves most. One of the tests that many of the greatest saints have shared is to suffer a negative reputation--to have others who love and serve God decide that you're suffering because God's displeasure is upon you. Jeremiah knew the sting of this reproach, as did our Lord Jesus. We must be very careful that we not find ourselves coming against someone who is silently favored of the Lord.

## Theological Crisis

It's interesting to see how God brings some of His servants to a point of theological crisis. God certainly did this with Abraham when He said, "Sacrifice your son to Me" (Genesis 15). Such a request didn't fit Abraham's theology of God. Abraham knew that God had given specific commands to Noah regarding murder — whoever kills his fellow man must himself be killed. But now God blows Abraham's theological circuits and asks him to kill his son. Abraham had the choice: follow the voice he has come to know, or follow his theology. Although he must have known great inner turmoil, the Bible doesn't suggest that Abraham hesitated even for

> **Abraham had the choice: follow the voice he has come to know, or follow his theology.**

a moment. He had tasted of the living words that proceed from the mouth of God, and he chose those words of life.

God also brought Job to a place of theological crisis. His three friends had pulled out the systematic theology of the day, and Job couldn't even come back with a better theological explanation. I can hear Job saying, "Listen, guys, I **wrote** the book on systematic theology! I know all your arguments because I firmly believed them myself. But God has done something in my life that has blown my theology out of the sky. I can't explain what's happening to me; I don't know why God has afflicted me, but I'm telling you it's not because of sin. All I can tell you is that God is not working in my life the way my theology said He was supposed to work."

Joseph must have had a theological crisis of sorts as well. He was serving the God of his great-grandfather Abraham, and God had revealed Himself to Abraham as the rewarder of those who seek Him. The theology that Joseph had received from his fathers went something like this, "Honor and obey God, and He'll honor and bless you." So Joseph honored and obeyed God — and ended up in prison! At that point Joseph faced a hard choice: either harbor resentment toward God for not honoring His promises, or hold to the voice of God that had come to him (God had spoken clearly to Joseph by means of some dreams). Joseph's question was, "How is it that you can serve and obey God, and get punished for it?" He didn't have an answer to that question, at least not yet, but he chose to serve God anyways and hold to the voice he had come to know.

Jesus also brought his twelve disciples to a point of theological crisis. Jesus had said to them, "'Most assuredly, I say to you, unless you eat the flesh of the Son of Man and drink His blood, you have no life in you'" (John 6:53). His critics charged Him with advocating cannibalism. The Twelve didn't understand this statement of Jesus either and found themselves greatly torn. The multitudes turned away from Jesus at this point, and so Jesus asked the Twelve if they wanted to leave Him as well. It's interesting to notice Peter's response: "Peter answered Him, 'Lord, to whom shall we go? You have the words of eternal life'" (John 6:68). The disciples were at a crossroads: follow their present theological understandings, or follow the voice they had come to recognize as the very voice of life. Peter was saying, "Lord, You're frying my theological circuits, but I've got to follow Your voice because You have the words of eternal life."

Notice what Peter **didn't** say. He didn't say, "You alone raise the dead and walk on water." He didn't point to the power that attended Jesus' ministry, but instead he pointed to the gracious words that flowed from His mouth. Once those words of life have touched your soul, and you've beheld the beauty of His face through the words He's spoken, you're hooked. You'll walk through the theological crisis because you've seen His face. You've tasted; you've beheld; you know too much to quit now. And what appears to be a theological mess will eventually prove itself to illustrate the true ways of God. So don't be disconcerted when you find yourself framing questions like, "Lord, what is happening in my life? Why is nothing working the way it used to work? Why have You abandoned me?" Just live by every word that proceeds from God's mouth, and you'll come through. In the meantime, realize you're in good company.

> **You'll walk through the theological crisis because you've seen His face. You've tasted; you've beheld; you know too much to quit now.**

Jesus doesn't lead you into theological crisis until He's first given you His voice. Then it's your choice: stay with the safety net of the verses you've always believed, or go with the voice that's leading you forward. Go with His voice, and you'll discover with the disciples that they are words of life!

By the way, the disciples that no longer followed Jesus at this moment weren't necessarily making a salvation decision. I'm sure many of them had opportunity after Pentecost to hear the gospel and did in fact respond to it. This wasn't so much a heaven-or-hell decision for them as it was a maturity decision. Those disciples who stayed with Jesus through the theological crisis were led into a dimension of maturity and fruitfulness in Christ that others forfeited.

## My Own Theological Struggles

Like Job, when calamity hit my life, I found myself with my own set of theological struggles and questions. Here are some of the issues that I have personally had to work through in recent years:

- I used to believe that God didn't use physical infirmity to bring His saints to greater maturity. Then, when infirmity hit my own life, I had to wrestle through to a new understanding of God's ways.
- I used to think that God intended that we always have joy (as per Romans 14:17). I preached and practiced that, as I was quite stable in the joy of the Lord. And then I took a knockout punch. Suddenly I found myself with absolutely no joy. Somebody might say, "Bob, you still had joy. You just didn't understand that joy goes much deeper than feelings." No, I'm telling you, I had no joy. All I had was depression. I hadn't done anything to bring the depression on, and I couldn't do anything to get out of it. I had no kingdom joy, and yet I knew I was still in the kingdom. This forced me to wrestle with God and to adjust my "joy theology." Now I can see that a pruned vine doesn't feel any joy. I had a happy childhood, but when I got spanked I was not a happy child. You may have a joyful walk in Christ, but when He prunes and disciplines, you have no joy for the moment because of the pain. But joy follows weeping just as surely as morning follows night. (See Psalm 30:5.)

> **But joy follows weeping just as surely as morning follows night.**

- Another verse I struggled with: "For the gifts and the calling of God are irrevocable" (Romans 11:29). I've always believed that when God calls He enables, and that when He calls you to a ministry He doesn't later change His mind and revoke that calling. My struggle, when infirmity hit me, was this: "God, you called me to lead worship, and now you've taken away my ability to sing and lead worship. I don't understand." Why would God call and enable me with giftings and then remove my ability to function in that calling? It took me many months to come to the conviction that my present inability is only for a season and that He will restore me to full function in His time.

- Another one: After I have been faithful to teach and train my children in the word of God, why would He severely limit my ability to continue to do so?

- Another one: "And nothing shall by any means hurt you" (Luke 10:19). How do I reconcile that promise of Jesus with the fact that Satan was given permission to injure me at a time when I was coming against Satan's kingdom with high praise? How can Satan take a shot at a saint when he's walking in obedience and living in the presence of God? (I deal with that question in Chapter Seven.)

The purpose of the theological crisis is not to change your theology (although that will happen) but to change you. Instead of viewing the Christian life through your lens of selected Bible verses (God's **acts**), you will begin to view the king-dom with a fresh appreciation for and understanding of God's **ways**. In the end we discover that His voice does not contradict His written word, even though for a time we couldn't reconcile them. The problem wasn't in His word but in our boxed-in understanding.

> **The purpose of the theological crisis is not to change your theology (although that will happen) but to change you.**

## Noah, Daniel, and Job

When the Lord was looking for three men to use as examples of great personal piety, He chose Noah, Daniel, and Job as His foremost examples:

> The word of the LORD came again to me, saying: "Son of man, when a land sins against Me by persistent unfaithfulness, I will stretch out My hand against it; I will cut off its supply of bread, send famine on it, and cut off man and beast from it. Even if these three men, Noah, Daniel, and Job, were in it, they would deliver only themselves by their righteousness," says the Lord GOD... "even though these three men were in it, as I live," says the Lord GOD, "they would deliver neither sons nor daughters, but only they themselves would be delivered. Or if I send a pestilence into that land and pour out My fury on it in blood, and cut off from it man and beast, even though Noah, Daniel, and Job were in it, as I live," says

the Lord GOD, "they would deliver neither son nor daughter; they would deliver only themselves by their righteousness" (Ezekiel 14:12-14,18-20).

Spiritual conditions in Judah had deteriorated to the point that even these three great men of God would be able to deliver only themselves by their righteousness, and no one else. The inference is that in their own generation, they **had** been able to deliver others through their piety. Noah, for example, delivered his family from the flood and, in so doing, delivered the entire human race from extinction. Daniel delivered the Babylonian wise men from being cut in pieces because he was able to tell Nebuchadnezzar his dream. Because of the favor he gained with the king, he was also able to gain favor for his fellow Israelites who lived in Babylon. So it's easy to see how Noah and Daniel were able to save others because of the holy lives they lived.

But how about Job? In what way did Job deliver others through his righteousness? We could point to the way he customarily sacrificed burnt offerings on behalf of his children, but this doesn't really answer the question because his children were all killed under the collapsed house. We could also point to the prayer he offered to God on behalf of his three friends, thus delivering them from God's judgment. But I think there's an even more significant way in which Job's righteousness delivered others. Because of his patience and example, his suffering has enabled countless thousands of saints over the centuries to gain comfort to persevere unto their own deliverance.

## Notes On Job

I do not have space here to comment on the entire Book of Job. But let me present just a few miscellaneous thoughts about the book for those who find his book fascinating.

As time went on, Job slowly began to realize that God had placed him in the refiner's fire and that God was perfecting something very precious in him. He finally gave expression to this in Job 23:10, "When He has tested me, I shall come forth as gold." (See also 28:1-19.) Understanding this doesn't lessen the pain, but it does give it significance. Job thought God had taken away his justice (27:2) because he felt like he didn't do anything to deserve such trauma and pain. It's true that he had done

> God doesn't bring people into crisis simply because they're disobedient. He also brings crisis into the lives of the obedient, but as in the case of Job, He has a special purpose for doing so.

nothing to deserve it, but God doesn't bring people into crisis simply because they're disobedient. He also brings crisis into the lives of the obedient, but as in the case of Job, He has a special purpose for doing so. God's purpose was to do such a deep work in Job that every generation after him would benefit from it.

So Job knew he was in the fire, and he knew God had delayed the answers to his prayers. At times he would be overwhelmed with his present despair, but at other times he would rise up with prophetic insight and see that God was going to visit him. "All the days of my hard service I will wait, till my change comes" (14:14). He was waiting for the delayed answer. The vacillation between overwhelming darkness and prophetic insight is quite typical of the valley experience.

The dealings of God are amazingly similar with God's saints, even though the means of His discipline varies with each person. For example, Job cries, "My purposes are broken off" (Job 17:11). The goals and purposes that Job had come to accept for his life were completely obliterated by God. His life vision was stopped in its tracks. This is a common experience of the wilderness season. God breaks off the purposes we've known for our lives in order that He might call us to His higher purposes. It involves a total rebuilding of life vision.

> **God breaks off the purposes we've known for our lives in order that He might call us to His higher purposes. It involves a total rebuilding of life vision.**

One of the necessary ingredients in breaking our purpose is found in Job 30:11, "He has loosed my bowstring and afflicted me." Job is saying, "He has taken my weapon of war, the very thing that I used to do exploits against the kingdom of darkness, and disarmed it. He has dismantled my ability to fight." When God takes us through Job's valley, He removes from us every ability to fight, to thrust forward, to push back the enemy lines. Our first response is frantic: "Oh no! I'm under severe attack, and I have no strength to fight back!" But the Lord gently shows us that in this season the enemy is God's tool, and we don't need to give him a second thought. Our preoccupation in this season needs to be exclusively with the face of Christ.

## Elihu

One of the more controversial figures in the Book of Job is a young man by the name of Elihu. After Job's three friends give up trying to correct Job, and after Job finishes his discourses, Elihu speaks up (chapters 32-37). We're not told what God thinks about Elihu. God rebukes

Job's three friends, and He honors and restores Job, but He doesn't say anything about Elihu. So commentators have a variety of opinions on Elihu, and for what it's worth, I'll give you mine.

I see Elihu as a young whippersnapper who doesn't have enough sense to keep his mouth shut. He thinks he's making a weighty contribution to the discussion, when in fact he's adding nothing. Not only does he have an inflated view of his own wisdom (36:4), but he runs off at the mouth (six chapters!) — which is typical of youth. His analysis of Job is this: "Oh, that Job were tried to the utmost, because his answers are like those of wicked men! For he adds rebellion to his sin; he claps his hands among us, and multiplies his words against God" (34:36-37). Elihu misses it by a mile.

Why does Job not answer him? Because Elihu's arrogance and naivete don't deserve a response. Why doesn't God rebuke him? God winks at his youth and in His mercy chooses not to hold him responsible for his error.

## The Turning Point

Everything changes for Job with chapter 38. Finally, God speaks. For this Job has been panting. He's been crying, "Lord, I don't care if you rebuke me or if you correct me — just talk to me! Be no longer silent to me!" God reveals Himself to Job "out of the whirlwind," and what a glorious visitation this is! The long delay is finally worth it. By coming in a whirlwind, God is dramatically reinforcing His message with a natural sign.

At first glance, God's opinion of Job appears to be contradictory. God seems to be talking out of two sides of His mouth with the following statements:

* "Who is this who darkens counsel by words without knowledge?" (38:2)
* And so it was, after the LORD had spoken these words to Job, that the LORD said to Eliphaz the Temanite, "My wrath is aroused against you and your two friends, for you have not spoken of Me what is right, as My servant Job has" (42:7).

So which is it, Lord? Did Job darken Your counsel, or did he speak rightly of You? The answer is seen in the one to whom God is talking. To the man's face, God speaks correction; but in speak-

> **To the man's face, God speaks correction; but in speaking of him to others, God vindicates him as a devout servant who has come to understand the greater mysteries of godliness.**

ing of him to others, God vindicates him as a devout servant who has come to understand the greater mysteries of godliness.

When we're in the crucible, God doesn't expect all of our responses to be perfect. The purpose of the crucible, after all, is to bring imperfections to the surface. God is big enough to handle our fears, frustrations, yearnings, anxieties, depression, anger, and self-pity. Job wasn't perfect, and God had plenty of correction to bring to him. But God's final verdict on Job is that he was a loyal and righteous servant. God's pleasure is very evident in this man who had kept his face toward God through the greatest trial of his life.

In chapters 38-41, God asks Job a myriad of questions, and thus all of Job's questions are silenced. Somehow in the midst of these questions Job is overwhelmed with a revelation of God Himself. When we see God, we have no more questions.

## The Creator God

When God comes to Job, He reveals Himself as the Creator (read chapters 38-41). It was the revelation of God as Creator that ultimately turned Job's captivity. It is doubtless this truth which Peter had in mind when he wrote, "Therefore let those who suffer according to the will of God commit their souls to Him in doing good, as to a faithful Creator" (1 Peter 4:19). Peter dwells on the subject of suffering at some length in his first epistle, and he clearly connects this with the truth Job learned, that we triumph through suffering by beholding our Creator.

Peter is giving counsel to the one who is suffering in a Job kind of way. His first counsel is that they "commit their souls to Him." In other words, God is doing a work that He alone can do, and instead of trying to speed up the process, we should instead commit our souls to God and trust His ability to complete His purposes in our lives.

Peter's second piece of advice is: continue "in doing good." Keep yourself from sin, apply yourself to seeking the face of Jesus, and maintain good works. This is powerful advice, and in the time of crisis it is all that God asks of us.

> **Keep yourself from sin, apply yourself to seeking the face of Jesus, and maintain good works. This is powerful advice, and in the time of crisis it is all that God asks of us.**

Peter's third point of counsel is: Place your confidence in God the "faithful Creator." As we meditate upon God as our Creator, we begin to see many wonderful things, such as:

1. We begin to realize that He who fashioned such an intricate and complex creation can surely oversee and bring to comple-

tion the complexities that afflict us in our present suffering.
When we see the Creator, we see one who is big enough to
handle any challenge we might face. Our soul can find its
proper posture of simultaneous rest and intensity ("quietness
and confidence") only as we gain insight into the all-capable
wisdom of our Creator Father.

2. He is a "faithful" Creator. When God creates something or
someone, He is always faithful to that creation. He doesn't
create and then abandon. Whatever He creates He faithfully
oversees, guides, helps, and nourishes. Since I am "twice cre-
ated" by God — created the second time when He made me a
new creature in Christ —
God is "doubly faithful" (if
that is possible) to me as
one of His precious saints.
All of God's promises of
faithfulness spring alive at

> **He doesn't create and then abandon. Whatever He creates He faithfully oversees, guides, helps, and nourishes.**

this point, including that precious assurance, "Being confi-
dent of this very thing, that He who has begun a good work in
you will complete it until the day of Jesus Christ" (Philippians
1:6).

3. Psalm 139:16 asserts that when God creates us, He establishes
and numbers our days. So in the time of delayed answers I
can abandon myself to my Creator, who will grant me every
day for which He has fashioned me.

4. Psalm 95 expresses most beautifully what our attitude should
be in the presence of our Creator: "Oh come, let us worship
and bow down; let us kneel before the LORD our Maker. For
He is our God, and we are the people of His pasture, and the
sheep of His hand" (Psalm 95:6-7). As our Maker, we should
kneel adoringly before Him, bowing to His will in our lives.
If He purposes that we suffer for a season, we bow to that in
reverance. Furthermore (together with Psalm 100:3), these
verses link the truths of God as Creator and God as Shepherd.
What God creates, He shepherds. So even though you may be
suffering, dear saint, your Creator is shepherding you, feed-
ing you, and leading you toward His eternal city. Hallelujah!

## Judgment Begins At God's House

The context of 1 Peter 4:19 is most instructive:

> For the time has come for judgment to begin at the house of
> God; and if it begins with us first, what will be the end of
> those who do not obey the gospel of God? Now "If the righ-
> teous one is scarcely saved, where will the ungodly and the
> sinner appear?" Therefore let those who suffer according to
> the will of God commit their souls to Him in doing good, as to
> a faithful Creator (1 Peter 4:17-19).

> **God works the same way to-
> day, sending His fire first of all
> to His choicest saints.**

Judgment begins at God's
house, with God's people. The
earth was full of wicked men in
Job's day, but where did God
send His refining fire? To the most godly man on earth! God works the
same way today, sending His fire first of all to His choicest saints.

"If the righteous one is scarcely saved" has new meaning to me
because I almost didn't survive spiritually. When my crisis hit, and all
the lights went out, I lost all my spiritual bearings, and almost turned
away from God. The only thing that kept me was His awesome mercy
and grace. I literally felt like I was saved for the second time! I was
raised in a Christian home and had never really known the ways of the
world. I accepted Christ at such a young age that I can't even remember
doing it, and my heart has always been tender toward the Lord. So when
my crisis hit, for the first time in my life I experienced what it felt like to
be truly lost. My heart gave out. I collapsed. I was lost in my despair.

When I recall this, great fear seizes me. Because I think, "If I al-
most lost it when God's fire touched me — someone who had walked
with God for many years and been in full-time ministry for over ten
years — what will happen to others when the fire of God touches them?
What will happen to the complacent in Zion? What will happen to the
sinners in Zion?"

This is the riveting question of Scripture: "If the righteous one is
scarcely saved, where will the ungodly and the sinner appear?" Are you
ready, dear reader, for the fire of God? Because Jesus made it very clear,
"Everyone will be seasoned [salted] with fire" (Mark 9:49). Everyone.
Job — me — you. Everyone. His burning begins with His people.

And yet, it is a merciful fire! It is a fire we should invoke. It is a fire
we should desire and invite. It is a fire that confirms our standing in
Christ and directs our hearts into greater dimensions of kingdom fruit-
fulness.

## Sharing Christ's Afflictions

One of the big questions I've worked with is this: "Is my physical infirmity a sharing in the sufferings of Christ? Is it a participation in Colossians 1:24?" Colossians 1:24 reads, "I now rejoice in my sufferings for you, and fill up in my flesh what is lacking in the afflictions of Christ, for the sake of His body, which is the church." Is my affliction an affliction of Christ?

Peter writes, "But rejoice to the extent that you partake of Christ's sufferings, that when His glory is revealed, you may also be glad with exceeding joy" (1 Peter 4:13). I thought, "It would be much easier to rejoice if I knew that my present suffering was in fact partaking in Christ's sufferings." Christ never had a physical infirmity like I have. So how can I know if my suffering is actually a partaking of His sufferings? After all, there is such a thing as "stupid suffering" — tolerating something that Jesus never intended we tolerate. So should I rebuke, or should I rejoice? I don't want to try to circumvent the cross, but I also don't want to accept something that I should resist.

The answer came for me in this tiny phrase of 1 Peter 4:19, "suffer according to the will of God." If I am suffering **according to God's will**, then it's part of the sufferings of the cross. To take up your cross is to be willing to suffer **according to God's will**. For Jesus, that was a literal cross at Golgotha. For Job, it was the devastation of all he owned and held dear. And if your present suffering is according to God's will, beloved, then it is a filling up in your "flesh what is lacking in the afflictions of Christ."

> If I am suffering according to God's will, then it's part of the sufferings of the cross.

To "partake of Christ's sufferings" is to "suffer according to the will of God."

## Deciphering God's Will

So the real question is, "Is it God's will for me to suffer in this way at this present time?" In my own case, the answer came through very clearly: yes.

Again, not all affliction is suffered according to the will of God. Just like not all persecution happens according to God's will — some persecution we incur upon ourselves because of our stupid behavior. Much of our affliction is suffered according to the devil's will, and we should make every effort to see the advance of the kingdom against all such evil suffering.

Most physical affliction is not suffered according to the will of God, but some is. Job is a primary example of the latter. So is Paul, with his thorn in the flesh. In both cases, it was an affliction that happened in the full will of God, to accomplish a kingdom purpose. So when afflicted, one of our chief concerns becomes, "Is this something I should suffer according to God's will, or is this something that I should resist and war against?"

My advice would simply be this: war against it, unless the Lord tells you to cool your jets. If you've got grace to fight, then rise up in faith against that affliction.

> **My advice would simply be this: war against it, unless the Lord tells you to cool your jets.**

But when the witness of the Spirit is clear that your present infirmity is designed by God to accomplish His kingdom purposes, then you must "commit [your] souls to Him in doing good, as to a faithful Creator" (1 Peter 4:19). It is my unequivocal contention that all such affliction, when suffered according to the will of God, is intended by God to temper us in the fires of delayed answers and that He has designed a moment of deliverance in His time. "My times are in Your hand; deliver me" (Psalm 31:15).

## Why Did Job Suffer?

God had a very specific purpose in allowing Job to suffer as He did. His purpose was that Job would be a model for all generations after him of how God's ways are beyond comprehension, of how the righteous do suffer, and of God's designs to bring them through to victory.

Job was traumatized in all three of the main areas that God uses to refine His servants: personal deprivation (business loss, financial loss, material loss), grief (loss of children or loved ones), and physical infirmity. To be hit in one area by itself is sufficiently devastating, but Job endured loss in all three areas. This is the thing that makes him such a great spiritual father to those who experience God's hand of adversity. So many people can relate to at least one aspect of his life. Because of his great pain he carries great influence, even to this day.

A sister in Christ wrote me a note recently, and in it she asked this passionate question, "Can you find a loving merciful God in the book of Job?" My answer to her was yes, and here's why. God could have left Job alone, and he would have been confined to his little, happy world. **But God chose Job for a far higher privilege: to impact his generation, and all generations since, with the example his life affords.** The choice was, be a father to his immediate family, or be a spiritual father to many generations of saints. Saints of every age have walked in his steps and gained encouragement from his example of perseverance. That kind of spiritual impact is gained only through great trials and the sharing in the sufferings of Christ. So it was God's love and mercy that elevated Job to a dimension of ministry that is touching the entire world, from his time till ours. I've observed the following principle: The greater the suffering, the greater the glory God can derive from it. Calvary is the ultimate illustration of that truth.

To see how Job impacted his generation after his suffering we need to look at the contrast between Job's first and second sets of children. Both sets of children were comprised of seven sons and

> **The greater the suffering, the greater the glory God can derive from it.**

three daughters. His first ten children were party animals, requiring him to constantly offer sacrifices on their behalf, lest they had cursed God in their hearts. Although Job was an upright man, he had somehow failed or been unable to impart his heart for God to his children.

Job's second set of ten children were totally different, and the difference is doubtless due to the radical changes in Job himself. He had truly entered into a new dimension of spiritual fatherhood. He had become a 100-fold garden. Being pruned had made of him an exceedingly fruitful vine. His three daughters were stunningly beautiful, not only physically, but also in character. This is seen in the beauty of their names, which in those days were always symbolic of character. Their names translate as follows: "Handsome As The Day," "Cassia" (a fragrance), and "The Colorful Ray." They were of such stature and beauty that they received an equal inheritance with their brothers. Job's suffering turned him into a profoundly changed man, evidenced first of all in the impact he had on his second set of children, and evidenced secondly on the heritage he continues to pass along even up to this present generation.

Was the pain worth the gain? Those with an eye for true spiritual riches would respond with an unhesitating, "Yes!"

"Can you find a loving merciful God in the book of Job?" Oh yes, my friend, I can!

## How God Changed Job

After the Creator revealed Himself to Job, Job made a final utterance which is very intriguing because it offers us insight into how God changed him. Job had declared, "When He's finished with me, I will come forth as gold" (23:10). His responses in the last chapter reflect the culmination of the work God had performed in him, bringing him out as pure gold. As we look at his final words, we see what Job was like on the other side of his experience:

Job 42:1, Then Job answered the LORD and said: 2 "I know that You can do everything, and that no purpose of Yours can be withheld from You. 3 You asked, 'Who is this who hides counsel without knowledge?' Therefore I have uttered what I did not understand, things too wonderful for me, which I did not know. 4 Listen, please, and let me speak; You said, 'I will question you, and you shall answer Me.' 5 I have heard of You by the hearing of the ear, but now my eye sees You. 6 Therefore I abhor myself, and repent in dust and ashes."

a) "I know that You can do everything" (v.2)

Job had always been a man of faith, but at the conclusion of his ordeal he had a faith that was purer and stronger and deeper than anything he had previously known. He was awakened to a new awareness of God's overwhelming omnipotence. Discern the heart conviction in his words, "I know!" His faith had survived the crucible, and now he owned an intimate knowledge of God that would radiate to others a profound confidence in his Lord.

> **Job had always been a man of faith, but at the conclusion of his ordeal he had a faith that was purer and stronger and deeper than anything he had previously known.**

You can't help but see Job's likeness to Christ here at this point. There are several times in the gospel stories when the Lord Jesus is specifically said to have **looked** at someone before He spoke. When it says, "He looked at them and said," we are to realize the passionate intensity with which He spoke the words that would follow. With that as a backdrop, let me direct your attention to Matthew 19:26, "But Jesus looked at them and said to them, 'With men this is impossible, but with God all things are possible.'" Jesus makes this statement with fiery passion that burns with conviction and confidence. Jesus, more than anyone, knew the truthfulness of this statement. Even now, His eyes of fire are looking at you — and He is saying something to you. Hear the force of His words: "With God all things are possible."

Job's life exemplifies that there is a dimension of faith in the power of God that opens to those who persevere through the fiery test of God's delays.

b) "and that no purpose of Yours can be withheld from You" (v.2)

The key word in that statement is "purpose." Job came away

with a profound appreciation for and understanding of God's **purposes**. He owned the reality that God is going to do what God is going to do. He had been schooled in the ways of God.

God wants to awaken us to the fact that He is a God of purpose. God doesn't set goals for your life and hope they come to pass. God doesn't have a vision for what He'd like your life to become. God only has purpose. He has a purpose for your life, and when He purposes to do something, it is impossible for anything to hinder that purpose. Once you've been purified by the fire, that little word "purpose" will become a greater part of your vocabulary because it reflects the character of God.

c) "I have uttered what I did not understand, things too wonderful for me, which I did not know" (v.3)

Having seen God in the sovereignty of His ways, Job owns an entirely fresh awareness of his own puny understanding. He realizes that even if God were to explain everything He's doing, down to the most minute detail, that he still wouldn't be able to comprehend God's ways. Job came through his trial with a living revelation of what Isaiah would later write about — that God's thoughts and ways are a universe above ours (Isaiah 55:8-9).

From this point on, Job probably made statements like this: "I don't need to know why; I just need to be obedient."

> **"I don't need to know why; I just need to be obedient."**

d) "I have heard of You by the hearing of the ear, but now my eye sees You" (v.5)

Job's relationship with God became intensely personal because of what he went through. He had been a devout and faithful servant of God, but now he talked about a first-hand revelatory encounter with God Himself.

Job entered into the promise Jesus left us, "Blessed are the pure in heart, for they shall see God" (Matthew 5:8). Job had kept himself pure, even in his distress, and he was rewarded with the greatest gift any man can possibly receive in this life: a vision of God.

This is what Job longed

> **This is what Job longed for, and this is what caused everything in his life to change: a personal revelation of God!**

for, and this is what caused everything in his life to change: a personal revelation of God! Oh, doesn't your heart burn for a similar experience?

"I'm not sure I like the pricetag," someone might say. "Seems like Job paid a terribly steep price before he received this revelation of God." Well, Jesus did tell us to count the cost before asking for these things (Luke 14:27-33).

Have distressing circumstances suddenly come into your life? Then you face a very weighty choice. Satan wants your pain to get you offended at God; God wants your pain to press you into His face with a fervency that will produce change in you. The very thing that Satan wants to use to cause you to pull away from God, God will use to cause you to get to know Him more intimately than ever before.

> **The very thing that Satan wants to use to cause you to pull away from God, God will use to cause you to get to know Him more intimately than ever before.**

e) "Therefore I abhor myself, and repent in dust and ashes" (v.6)
   When God truly revealed Himself to people in the Bible, this was their common response: an overwhelming sense of personal unworthiness and inadequacy. See the incredible contrast of statements in this final chapter:

◆ God's statement: God declares that Job is upright, blameless, and that he has spoken correctly about Him even in the midst of great pain.

◆ Job's statement: Job, however, testifies that he is abhorrent to himself and worthy only of groveling in dust and ashes.
   Now, this was not simply a one-time act of repentance on Job's part. He wasn't simply saying, "I'm sorry, Lord, for my brash words and bad attitudes." Job was saying that he had come away from his trial with a profound awareness of his own weakness, inadequacy, insignificance, emptiness, and absolute nothingness apart from God. He was a broken man. This sense of personal bankruptcy would never leave him because it was purchased in the fire, and it would enable him to walk in true dependence and humility before the Lord for the rest of his life.

## Greater Fruitfulness

When we look at Job's final declarations, we realize that he had great attainments in all those areas before his trial came along. He knew God was all-powerful; he knew nothing could stop God's sovereign purposes; he knew God was far wiser than he was; he knew God in a personal way; and he knew what it was to walk in repentance and humility before God.

But even though Job had attainments in all those areas, he was living in a dimension of limited fruitfulness spiritually. He had a personal faith in God, but somehow he was never successful in igniting his own children with his love for God.

God didn't do anything new in Job, He just did something very deep in him. Through the fiery season of delayed answers, God burned something into the depths of Job's heart that changed him irrevokably.

> **God didn't do anything new in Job, He just did something very deep in him.**

God continues to raise up fathers in the faith who, like Job, persevere through the pain and perplexity and come out on the other side with a fire in their eyes and a breadth in their hearts that will produce great fruitfulness in the kingdom, to the glory of God. May God give us more men like Job who will not quit when the heat gets turned up.

This is the hour of training for such fathers. Will you be one of them?

# PRISON THEOLOGY

*"For the LORD hears the poor, and does not despise His prisoners" (Psalm 69:33).*

There is an incarceration that is ordained of God. God has His own prison block where He confines His servants with chains in order to prepare them for greater works of service.

I've discovered that if God has ordained a prison cell with your name on it, you are powerless to get yourself out. When He shuts a door, no man can open it. "If He imprisons a man, there can be no release" (Job 12:14).

To get our "prison theology" right, we must clearly delineate between godly imprisonment and demonic imprisonment.

## Satanic Bondage

There is a satanic bondage that ultimately leads men and women to hell, and it is the consequence of Adam's sin (Romans 7:23). Sin imprisons. The Scriptures say that Satan takes people captive in order to do his will (2 Timothy 2:26).

Jesus came with an anointing, however, "to proclaim liberty to the captives" (Luke 4:18). With great compassion he loosed a woman who had been bound by Satan with a physical infirmity for eighteen years (Luke 13:16). Jesus administered this kind of freedom because of the work of His cross, by which He destroyed the devil's power to subject people to bondage (Hebrews 2:14-15).

The witness of Scripture is clear: Jesus released power to His body through His death and resurrection to minister liberty to Satan's captives. Satanic bondage is not to be endured or tolerated; it is to be broken in Jesus name.

Much could be said about releasing people from satanic bondage, but that is not the scope of this book. This chapter deals with those who are the Lord's prisoners. I felt it necessary, though, to establish from the start that we are not talking about the satanic bondage of sin and death.

## A Divine Prison

God strategically imprisons some of His servants in order to prepare them for His purposes.

The apostle Paul was imprisoned by God, and in his case it was a literal civic prison. It's interesting to note that he never gave the Romans the credit for his capture. Never once did he say, "I'm a Roman prisoner." In his letter to the Ephesians, he used three phrases to describe himself: "I, Paul, the prisoner of Christ Jesus" (3:1); "the prisoner of the Lord" (4:1); "I am an ambassador in chains" (6:20). Paul clearly understood that even though the Romans had arrested him, it was God who had planned his imprisonment, and as such he insisted that he was God's prisoner.

Many who are imprisoned by God do not find themselves in a literal prison cell, however. Some are imprisoned by circumstances, by financial constraints, by physical infirmity, by family limitations, and so forth. The common denominator is limitation and restriction, along with an absolute helplessness to change anything, or a divine mandate to do nothing to initiate change. The shackles may not be literal iron chains, but they are just as real. The initial pain when first restricted by God is seen in the cry of these verses:

> **The common denominator is limitation and restriction, along with an absolute helplessness to change anything, or a divine mandate to do nothing to initiate change.**

- Why is light given to a man whose way is hidden, and whom God has hedged in? (Job 3:23).
- You have put away my acquaintances far from me; You have made me an abomination to them; I am shut up, and I cannot get out (Psalm 88:8).
- He has hedged me in so that I cannot get out; He has made my chain heavy. Even when I cry and shout, He shuts out my prayer. He has blocked my ways with hewn stone; He has made my paths crooked (Lamentations 3:7-9).

The length of the incarceration varies with each instance. On one occasion, Peter was in prison for only a few hours before an angel released him (Acts 5:18-19). Another time, Peter was in jail for a few days before the angel delivered him (Acts 12:4-10). It seems as though John the Baptist was imprisoned for several weeks before his decapitation. During his first imprisonment, Paul was a prisoner for well over two years.

God's affection for His prisoners is clearly seen in Scripture. They are honored with these crowning words: "of whom the world was not worthy" (Hebrews 11:38).

Most of God's prisoners in the biblical record were released at some point in time, and their incarceration and subsequent release are filled with meaning and kingdom purpose. Occasionally, some of God's prisoners are killed. For example, Paul was killed during his second imprisonment. John the Baptist was killed in prison. But when we study God's prisoners in the Bible, and how He deals with them, there is one category of prisoner that is glaringly absent: God never leaves a prisoner to rot in jail until his death. Some are martyred, and the rest are eventually released unto God's purposes. **This is comforting for God's prisoners, to know that God intends one of two options for them: martyrdom or release.**

## The Church At Smyrna

Jesus spoke some very sobering words to the believers in Smyrna, "Do not fear any of those things which you are about to suffer. Indeed, the devil is about to throw some of you into prison, that you may be tested, and you will have tribulation ten days. Be faithful until death, and I will give you the crown of life" (Revelation 2:10).

Even though the devil is the one who throws into prison, the Lord is behind it, and purposefully allows it to happen. This is why we don't have to fear the things we suffer. The Lord oversees our suffering from beginning to end, and after ten days He will deliver us.

Interestingly enough, the number ten is associated elsewhere in Scripture with testing and trials (Job 19:3; Daniel 1:12). In saying the believers of Smyrna will be tested for ten days, the Lord is preparing them for a season of suffering, but He's also telling them it won't last forever. In fact, in the scheme of things, it will be a comparatively short period of time. When you're in prison, it can feel like it's lasting an eternity, but the Lord assures us that the time of imprisonment is measured, and it will come to an end in the Lord's purposes.

## Imprisoned With A Purpose

When God allows one of His people to be imprisoned, He always has a redemptive purpose in mind. Prison is incredibly lonely, and the Lord uses that season to cause us to find our companionship in Him.

> **One of the purposes of prison is to give the prisoner great quantities of time to spend with the Lord.**

One of the purposes of prison is to give the prisoner great quantities of time to spend with the Lord. If we were free, we would be quite distracted with the affairs of life. But with little else vying for our attention, the prison becomes a time when we can establish an extraordinary connection with Jesus. If you're in prison, dear reader, don't be so distressed over your condition that you succumb to despair. Maximize this time — the Lord is waiting to reveal Himself to you in a most singular way.

Samson's prison changed him dramatically. When the Philistines plucked out his eyes and incarcerated him (Judges 16), Samson was totally broken. The brash cockiness was knocked out of him. "So they called for Samson from the prison, and he performed for them" (Judges 16:25). Out of the prison he came, broken, humbled, weak, and dependent. He cried out to God, and by God's mercy was able to kill more Philistines in his death than he did during his strength. Not only did Samson's imprisonment change and soften him, but it prepared him for the greatest victory of his life.

> **Not only did Samson's imprisonment change and soften him, but it prepared him for the greatest victory of his life.**

The Scriptures make an interesting comment about what happens when we don't experience the benefit of this kind of captivity: "Moab has been at ease from his youth; he has settled on his dregs, and has not been emptied from vessel to vessel, **nor has he gone into captivity**. Therefore his taste remained in him, and his scent has not changed" (Jeremiah 48:11). Jeremiah is describing the nation of Moab with a very vivid metaphor. In speaking of "vessel to vessel," he is referring to the process in winemaking where wine is allowed to settle in a container and then is poured off into another container, while the dregs that have settled at the bottom of the first container are thrown away. If wine is not removed from its dregs, it will not ferment and mature properly but will become bitter and distasteful. The process of being poured from vessel to vessel, while unsettling, is thus absolutely necessary if the wine is to be pleasing. God is saying of Moab that the nation is very distasteful to Him because they haven't been poured from vessel to vessel, and they haven't gone into captivity. In other words, it's the going into captivity that is the equivalent of being poured into another vessel. God wants His people to mature before Him as fragrant wine, and in order to complete the maturing process there are times that He must send us into captivity.

What might this captivity look like? Well, you might feel like a captive on your job. You could feel trapped by your family circumstances. You may become bound by financial debt. Perhaps you would come under the constraints of a physical infirmity. Whatever the nature of the confinement and restriction, you feel totally out of control and bewildered about why God has you here. If your heart is right, then you are a prisoner in the order of Joseph. God is using your imprisonment to perfect the wine of your love and to prepare you for greater fruitfulness.

> **God is using your imprisonment to perfect the wine of your love and to prepare you for greater fruitfulness.**

To be pitied, rather, are those who never go into captivity, for their "scent has not changed," and they will not know the joy of being a delightful fragrance to the Father.

## Paul The Prisoner

Paul makes a few interesting statements about his imprisonment:

- What God was doing in and through Paul during his imprisonment was such a clear testimony, that Paul said it became clear to the whole palace guard and all the other prisoners that he was a man of God who had been chained by Christ (Philippians 1:13).
- The witness of Paul's life in the midst of prison had such an effect on the body of Christ that many of the saints who were not in prison were gaining boldness "to speak the word without fear" (Philippians 1:14).
- Paul appealed to the church that they not forget his chains (Colossians 4:18). I believe this was primarily an appeal for prayer support, as he felt a profound need for God's grace to enable him to endure. God's prisoners carry a great awareness of their need for the prayers of God's people. "Remember the prisoners as if chained with them" (Hebrews 13:3).
- Paul pled with Timothy that he not be ashamed of his imprisonment. God's prisoners live in rather ignoble conditions. On the surface, they appear to be punished by God, which is

how many people read it. It's usually not a very popular posi-
tion to stand up and say, "Hey, I think this guy is a prisoner of
the Lord, and he's not in this condition because of sin in his
life. I think God's doing a holy work in his life, and I'm hon-
ored to identify with it." Prison can be lonely, and Paul de-
sired this kind of solidarity and support from Timothy.

## Cut Off From The Mainstream

One of the most painful dynamics of the prison season is the feeling
of being excluded from everything that God is doing around you. You sit
and watch others progressing in God, rejoicing in the Lord, moving about
with great freedom and fruitfulness. And here you sit.

Sort of like John the Baptist. There's revival happening, the crowds
are following Jesus of Nazareth, the reports are incredibly exciting, but
John is in chains. How his heart must have yearned within him! How he
must have longed to be able to participate in the revival meetings. But
instead he's a total non-participant, languishing in prison. When John
sent his disciples to ask of Jesus, "Do we look for another?" I hear the
pain of a man who is disoriented because he has been cut out altogether
from the flow of what the Spirit is doing. God wasn't calling him to
follow the blessing but to follow His voice.

I reckon that John the Baptist never was able to figure out why he
was in prison. One of the baf-
fling dynamics to being a pris-

> **One of the baffling dynamics to being a prisoner of the Lord is the sheer wastefulness of it all.**

oner of the Lord is the sheer
wastefulness of it all. Not only
is nothing being accomplished
(at least that's how we feel), but we're looking at a whole lot of untapped
potential, just frittering away in jail. There was a mighty anointing on
John the Baptist, and God wasn't even using it!

We see the same thing in Joseph. Here's a young man who is in-
credibly talented and gifted, very bright, exceptionally creative, equipped
and ready, willing to serve, walking in obedience and faith, and he's just
sitting in prison and wasting away. Talk about squandered resources!
**Joseph was in an enforced barrenness in the height of his best years.**
I would have thought Joseph was too valuable a player to have him just
sitting on the bench. But God has a different perspective on these things.
God had a purpose in Joseph's captivity, but for the longest time Joseph
couldn't see it, and his vexation of soul must have been most grievous.

## Joseph's Jail

God put Joseph in jail. Sure, Satan no doubt played a role in it (he's always a willing accomplice when it comes to harassing God's people). But from beginning to end God was in it, taking what the enemy had intended for evil and turning it around for the good (Genesis 50:20). Joseph himself testified that God did it to him: "And God sent me before you to preserve a posterity for you in the earth, and to save your lives by a great deliverance. So now it was not you who sent me here, but God; and He has made me a father to Pharaoh, and lord of all his house, and a ruler throughout all the land of Egypt" (Genesis 45:7-8).

God crucified Jesus; God made Sarah barren; God afflicted Job; God sent Moses to the desert for 40 years; God orchestrated David's wilderness wanderings; God took Naomi's husband and two sons. When God does something to you, all you can do is submit and pray and wait for God to fulfill His purposes.

In each of these cases just mentioned, however, the pain was in actuality a gift of God, an expression of His love. When you're in prison, it's difficult to keep this perspective, but the fact is that God has you where He has you because He loves you so much. Your pain may be greater than your neighbor's, but it's because of His special affection for you. In all candor, there have been times when I've felt, "If this is Your love, who wants it?" At those times I remind myself that God imprisoned Joseph because He loved him. God loved him so

> **God imprisoned Joseph because He loved him.**

much that He bound him up in affliction and darkness, in order to prepare him to be a vessel who would be able to lead an entire nation without self-destructing. In order to be able to handle the promotion he would experience, Joseph's heart had to be purified in the fiery crucible of an Egyptian dungeon.

Do you feel helpless, totally incapable of doing anything to change or control the circumstances that restrict you? God loves you so much, He intends to bring great blessing out of your affliction. "He brings out those who are bound into prosperity; but the rebellious dwell in a dry land" (Psalm 68:6). This verse reveals that the Joseph prison is intended of the Lord to root out all rebellion and inculcate a profound humility of heart and dependence of spirit. Truly this is the spiritual "prosperity" the Lord wants to bring to His prisoners.

## Imprisoned For Obedience

When we see someone in prison, our first question is, "What did he do wrong to end up in such a mess?" It's possible to find ourselves imprisoned because of disobedience or rebellion. In such cases, we're not so much prisoners of the Lord as we are prisoners of our own sin. Even that the Lord can use, however, as He did in the case of Samson.

On the other hand, we might find ourselves in prison without having done anything wrong. If you search your heart before God and can't come up with any reason why you're in prison, you may very well be a prisoner of the Lord. It's a prison of obedience. That's what happened to Jeremiah. He was faithful to deliver the words God had given him, and he ended up in prison for it. But God knew that Jeremiah was addressing people who were themselves going to be taken captive by the Babylonians. People are more open to receive from someone who has shared their pain, and so God ordained an imprisonment for Jeremiah so that he would be able to speak into the lives of his fellow Israelites. Sometimes God imprisons His servants in a prison of obedience so that they have a platform to speak into the lives of those in a prison of disobedience.

> **Sometimes God imprisons His servants in a prison of obedience so that they have a platform to speak into the lives of those in a prison of disobedience.**

"But I didn't do anything to deserve this," I can hear Joseph crying. The first response of God's prisoner is to feel like God has acted unfairly toward him. The fact is, you're not in prison because of something wrong you've done but because of something right you've done. You've asked God to lift you to a higher plane. You've asked God to increase your fruitfulness. He's answering your prayer. You'll notice that Joseph and Jeremiah ended up in the blackness of prison after doing everything right.

But even in Joseph's case, God did not deal with Joseph according to his righteousness, but according to His righteousness. For it says the Lord "showed him mercy" in prison (Genesis 39:21), which means God dealt with him not according to his perfect responses but according to His own goodness. That little phrase reveals that Joseph didn't handle himself perfectly in every test. He had some bad attitudes, and he struggled with sinful thoughts. But God was merciful to him and delivered him from prison. **That's the definition of mercy: God doesn't deal with us according to our level of perfection but according to His loving grace and redemptive plan for our lives.**

We want God to deal with us in accordance with who He is, which is why David cried from his emotional prison, "Revive me, O LORD, for **Your** name's sake! For **Your** righteousness' sake bring my soul out of trouble" (Psalm 143:11). We seek release, not simply for our own personal relief, but in order that God's reputation might be promoted throughout the earth.

## The Word Of The Lord Tested Him

Psalm 105 gives us a most delightful angle on Joseph's life:

> We seek release, not simply for our own personal relief, but in order that God's reputation might be promoted throughout the earth.

Psalm 105:16, Moreover He called for a famine in the land; He destroyed all the provision of bread. 17 He sent a man before them — Joseph — who was sold as a slave. 18 They hurt his feet with fetters, he was laid in irons. 19 Until the time that his word came to pass, the word of the LORD tested him. 20 The king sent and released him, the ruler of the people let him go free. 21 He made him lord of his house, and ruler of all his possessions, 22 to bind his princes at his pleasure, and teach his elders wisdom.

Are you aware that the God we serve is still the same God that is described in these verses? There are seasons today when God will call for a famine and will destroy "all the provision of bread." That could apply physically, but also spiritually — a time when we seem to be starving spiritually from lack of spiritual food. God used the famine in Joseph's day for His purposes, and He still stirs up spiritual hunger by cutting off the channels of supply for a season.

The margin of my Bible has an alternate reading of verse 18 that is also reflected in the Amplified Bible: "His soul came into iron." Joseph's imprisonment wasn't simply physical in its dynamics, but he literally felt chained in his soul. These words depict great mental anguish.

"Until the time that his word came to pass, the word of the LORD tested him." What was this word of Joseph's that was being delayed in its fulfillment? It was the word he spoke based upon the dreams he received: "My father, my mother, and my brothers will all bow down before me." He carried a dream — a word from God — in his heart. While the manifestation of that word was delayed, that word "tested him." It was the fire of delayed answers.

> He carried a dream — a word from God — in his heart. While the manifestation of that word was delayed, that word "tested him." It was the fire of delayed answers.

I wonder if Joseph ever regretted telling his brothers about his dreams. "If I had just kept my mouth shut, I could have saved a lot of face. But no, I just had to blab it to everybody, and now look at the mess I'm in!"

Joseph's declarations of his dreams were an expression of faith, how-
ever. A confidence rose up in his soul, and he just had to speak forth
what he knew was from God.

But then the word tested him. I can certainly imagine him sitting in
his prison cell and thinking to himself, "What were those dreams all
about? I was so sure they were from God. Am I delusionary? Maybe
I'm deceived, maybe God doesn't talk to me at all. But no...it **had** to be
God! I'm prepared to bet my life on it. God spoke to me, and I'll never
let go of that." The fire on his life during this season must have been
incredible.

By the time God was finished with Joseph, he was an entirely differ-
ent person. No longer the impetuous lad who had to blurt everything he
was seeing and hearing, he had matured to the place where he was will-
ing to wait nine years for his family to finally arrive. (Nine years elapsed
between the time Joseph ascended to power and the arrival of his broth-
ers to Egypt.) It would have been quite tempting, during those first years
in power, to send a memo to his father in Canaan, "Hey, dad, I'm alive!
And I'm Prime Minister of Egypt! Come on down to Egypt, dad, and
see me." But by now he could
see God's purposes in the years

> **So he waited patiently for God
> to fulfill His purpose. He had
> become a mature co-worker
> with God.**

of plenty, and he knew the fam-
ine would eventually draw his
brothers to Egypt. So he waited
patiently for God to fulfill His
purpose. He had become a mature co-worker with God.

After being raised up by Pharaoh, verse 22 says this of Joseph: "To
bind his princes at his pleasure." Now Joseph has the authority to bind
and put into prison. Because he was once a prisoner, Joseph would now
be able to judge righteously and pronounce righteous judgment mixed
with empathy. He was equipped for righteous but yet compassionate
leadership. At the same time, he would not shrink back from consigning
to prison in righteous judgment because he understood the value of the
prison season.

## Wisdom Is Fruitful

One day Jesus spoke to the crowds that followed Him, saying, "For
John came neither eating nor drinking, and they say, 'He has a demon.'
The Son of Man came eating and drinking, and they say, 'Look, a glut-
ton and a winebibber, a friend of tax collectors and sinners!' But wis-
dom is justified by her children" (Matthew 11:18-19). Jesus was ad-
dressing the fact that spiritually hardened people will not accept God's
servants, no matter how they make their appearance. God told John the

Baptist to live a life of asceticism and strict self-denial, but they didn't accept him. Jesus came with a different style, and they didn't accept Him either. And then Jesus added this poignant statement: "But wisdom is justified by her children."

In saying that wisdom has children, Jesus was saying that wisdom is fruitful. Jesus was basically saying to His critics, "The wisdom of My words will inevitably bear fruit, and the harvest they produce will vindicate the validity of My message." One of the characteristic marks of true godly wisdom is that it is **fruitful**. It produces a harvest that is obvious to all, thus vindicating the one who bore witness to that wisdom. Godly wisdom is often criticized and assailed, as was Jesus' wisdom, but in the end the weight of the fruit from His wisdom was indisputable.

The Scriptures draw an interesting connection between wisdom and fruitfulness. Look at James 3:17, "But the wisdom that is from above is first pure, then peaceable, gentle, willing to yield, full of mercy and good **fruits**, without partiality and without hypocrisy." James affirms that godly wisdom bears good fruit. This is the thing that vindicates godly leaders. When their wisdom proves fruitful, others cannot deny that they are hearing from God.

Joseph was such a man. The wisdom he carried was a witness to the fact that God was with him, and it was this wisdom which made Joseph exceedingly fruitful in Egypt. Let's look at this dimension of his life very briefly.

## Joseph's Wisdom

It all started with Pharaoh's dream. Joseph had been in prison for well over two years when God visited Pharaoh with a prophetic dream. Pharaoh knew the dream had special significance, but none of his wise men or magicians could interpret it for him. Then Pharaoh's chief butler recalled that while he was in prison Joseph had correctly interpreted one of his dreams. So the butler mentioned Joseph to Pharaoh, Pharaoh sent for Joseph, and in an instant Joseph found himself out of his prison and getting bathed and dressed so he could appear before the king. (Your release from prison can happen just that fast, too!)

When Pharaoh told Joseph the dream, Joseph was able to interpret it on the spot. This in itself serves to illustrate the fact that Joseph's heart was right before God. He had not allowed his innocent imprisonment to embitter his soul, but he had kept his heart pure before God. Thus, he was able to

> **He had not allowed his innocent imprisonment to embitter his soul, but he had kept his heart pure before God.**

hear from God in the moment of necessity.

Joseph didn't simply interpret the dream. He also went on to give Pharaoh concise instructions on what Pharaoh's response should be to the interpretation. Joseph said:

> Genesis 41:33, "Now therefore, let Pharaoh select a discern-ing and wise man, and set him over the land of Egypt. 34 Let Pharaoh do this, and let him appoint officers over the land, to collect one-fifth of the produce of the land of Egypt in the seven plentiful years. 35 And let them gather all the food of those good years that are coming, and store up grain under the authority of Pharaoh, and let them keep food in the cities. 36 Then that food shall be as a reserve for the land for the seven years of famine which shall be in the land of Egypt, that the land may not perish during the famine." 37 So the advice was good in the eyes of Pharaoh and in the eyes of all his servants. 38 And Pharaoh said to his servants, "Can we find such a one as this, a man in whom is the Spirit of God?" 39 Then Pha-raoh said to Joseph, "Inasmuch as God has shown you all this, there is no one as discerning and wise as you."

Pharaoh appointed Joseph as viceroy over the entire land of Egypt for one reason: because of his outstanding wisdom (verse 39). As the number one man under King Pharaoh, Joseph quickly established him-self as extremely judicious and brilliantly administrative. Joseph's God-given wisdom won him incredible favor before the entire nation of Egypt.

I found myself asking, "How did Joseph get all that wisdom?" Well, it wasn't by reading the Scriptures — because he had no Scriptures to read! (The Bible wasn't written yet.) The answer is, he received wis-dom directly from "the Spirit of wisdom," the Holy Spirit. "Can we find such a one as this, a man in whom is the Spirit of God?" Joseph moved in wisdom because he was full of the Spirit of God. Wisdom isn't to be found in a book but in the Person of Jesus Christ.

Now let's connect Joseph's wisdom with his fruitfulness.

## Fruitfulness

It was the practice in those days to give children a name that meant something special. Joseph named his two sons in a very purposeful manner:

> Joseph called the name of the firstborn Manasseh: "For God has made me forget all my toil and all my father's house."

And the name of the second he called Ephraim: "For God has caused me to be fruitful in the land of my affliction" (Genesis 41:51-52).

Joseph named his second son "Ephraim" because that name literally means "Fruitfulness." Joseph was celebrating the realization that because of the wisdom God had given to him, he had become abundantly fruitful in the land of Egypt. That wisdom inevitably produced fruit. When we have the wisdom of God flowing through us, we too will be fruitful.

This was God's purpose in incarcerating Joseph. God designed the confinement of prison to perfect Joseph in wisdom and in the Spirit of God so that He might make him exceedingly fruitful over the entire nation.

> **God designed the confinement of prison to perfect Joseph in wisdom and in the Spirit of God so that He might make him exceedingly fruitful over the entire nation.**

Joseph became responsible single-handedly for saving the entire nation from starvation. The prison was successful and had produced a man who would be a faithful and humble servant in the midst of great promotion.

## Breaking Off The Yoke

The righteous cries, "Bring my soul out of prison, that I may praise Your name" (Psalm 142:7).

The Lord answers, "Though I have afflicted you, I will afflict you no more; for now I will break off his yoke from you, and burst your bonds apart" (Nahum 1:12-13).

The righteous responds, "You have loosed my bonds" (Psalm 116:16).

Is there anything the Lord's prisoner can do to effect or hasten his deliverance? Isaiah 10:27 is helpful here: "It shall come to pass in that day that his burden will be taken away from your shoulder, and his yoke from your neck, and the yoke will be destroyed because of the anointing oil." The prisoner's yoke will be broken from his neck because of the anointing on his life. This is what happened to Joseph. There was such an anointing on his life

> **The prisoner's yoke will be broken from his neck because of the anointing on his life.**

that the prison could not hold him. Here's some advice for God's prisoners: Give yourself to the anointing oil of the Holy Spirit. "Anoint me, Lord!"

"The righteousness of the upright will deliver them" (Proverbs 11:6).

## A Prisoner Of Hope

It says of Joseph, "The king sent and **released** him, the ruler of the people let him go free" (Psalm 105:20). The word "released" is the Hebrew word "patach," which means to open, loosen, set free, release, unshackle, liberate. The related Hebrew noun, "petach," means door or gate.

It is this related word, "petach" (door), that is used in Hosea 2:

Hosea 2:14, "Therefore, behold, I will allure her, will bring her into the wilderness, and speak comfort to her. 15 I will give her her vineyards from there, and the Valley of Achor as a **door** of hope; she shall sing there, as in the days of her youth, as in the day when she came up from the land of Egypt. 16 And it shall be, in that day," says the LORD, "that you will call Me 'My Husband,' and no longer call Me 'My Master.'"

According to verse 14, God doesn't impose the wilderness on us; instead, He puts a desire within us for His higher purposes, and so He **allures** us into the wilderness. We weren't asking for the wilderness; we were asking for more of Christ. But God knew the wilderness would be the place where we'd gain more of Christ. "And speak comfort to her" is literally "And speak to her heart."

Then the Lord says, "I will give her her vineyards from there." He is assuring us that He will use the wilderness as a springboard for new dimensions of fruitfulness.

"And the Valley of Achor as a door of hope" — Achor means "Trouble." The Lord is saying He will turn the Valley of Trouble into an opportunity for hope. It's a doorway of hope that opens up to release and liberation. Hope is a key ingredient for the Lord's prisoner to maintain his focus. We'll see that in Zechariah in just a moment.

But first, look again at verse 16, "'And it shall be, in that day,' says the LORD, 'that you will call Me "My Husband," and no longer call Me "My Master."'" This verse describes another byproduct of the wilderness prison. During the season of dryness and confinement, the Lord transforms our relationship

> **During the season of dryness and confinement, the Lord transforms our relationship with Him from a Master/servant relationship to that of a Husband/wife relationship.**

with Him from a Master/servant relationship to that of a Husband/wife relationship. God intends the prison to awaken deep bridal affections for the Lord Jesus Christ.

The Spirit of the Lord prophecied through Zechariah, "I will set your prisoners free from the waterless pit. Return to the stronghold, **you prisoners of hope**. Even today I declare that I will restore double to you" (Zechariah 9:11-12). A prisoner of hope is a prisoner of the Lord who has his hope set on the certainty that God is going to deliver him, and even restore double to him. He carries the hope of eventually being doubly blessed.

How does a prisoner gain this hope?

## The Source Of Hope

The pathway to hope is very clearly delineated in Paul's letter to the church at Rome:

> Romans 5:3, And not only that, but we also glory in tribulations, knowing that tribulation produces perseverance; 4 and perseverance, character; and character, hope. 5 Now hope does not disappoint, because the love of God has been poured out in our hearts by the Holy Spirit who was given to us.

It all starts with "tribulations." This New Testament word ("thlipsis") means "pressure." One definition of "thlipsis" says the word means "putting a lot of pressure on that which is free and unfettered." In other words, it describes an imprisonment of sorts, being bound by unpleasant circumstances. There can be no hope unless there is first of all an imprisonment to pressure.

"Tribulation produces perseverance" — to those who respond properly to tribulation, that is. It is incredibly tempting to give up when the pressure is on, but God designs that we persevere in the midst of the pressure. This is where the fire is. The heat is turned up when the pressure doesn't abate, and we're called of God to persevere. It's unabated heat and pressure, and it's the stuff of which diamonds are made.

> **It's unabated heat and pressure, and it's the stuff of which diamonds are made.**

Verse 4 goes on to say that perseverance in the midst of the fire produces character — the character of Christ. Character is Christlikeness. When character is being produced in us, it means we're being changed; we're looking more and more like Jesus. We often say, "Lord, make me more like Jesus." What we forget, though, is that the character of Christ is produced in us in only one manner: by persevering through pressure. So when you pray, "Change me, Lord," you're saying, "Lord, bring on the pain. I'm prepared to persevere in the midst of tribulation."

## Character Produces Hope

Verse 4 continues by saying that character produces hope. This, dear friends, is the key to hope. Hope is what happens when we see God changing us. Hope automatically rises in our hearts when we see that God is using the pressures of our circumstances to conform us to the image of Christ. Suddenly we realize, "Hey! God is working in my crisis! I couldn't see God in my situation, I didn't know why there was pressure on my life from every side, but now I see it. God has been using this fiery season to make me more like Jesus!"

You've got to see the grizzled nature of hope. Hope isn't a fluttery feeling or a wispy kind of wishful thinking. Hope is something that's been weathered and hardened by the elements and has proven itself genuine. **Hope has persevered; hope has suffered; hope has endured the crucible; hope has come through the fire; hope has trudged through the valley and gained the mountain, purified!** This biblical kind of hope does not disappoint because it's been bought at a price.

You've been persevering for weeks, or months, or possibly even years. You've known darkness, pain, perplexity, and fire. You don't understand why God is allowing all this. And then one day it's as though you awaken from a sleep, and it suddenly hits you: "I'm different! God has used this trial to revolutionize me. This tribulation is none other than the love of God for me." The Holy Spirit pours in to confirm that love, igniting a non-perishable confidence that God's purposes shall be fulfilled. It's one thing to see Jesus changing other people, but when you begin to see how He has changed **you**, it really is amazing! Hope is your natural response when you see the character of Jesus developing in yourself.

> **Hope is your natural response when you see the character of Jesus developing in yourself.**

Character produces hope because when I see God working in my life and changing me, I know that He's not going to do a half-baked job. What God starts He finishes. If He has started to make me like Christ, He's going to complete the project! Hope springs from the fountainhead of Philippians 1:6, "being confident of this very thing, that He who has begun a good work in you will complete it until the day of Jesus Christ."

Now I get it. God has imprisoned me in order to change me. I have this hope in the God who completes every good purpose He starts, that He will finish the work in my heart. Not only will he deliver me from my chains, but I will leap forth from the prison a changed person!

> Remember the word to Your servant, upon which You have caused me to hope. This is my comfort in my affliction, for Your word has given me life (Psalm 119:49-50).

# CHAPTER 4

# DAVID'S CAVE

*"They wandered in deserts and mountains, in dens and caves of the earth"* (Hebrews 11:38).

David is a great example of walking through the fire of delayed answers because: 1) he experienced many delays before his prayers were answered; 2) he successfully traversed the wilderness of delay, keeping his heart right before God and truly discovering God's heart in the process; 3) his life is described in more detail than any other Old Testament personality, giving us a wide window into his soul, and; 4) he wrote prolifically, prophetically, and transparently about his own personal struggles, heart attitudes, and supplications before God (recorded in the Psalms).

David's unabashed openness won the affection of God and continues to gain the gratefulness of saints who glean from the pathway David was willing to walk.

## David's Delay

To understand David's desperation, we need to survey David's history. David was quite possibly still a teenager when he killed Goliath, proving himself at an early age to be a warrior of faith and power. King Saul immediately brought him into his court, and David quickly endeared himself to the Israelite nation. Because Saul strayed from God's will, the Lord sent the prophet Samuel to anoint David as the next king of Israel. Soon after God anointed David, however, Saul became jealous and tried to kill David. David ended up having to run for his life. For a period of seven to ten years (we don't know the exact length), David was a fugitive from Saul, hiding in caves, forests, mountains, wilderness areas — wherever he could preserve his life.

At one point David lived in "the cave of Adullam," and that cave became something of a symbol of those years of nomadic distress. Imagine your mailing address being a cave! It was during these years of hiding that David penned some of his most passionate psalms. God anointed him and promised him the kingdom and then came "the great delay." The years of delay, from the time of promise to the time when he actually became king, were used as a refining fire by God to purify David and prepare him for the throne.

> **The years of delay, from the time of promise to the time when he actually became king, were used as a refining fire by God to purify David and prepare him for the throne.**

## David's Depression

If David were alive today, he would probably be diagnosed by modern psychoanalysts as suffering from "clinical depression." David didn't live in a constant state of depression, but he certainly had his ups and downs, and many of his psalms express his low moments of depression and despondency. This is why the Psalms are the primary prescription for saints who struggle with depression.

Why was David given to depression? Well, he was a very intuitive, emotive sort of person in the first place. You know, he was one of those creative, expressive musician types. (I can talk; I'm a musician as well.) He was both a theologian and an incredibly gifted songwriter. The love of his life was to get alone with God and worship with the harp. He was intensely passionate and had no qualms whatsoever about venting his feelings and love for God. In other words, David was secure enough in himself to give honest expression to his real feelings and emotions.

David, then, was given to depression because God put the squeeze on him. Wherever he turned, he faced malicious attempts on his life, betrayal, impoverishment, resistance, hassles, and misunderstanding. God determined that nothing would go David's way, and since He knew David inside and out, He knew exactly what it would take to press David into sore distress.

Look, for example, at the people that surrounded David. The men who came to David in the cave of Adullam were "in distress...in debt, and everyone who was discontented" (1 Samuel 22:2). The literal word for "discontented" is "bitter of soul," which meant they had faced great disappointment. Perhaps rather than "discontented," a better translation would be "depressed." David inherited a mess of manic depressives. No wonder so many of his psalms come from a place of depression — David not only had his own problems, but his company was depressing too.

One day, while I was particularly struggling with depression, I seemed incapable of rejoicing and celebrating in praise to God. I thought, "Lord, this is real bad. Here I wrote this book on worship (Exploring Worship), and after having written the book I can't even praise you now myself!" Then the Lord brought this psalm of David's to mind: "Bless the Lord, O my soul; and **all that is within me**, bless His holy name!" (Psalm 103:1). I sensed the Lord asking, "What's within you? What do you have to give?" I said, "Lord, all I've got today is tears." He said, "Then give me your tears." He doesn't ask us to give Him something that we don't have. When you feel empty, give Him whatever you have within you, little as it may seem.

## David's Loneliness

Four hundred men joined themselves to David at the cave of Adullam, and then the ranks grew over time to six hundred. So on the surface of things it would seem like, "Well, at least David had 400 men to keep him company." But they weren't great company. Not only did they talk of mutiny when Ziklag was invaded, but David's right-hand men were always giving him carnal advice. "God has delivered your enemy, King Saul, into your hand, David! It's God's will that I kill him right now!" There's only one thing that's lonelier than having no one with you, and that's being in the company of folks with whom you can't relate at all. David's in a crowd, but he feels all alone.

> There's only one thing that's lonelier than having no one with you, and that's being in the company of folks with whom you can't relate at all.

David's loneliness was compounded by the fact that none of his contemporaries understood him. They could never figure out what made him tick. They were constantly baffled at David's responses, and, in many cases, actually irritated and angered by them. They couldn't figure out why he wouldn't take matters into his own hands and just do something decisive. David was waiting on God alone, even when it was in his power to overthrow or kill King Saul. David's stance was, "God promised me the kingdom, and God will have to give it to me. I won't take it for myself." There is no evidence, however, that any of David's companions fully comprehended his position.

David sang it to the men who followed him with these words, "Wait on the LORD; be of good courage, and He shall strengthen your heart; wait, I say, on the LORD!" (Psalm 27:14). We don't know when David wrote Psalm 27, but it seems most reasonable to suppose that it was written during his years of hiding. He's waiting on the Lord, even though he's had opportunity to help things along in his own strength. (David had two opportunities to kill Saul, but he refused to kill the Lord's anointed.) David tasted of the blessing that comes to the one who does nothing but waits on God, but he struggled to impart that conviction to those who followed him.

David expressed his loneliness to the Lord in this way: "Turn Yourself to me, and have mercy on me, for I am desolate and afflicted" (Psalm 25:16). Although surrounded by hundreds of men, there was only one to whom David could pour out his heart: God. All David wanted to do during that season was get away from everybody and find a quiet corner where he could cry out to God.

My reason for pointing to David's loneliness and depression is this: If God has you in a place where you feel like you're living in a cave, and you never really had struggles with depression and loneliness

> **The loneliness and despondency are tools in God's hands to break, mold, and fashion you according to His plan.**

until you entered this wilderness, then take heart. You're sharing company with some incredible saints of God. The loneliness and despondency are tools in God's hands to break, mold, and fashion you according to His plan.

## Ministry Hiatus

David was called and anointed to full-time service. The anointing on his life was manifested early on in the way he killed the lion and the bear that attacked his sheep. It was manifested in the way he played the harp. And it was manifested in the way he killed Goliath. Samuel had anointed him, but now David was beginning to see that anointing bear fruit. He was watching God honor his faith. With each step, David was growing in confidence and faith before God. He became Saul's armor bearer, one of the captains in the army, and he served Saul as a musician in his court. David was one of those rising stars who had distinguished himself as "the most likely to succeed." When David was brought into King Saul's court, it was obvious to everyone that God's hand was on him. David was on the way up.

Then, BOOM. It happened just that fast. All of a sudden, Saul did a complete turnabout and began to suspect and hate David. He became so jealous that he even tried to kill David with a javelin. Eventually, David had to flee from Saul for his life. Saul not only demoted him, Saul hunted him.

David was anointed, talented, smart, faithful, bold, creative, winsome, strong, and upright in every way. He had followed God's will blamelessly. And suddenly he's totally removed from service, no longer free to minister among the people, and he finds himself in a desert cave. Talk about the death of a vision! It seemed that all of heaven and earth was against him, and he had no idea why.

I can hear David crying, "Why, God? Why me? What did I do? I don't understand why you would call me, and then kick me out of my inheritance." When he found himself ostracized from the nation, running for his life, living in destitute circumstances, there is no doubt that he began to scramble spiritually. God was not acting like the God David knew. David was in a spiritual crisis, so he went on a desperate search to understand the ways of God. What in heaven's name was going on here? Many of his psalms reflect his conclusions, and when he wrote them down the Holy Spirit said, "I'm going to put these songs in My holy Scriptures because they accurately reflect My ways."

One of the devices God uses to train His Davids is called "removal from ministry." Whether it's a forced removal or an inability to continue, the net effect is the same: cessation or limitation of ministry. His purpose is to test the heart motivations. God is wondering, "Are you in this thing for Me or for yourself? Do you love to serve Me because it meets an ego need in yourself or is it because you really love Me? Are you in ministry because it satisfies your need for feelings of significance? Are you Mine even if I let leaders who you honor touch you and test you?"

> "Do you love to serve Me because it meets an ego need in yourself or is it because you really love Me?"

## A Sense Of Significance

There is something in the heart of man that longs for significance. We want our lives to be meaningful and fulfilled. The temptation in the body of Christ is for believers to receive their significance from their area of service or ministry. The Lord desires, on the other hand, for us to gain our fulfillment from being in His presence and pleasing His heart.

If I derive my sense of fulfillment from what I accomplish for God, the Lord will surface that misplaced motivation by placing me on the shelf. Then, when I have nothing but my relationship with Him, I discover where my heart has really been. We're not capable of seeing it until the Lord removes us for a season from all ministry. This is what God was after in David's heart.

Jesus' followers struggled with the exact same thing:

> Luke10:17, "Then the seventy returned with joy, saying, 'Lord, even the demons are subject to us in Your name.' 18 And He said to them, 'I saw Satan fall like lightning from heaven. 19 Behold, I give you the authority to trample on serpents and scorpions, and over all the power of the enemy, and nothing shall by any means hurt you. 20 Nevertheless do not rejoice in this, that the spirits are subject to you, but rather rejoice because your names are written in heaven.' 21 In that hour Jesus rejoiced in the Spirit and said, 'I thank You, Father, Lord of heaven and earth, that You have hidden these things from the wise and prudent and revealed them to babes. Even so, Father, for so it seemed good in Your sight. 22 All things have been delivered to Me by My Father, and no one knows who the Son is except the Father, and who the Father is except the Son, and the one to whom the Son wills to reveal Him.'"

In verse 17, Jesus' disciples rejoiced. In verse 21, Jesus rejoiced. Interestingly enough, each party rejoiced for a totally different reason. The seventy rejoiced because evil spirits were obedient to them. They found their significance in accomplishing exploits for God. Jesus, on the other hand, rejoiced that the Father had "hidden these things from the wise and prudent and revealed them to babes." Jesus wasn't rejoicing because His students were learning how to move out in ministry but because God had chosen to glorify Himself by revealing His kingdom truths to simple babes. The things that excited Jesus and the things that excited the disciples, were miles apart.

I've been pondering the fact that Jesus never seemed to get excited when someone was healed or delivered. Miracles and healings never seemed to prime His pump. His passion was directed more toward prayer and preaching. In contrast, when someone is healed in our midst, we shout and dance and tell everybody about it. Nothing seems to energize us quite like seeing someone healed. I believe the Lord is preparing those who will be empowered to minister in the arena of divine healing, but instead of being energized by witnessing the miraculous, they will have learned to gain their significance from their relationship with Jesus and their obedience to His will.

> **Instead of being energized by witnessing the miraculous, they will have learned to gain their significance from their relationship with Jesus and their obedience to His will.**

## The Purpose Of The Wilderness

God did not take David into the wilderness for ten years to make him a man of faith. He already was a man of faith. It took remarkable faith to kill the giant. He was the only man in the entire nation with enough faith to kill Goliath. So if David's wilderness was not intended to refine his faith, for what was it intended?

The wilderness prepared David for more than just the throne. David didn't have to go through wilderness testings in order to take the throne; he was ready for the throne when he killed Goliath. But he wasn't ready for the throne God wanted to give him. David thought God was giving him the throne of Israel, but God wanted to give him an eternal throne (see Psalm 89). David was ready to be king of Israel at 23, but he wasn't ready to be the heir to God's eternal kingdom. He wasn't ready for God's promise, "I will establish your throne for ever."

David's seven years in the furnace were not to prepare him to be king, but to prepare him to receive an everlasting kingdom. The kind of promises God wanted to extend to David could be given only to someone who had been completely broken.

## A Broken Faith

The Bible commends David for having giant-slaying faith. He was strong in faith, and the Lord was pleased with him. His faith had made him a warrior, and although David was not arrogant, he was ready for war. His faith was not haughty — but it was unbroken.

> **His faith was not haughty — but it was unbroken.**

In order to produce the kind of brokenness in David that God desired, God had to break David's faith.

How did He do that? By leading David into a wilderness where no amount of faith posturings would effect any change. It didn't seem to matter how many times He claimed the promises of God, Saul still kept coming after him. I can imagine David crying, "Before, when I rose up in faith, God enabled me to accomplish great exploits. Now, when I rise up in faith, nothing happens. Lord, what's wrong?"

God taught David how to be a man of faith. And then God brought devastation into his life, and none of the lessons he learned previously was applicable anymore. In this way, God broke David's framework and understanding of faith and then began to totally rebuild it.

David would again rise up in faith, but this time it would be a faith that would be devoid of all self-confidence and trust in human strength. David didn't realize it, but some of his faith was rooted in the fact that he felt so strong and virile and anointed. He felt so great that it was easy to have faith. When God devastated him, and he felt horrible, he saw that his faith crumbled at the same time. Without realizing it, his faith had been built in part on the health and vigor of his natural youthfulness.

God was producing in David genuine faith in God. This faith would not come because he felt strong and confident but because of a deepened realization that the Lord is God. Until our faith is broken, we think it's pure — especially because of the great victories we've seen. But the Lord knows how to break every natural prop upon which our faith tends to lean. David could testify, "I was strong, I was serving the Lord, God was blessing through my life, everything was going great — until BOOM. God pulled my feet out from under me, He broke me, and now I'm totally disoriented. I've never walked this way before, and I have no idea what God is doing in my life. I feel so utterly dependent upon God for every breath." This is the dependence that delights the Father's heart.

In the place of brokenness, God will teach you what true faith is all about. It's incredibly challenging, when you feel totally empty, to have faith in God. But God wants us to see that our faith should not waver, whether we feel good in ourselves or whether we feel completely undone.

A faith that springs from brokenness smells different. It looks different. It sounds different. It **is** different. It's not marked by sweat and spittle and froth and pulpit-pounding because it's not trying to elicit a human response. Broken faith does not focus on getting people to respond because its confidence is truly in God alone. Broken faith has been tempered in the furnace, and it has a fortitude to endure great resistance. It is quieter, more durable, and more fruitful.

The greatest dimensions of faith can be entrusted only to broken vessels. Unbroken vessels have

> **The greatest dimensions of faith can be entrusted only to broken vessels.**

a tendency to misappropriate great faith. We see this in the brothers James and John, who were willing to call down fire from heaven, like Elijah did, to consume the Samaritans who wouldn't receive Jesus. Their faith had grown to the place where they were believing that God would send fire from heaven at their invocation. They thought they had great faith, but Jesus said to them, "You do not know what manner of spirit you are of. For the Son of Man did not come to destroy men's lives but to save them" (Luke 9:55-56). They didn't realize their zeal was rooted in racism (against the Samaritans), and in a boldness of faith that was not seasoned with brokenness. **Great faith that has not been broken turns into presumption.**

## Balancing Brokenness And Faith

The human tendency is to emphasize either brokenness or faith. The faith-speaking people talk about "taking our cities for God," and "doing great exploits." They're ready to take on the "principalities and powers" of darkness. They're bold; they're strong; they're undefeatable; they're more than conquerors.

Then you've got your brokenness people. Every time you ask them how they're doing, they say things like, "God is sifting His church. There's a breaking going on right now. He's shaking everything that can be shaken. God is really cleaning house. He's the Potter and I'm the clay."

To use different terminology, the faith-talkers focus on "the gifts of the Spirit," the outward manifestation of kingdom power and blessing. The brokenness-talkers focus on "the fruit of the Spirit," the inward working of Christlike character.

There's tremendous truth on both sides, but the Lord doesn't want us to end up on either side. He wants us to embrace both and find the balance of "a broken faith." This is one of the primary purposes of David's cave.

## The Lord's Deliverance

When David wrote Psalm 34:19, you get the impression that he was on the other side of his wilderness years. Look at it: "Many are the afflictions of the righteous, but the LORD delivers him out of them all." The casual observer would think David has experienced total deliverance when he writes those words. But a closer look at the psalm's title reveals that David wrote this after he escaped from Achish, king of the Philistines, by feigning madness. He escaped from Achish, but he was not yet delivered from his greatest trouble — Saul. In fact, his seven or so years of running and hiding were only just beginning. David didn't know what lay ahead, but in response to this small deliverance he writes these words that describe God's ways. David wrote under a strong prophetic anointing which saw beyond his circumstances. Even though he was still greatly troubled, he was able to declare God's ways with conviction and passion.

Isaiah talked about "the sure mercies of David" (Isaiah 55:3), and Paul quoted that passage (Acts 13:34), saying it referred directly to the resurrection of Christ. Christ rose from the dead because He was given "the sure mercies of David." God had proven His mercies to David — that after death there is resurrection, that after the cave comes the crown. For years the promise was delayed, but David held onto the fact that God is merciful. He refused to take matters into his own hands, but trusted God alone for deliverance. For those who will follow in the way of

David, and keep their faces only on the Lord in the darkness of their cave, He comes to say that His mercies are sure. His resurrection most assuredly comes to the one who thus waits on Him.

Psalm 31 gives two reasons why David asked the Lord to hear and answer him: "for Your name's sake" (v.3) and "for Your mercies' sake" (v.16). David doesn't cry, "O Lord, please save me because I'm so needy." Instead he prays, "Save me because of who You are." Don't simply pray, "Lord, heal me because I'm sick." Rather, touch the heart of God with this prayer: "Lord, be merciful and heal me for Your name's sake — that your reputation might be promoted."

## David And Achish

During his fugitive years, God was doing a deep preparatory work in David's heart. He had no idea how much longer he would have to run from Saul, but as time went on and his heart was being seasoned and perfected, the time of his release also drew near. At the time when God was just about to bring David to the throne, he had just one final test for him. As we look at this story, it's perhaps the most puzzling incident in David's life. I am referring to the events of 1 Samuel 29. David has taken up residence with the Philistines in order to find refuge from Saul, and the time has come for the Philistines to move out in war against Israel. David has been telling Achish that he raided some of the outlying communities of Israel when in fact he has been raiding remote enclaves of neighboring Gentiles. Achish, the Philistine king, thinks David has made himself abhorrent to Israel and figures he's got David as a servant for life.

So when Achish moves out against Israel, he invites David and his men to join him, which David does. The Philistine princes, however, got together and vetoed that idea. They said, "Make this fellow return, that he may go back to the place which you have appointed for him, and do not let him go down with us to battle, lest in the battle he become our adversary. For with what could he reconcile himself to his master, if not with the heads of these men?" (1 Samuel 29:4). They feared that David would turn against them in the battle. The exchange between David and Achish in the following verses is interesting:

> So David said to Achish, "But what have I done? And to this day what have you found in your servant as long as I have been with you, that I may not go and fight against the enemies of my lord the king?" Then Achish answered and said to David, "I know that you are as good in my sight as an angel of God; nevertheless the princes of the Philistines have said, 'He shall

not go up with us to the battle.' Now therefore, rise early in the morning with your master's servants who have come with you. And as soon as you are up early in the morning and have light, depart." So David and his men rose early to depart in the morning, to return to the land of the Philistines. And the Philistines went up to Jezreel (1 Samuel 29:8-11).

The big question here is, what was David really intending to do? Was he intending to help the Philistines slaughter off his fellow Israelites? Or was he planning to turn against the Philistines and fight for Israel? Some interpreters suggest that David was at a place of such cynicism, bitterness, and disorientation that he was actually about to move out and slaughter his own people. I disagree.

David was incredibly close to his summit. He didn't know it, but as events would transpire, he was going to be crowned king of Judah in just a few short days. That coronation represents the end of his wilderness wanderings — the moment of answered prayer. If he was that close to the culmination of God's purifying work in his life, it's inconceivable to think that he was still grappling with cynicism and anger. He was far past that. God had done a great work in his life, and his moment was almost here.

I believe David was deceiving Achish on this occasion. Even as he had deceived Achish by claiming to raid Israelite villages, so too he is now pretending to be fully supportive of Achish. But his heart is clearly with Israel (see 1 Samuel 30:26). I don't know what David was planning, but he definitely had something up his sleeve. God, however, had another pathway for David to take. My point here is that if you understand the nature of God's wilderness testings, and see the point David had reached in that process, you realize it would be impossible for David to still be in a place of great personal crisis, uncertainty, cynicism, and bitterness.

## Return To Ziklag

When David was denied participation with the Philistine armies, he returned home. And good thing he did, because he discovered that the Amalekites had raided his town, taken all their women and children captive, and plundered all their goods. David's men were so upset they spoke of killing him. But the grace of God on his life and the maturity in which he walked was made evident in his response: "Now David was greatly distressed, for the people spoke of stoning him, because the soul of all the people was grieved, every man for his sons and his daughters. But David strengthened himself in the LORD his God" (1 Samuel 30:6).

When you see the point David had attained in God's wilderness training seminar, you realize that the raiding of Ziklag by the Amalekites was David's final test before God gave him the throne. His men had followed him with genuine devotion, but now they spoke of killing him. He didn't fit with the Philistines; he didn't fit with the Israelites; the Amalekites are against him; no one is on his side — but God. Instead of succumbing to despair, anger, or bitterness, David went aside and encouraged himself in the Lord. When everyone was against him, he found his comfort in God. David had passed the test.

> **When everyone was against him, he found his comfort in God. David had passed the test.**

## Why So Much Pain?

When we read David's cries in the Psalms, we might wonder, "Why did David have to suffer so much? I can see the need for refining, but why so much pain?" Here's one answer: Had David never experienced as much pain as he did, he would have never been able to prophesy about the Messiah's passion as he did (Psalm 22 is the most compelling example of David's identification with the Savior's sufferings). Personal suffering opens to us the portal of identifying with God in His great passion for mankind.

> **Personal suffering opens to us the portal of identifying with God in His great passion for mankind.**

God had to take many of His prophets through grueling circumstances in order to prepare their hearts so that they would be able to carry God's kind of passion for His kingdom purposes. The prophets paid a great price personally to be able to process and reproduce the prophetic cry of God for His people. Jesus was called "the son of David," and we think, "Wow, what a distinction! David sure is blessed to carry that honor!" The fact is David had to experience the horror of Psalm 22 in order to qualify for that great privilege.

## David And Solomon

When we consider what David's wilderness years accomplished in him, it's interesting to compare him with his son Solomon. Solomon succeeded his father David to the throne of Israel, and he enjoyed forty years of unparalleled peace and prosperity. Solomon seemed to have so many advantages over David, so it's almost unbelievable to realize the ungodly state into which he deteriorated, even to the point of serving other gods. He had been crowned with supernatural wisdom and knew full well the deception of false gods. He had a great start — God loved him (2 Samuel 12:24), and Solomon loved the Lord (1 Kings 3:3). But in his latter years Solomon capitulated to idolatry. The big question is, why?

David and Solomon both had a heart for God, both were blessed by the Lord in their reigns, and yet Solomon pulled away while David remained true to his God. What was the difference? I'm convinced it was this: Solomon had no cave of Adullam. He knew no counterpart to David's years

> **What was the difference? I'm convinced it was this: Solomon had no cave of Adullam.**

in the wilderness. He didn't have the seven years David had, of pain and pressure and suffering and reproach and heartbreak. His lack of personal suffering became his downfall, and as a consequence he fell prey to eternal suffering. It's a scriptural principle: **We can't handle the glory unless we've first handled the pain.**

David hesitated in installing Solomon as king, so much so that Adonijah (another son of David) tried to take advantage of the delay. But David didn't hesitate to install Solomon as king because he had sticky fingers and couldn't release the throne. It was because he realized Solomon had no cave of Adullam training season, and he was concerned that Solomon was insufficiently prepared by God's Bible School (the wilderness) for the throne. As it turned out, his hesitation was well-founded. Since David knew that waiting and delay were part of God's dealings, he was probably hoping that the waiting season would produce something positive in Solomon's soul.

## Teaching Versus Training

Although Solomon lacked training through hardship, it seems that David attempted to fill that void through instruction. Solomon talks about how his father and mother instructed him. Solomon said, "Train up a child in the way he should go, and when he is old he will not depart from it" (Proverbs 22:6). That was not something Solomon got, that was something David got and passed along to Solomon. Because if Solomon had gained that principle first-hand, he would have never departed from God in his old age. But when he was old, he did depart — because he was insufficiently trained.

Instructing and teaching our kids will never be sufficient. We need to find ways to **train** our kids and to allow God to train them as well. How do we train our kids? The same way God does — by allowing them to experience difficulty, hardship, and crisis. We make the mistake as parents of trying to spare our kids those things, and thus don't cooperate with God in providing them with critical training. We try to replace

> **Wise parents would do well to permit their children cave experiences within God's purposes as well, rather than asserting the instinctive tendency to try to steer them clear of the pain.**

training with instruction, but even though instruction is vitally important, it is never a substitute for the cave of Adullam. God fashions caves for His choice sons; wise parents would do well to permit their children cave experiences within God's purposes as well, rather than asserting the instinctive tendency to try to steer them clear of the pain.

God gave Solomon incredible wisdom and a singular ability to analyze and philosophize on all areas of life. The Book of Ecclesiastes records some of Solomon's conclusions, the following being an excerpt:

> Ecclesiastes 2:18, "Then I hated all my labor in which I had toiled under the sun, because I must leave it to the man who will come after me. 19 And who knows whether he will be wise or a fool? Yet he will rule over all my labor in which I toiled and in which I have shown myself wise under the sun. This also is vanity. 20 Therefore I turned my heart and despaired of all the labor in which I had toiled under the sun. 21 For there is a man whose labor is with wisdom, knowledge, and skill; yet he must leave his heritage to a man who has not labored for it. This also is vanity and a great evil."

Verse 20 may well be Solomon's great error: "Therefore I turned my heart and despaired." He allowed his great insight into the futility of living at the natural level to cause him to turn his heart away from God. He turned his heart in unbelief and despair, and that was the beginning of his ruin. This is where Solomon left his first love. God can handle your despair, but He can't help you if you turn your heart away from Him.

> **God can handle your despair, but He can't help you if you turn your heart away from Him.**

It's as though God used Solomon as a test case. Perhaps God was thinking something like this: "Usually I lift My godly ones to higher understandings in Me by bringing them through seasons of great testing; but I will try it a different way with Solomon. I will give him the wisdom to see all these things without the pain of the crucible. I'll give him the understanding without the suffering." If God intended Solomon as a test case, it's clear that he failed. Solomon demonstrates the fact that when God lifts us to higher dimensions through increased understanding alone, through greater insight into the Scriptures, through teaching and instruction, that it backfires. We need more than instruction — we need training. And training means pain. He gives us the pain out of His merciful intention to preserve our souls to the coming of the Lord Jesus.

## David And Doeg

Doeg the Edomite provides an interesting contrast to David. When David was fleeing from Saul and had come to Ahimelech the priest, Doeg happend to be there in Nob at the same time, detained before the Lord. Ahimelech thought David was doing the king's business, so he sent David and his men off with provisions and with Goliath's sword. Later, however, Doeg reported this incident to King Saul, and as a result Saul killed all the priests at Nob in a vengeful act of cruel hatred. In fact, Saul commanded Doeg to kill the priests. The other warriors wouldn't touch the priests of the Lord, but being an Edomite, Doeg didn't seem to have the same respect for that office, and he implemented the king's order to kill the priests.

Being an Edomite, Doeg probably struggled to feel accepted as one of the people of God. He longed for approval and had natural ambitions for greatness in the system. Although killing the priests would not have been his preferred way to gain a higher position, he found in the reporting and killing of the priests a way to gain the favor of Saul. Instead of allowing God to bring him into greatness, he manipulated it for himself wickedly.

> **Instead of allowing God to bring him into greatness, he manipulated it for himself wickedly.**

The antithesis of that is found in David's response in Psalm 52. The title to that Psalm reads, "A Contemplation of David when Doeg the Edomite went and told Saul, and said to him, 'David has gone to the house of Ahimelech.'" So David is responding directly to that situation when he writes in verses 8-9 of that Psalm, "I trust in the mercy of God forever and ever. I will praise You forever, because You have done it; and in the presence of Your saints I will wait on Your name, for it is good."

"I trust in the mercy of God" — David is casting himself upon the mercy of God, and deciding that if anything is going to happen on his behalf, God is going to have to do it in His mercy.

"Because You have done it" — David is saying, "I'm not going to try to maneuver my way like Doeg did. If I am to gain any promotion at all, it will have to be because You do it, Lord."

"I will wait on Your name" — David has only one option left, then, and that is to wait on God. It's the waiting that's so hard. David had to wait for years and years, but finally David was raised up by God to a place of greatness in the nation. Doeg wanted it, but he refused to wait for it. David waited, and God came through in time and gave David an everlasting kingdom. As for Doeg, he is never again mentioned in the Bible.

# WHEN THE LIGHTS GO OUT

*"For You will light my lamp; the LORD my God will enlighten my darkness"* (Psalm 18:28).

When God allows a crisis to come our way for the purpose of maturing us and forming godly character in us, the first response we often have is, "Lord, why is this happening to me?" We don't understand what God is doing, and as much as we seek Him about it, the heavens seem to be like brass. We don't understand why God won't talk to us right now.

This is the darkness that God allows some of His servants to go through (Isaiah 50:10-11). In my previous book, <u>In His Face</u>, I referred to this darkness of Isaiah 50, and so will avoid repeating myself here. But I would like to add some further thoughts regarding the dark valley season, God's purposes in it, and how He leads us out.

## Walking Through The Valley

David wrote, "Yea, though I walk through the valley of the shadow of death, I will fear no evil; for You are with me" (Psalm 23:4). David himself knew what it was like to walk through the darkness of the valley season when you don't know where God's taking you and you can't see past your nose. God doesn't lead us into the valley, however, to keep us there. His purpose is to refine us in the valley of delayed answers and then bring us forth into the sunlight of maturity and fruitfulness. His purpose is always that we walk **through** the valley.

There are two kinds of people in the valley: those who are submerged under the river, and those who have tapped into the fruitful soil of the valley. When you first land there, you may very well feel submerged in deep waters. But if you seek the Lord fer-

> **You don't go out of the valley; you grow out of the valley.**

vently, He will give you the grace to find the bank and sink your roots into the valley's rich soil. You don't **go** out of the valley; you **grow** out of the valley.

## The Valley's Purpose

Isaiah points to the purpose of the valley, indicating that it prepares us to embrace the fullness of Christ:

> The voice of one crying in the wilderness: "Prepare the way of the LORD; make straight in the desert a highway for our God. Every valley shall be exalted and every mountain and hill brought low; the crooked places shall be made straight and the rough places smooth" (Isaiah 40:3-4).

"Make straight in the desert a highway for our God" — The purpose of the desert (valley) season is that we be given the opportunity to build a highway in our hearts for God. If we build Him a highway, it will be the pathway upon which He will lead us out of the valley. Here's how the highway is built.

"Every valley shall be exalted" — Typically we view the valley as an unhappy season, a time to be avoided, a hole to crawl out of as soon as possible. But the Lord will exalt those who allow the fullness of the valley to season their souls. The New Testament quotes this verse in this way, "Every valley shall be filled" (Luke 3:4). Jesus brings this assurance to those who persevere in their valley season, that He will fill them with a fresh fullness of His Spirit and exalt them to a higher plane of Christian experience.

"And every mountain and hill brought low" — Ministries that have known great prominence and high visibility will be brought down, and not only through scandals or moral failure. Some of them will come down through no fault of their own, but through circumstances totally outside of their control. The purpose will be to introduce the valley season, in order that the truest ways of God might be gained.

> **The Lord will take great pains to straighten out what we have not even thought to question.**

"The crooked places shall be made straight" — The crooked places are areas in our lives and understanding that are not correct but which we think are straight. The Lord will take great pains to straighten out what we have not even thought to question.

"And the rough places smooth" — This is a reference to personality and character — personal qualities and attributes that are abrasive and counterproductive to the Kingdom. We are helpless to change these things in ourselves, so the Lord will bring others into our lives who will be like iron sharpening iron. Only smooth stones will find their mark in the giant's forehead.

## Learning To Listen

One of the reasons we can't hear from God, when the darkness descends, is that God wants to re-train the way in which we hear from Him. Look again at this beloved Psalm: "Yea, though I walk through the valley of the shadow of death, I will fear no evil; for You are with me; Your rod and Your staff, they comfort me" (Psalm 23:4).

When I entered the darkness, it became very difficult for me to know whether I was hearing God accurately, and so I would strain at hearing Him. I can see now that that's what He wants. At the time, the Lord reminded me of Psalm 23:4. A sheep is normally accustomed to following the shepherd by both sight and sound — seeing where he's going, hearing his voice, and following the sounds of his feet. But in the darkness of the valley, when the sheep can't see where the shepherd is going, he has to rely totally on the sense of hearing. One of the things the sheep strains to hear is the shepherd's staff. The shepherd will use it as a walking stick, and the tapping of the staff on the ground or on rocks enables the sheep to know where the shepherd is going. So even though you may feel like you can't see where Jesus is in the darkness of the valley, if you'll listen carefully, He'll guide you via the sense of hearing.

The Lord showed me that I had ministered almost exclusively according to spiritual perception — by the ability to see spiritually. It's easy to do because the sense of sight is so very powerful. I began to see that He was wanting to cultivate my sense of spiritual hearing, and to do that He shut down my ability to see spiritually by introducing a season of darkness. I do not mean to imply that I have had outstanding spiritual sight, but only that most of my energies have gone into cultivating that spiritual sense, to the neglect of the other. I have relied upon my ability to see things, to the neglect of the cultivation of the spiritual ear. There's nothing wrong with seeing things in the Spirit, but there's more to the spiritual realm than what can be discerned with the spiritual eye.

> **There's nothing wrong with seeing things in the Spirit, but there's more to the spiritual realm than what can be discerned with the spiritual eye.**

Even as the ear detects things the eye cannot detect, the sense of spiritual hearing picks up spiritual realities that are not perceived by the sense of spiritual seeing. For example, God calls things that are not as though they were (Romans 4:17). The spiritual eye would see nothing, but the spiritual ear would hear God calling it into being.

Jesus said, "My sheep hear My voice, and I know them, and they follow Me" (John 10:27). This is how Jesus guides His sheep through the dark valley. He wants to guide us by way of the sense of hearing and not just sight.

The time of darkness is somewhat deceiving in this: You think God's not talking to you, but when you stop and look back, you realize He's actually spoken a lot of things to you. When you're walking in a season of darkness, be on the alert for what God is saying to you and even write things down in a journal. Although God may be silent regarding the things you want Him to talk about (namely, the darkness itself), He will

> **Jesus assured us that the dark times would be times when He would speak to us.**

be speaking to you the things that are on His heart. Jesus assured us that the dark times would be times when He would speak to us: "Whatever I tell you in the dark, speak in the light" (Matthew 10:27). So when you're in the dark, take note; He's going to speak to you. And what He gives you, you will declare when your night is past.

Be careful to note, also, the things that the Lord will speak through others in the body of Christ. Personally, I don't know how I would have come through my night season had it not been for the words from God that brothers and sisters spoke to me. At one point, as I was reviewing a certain prophecy that had been given to me, I began to wonder in my heart, "How much weight should I give something like this?" Then the Scripture came to mind: "Believe in the Lord your God, and you shall be established; believe His prophets, and you shall prosper" (2 Chronicles 20:20). If the Spirit bears witness that the prophecy you've received is from Him, then hold to it — and you shall prosper.

### Five Phases Of The Valley Journey

There is a fairly standard cycle through which the believer walks as he goes through the valley. Many of the Psalms chronicle this progression in the life of the believer. Certain Psalms are written as landmarks along the journey. There are five phases to this progression:

Phase I: The believer is doing great, rejoicing in God, delighting in serving Him.
Phase II: The crisis hits, and the believer plummets to the depths of the valley.
Phase III: The believer seeks God fervently for answers and doesn't

understand God's purposes in the crisis.

Phase IV: The believer begins to gain increasing insight into the purposes of God for this season and begins to see how God is bringing him into higher dimensions of life in the Spirit.

Phase V: God brings deliverance, after the refining process is complete, and the believer rejoices in answered prayer.

Following is a diagram of sorts, which represents these five stages of progression. The numbers represent their respective Psalms. A couple other Scripture references have been added for comparison, but basically we're looking at this progression through the eyeglasses of the Book of Psalms.

## Through The Valley With The Psalms

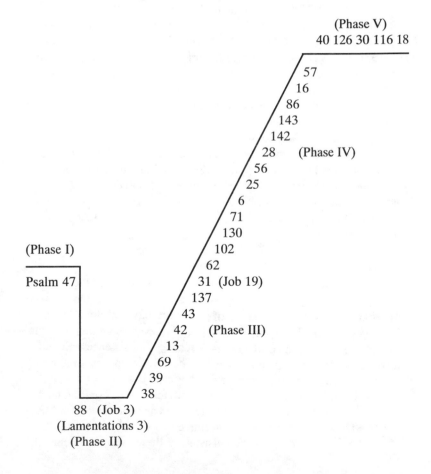

**Phase I**

In Phase I, the believer is really enjoying God. He's got the Psalm 47 shout of victory in his mouth. Life is great, activity in the kingdom is fruitful, faith is strong, and the believer is busy and fulfilled. There is, however, a nagging sense of having reached a spiritual impasse. The believer knows there must be greater heights in God, but he has no idea how to access them. So a cry begins to develop for more of God.

> **The believer knows there must be greater heights in God, but he has no idea how to access them.**

**Phase II**

Suddenly, seemingly out of nowhere, disaster strikes. Calamity hits, the believer crumples, and then he falls headlong into the valley of the shadow of death. Thud. Welcome to the Psalm 88 valley.

When you read Psalm 88, your first thought is, "This is depressing!" You may notice that the Psalm begins and ends with a sense of hopelessness. There is not a single statement of faith in the entire Psalm. Because when you splat onto the bottom of the valley, there is no hope; there is no faith; there is no joy; there is no light.

You may think Psalm 88 is morbid, but let me assure you, when you hit the darkness of the valley, it's deeply comforting. It's very comforting to know that it's okay to be in a place where all you see is blackness, where all you have are questions, and where all you feel is pain. Psalm 88 was endorsed by the Holy Spirit to be placed in the Scriptures, so we would understand that such a place of depression and discouragement is a necessary part of the process.

(You'll notice that two sister passages are Job 3 and Lamentations 3.)

**Phase III**

In utter desperation, the believer clings feverishly to the word of God. To meditate upon the word of God day and night becomes the believer's sole source of sustenance, subsistence, and sanity. The search for understanding begins.

> **To meditate upon the word of God day and night becomes the believer's sole source of sustenance, subsistence, and sanity.**

Slowly the believer begins to ascend, but the climb is so gradual that the believer is not aware of any change. A general sense of blackness persists. The depth of the crisis determines how long it takes to get to Psalm 31. Generally, the more devastating the crisis, the deeper the work intended by God; and the more devastating the crisis, the longer it takes to attain Psalm 31. It's around Psalm 31 that light is beginning to dawn. Early insight comes, and the saint begins to realize that already God has lifted him a considerable way from the depths of the valley. But there's still no sense of having attained higher ground.

The grief continues to be very intense, but it is joined now with a hopeful expectancy of God's salvation.

**Phase IV**

The believer is increasingly gaining understanding into God's purposes for this season. As the understanding grows, so does the faith and confidence that God will complete His purposes.

What is most encouraging is that the believer is experiencing recurring vantage points, breaks in the trees where he gets another look at where he once was and how high he has climbed. He sees down into the valley and realizes that although he thought he was walking in a valley, he's really on a mountain pass. It's the valley that wends its way upward between two mountains, but there is no question that he is slowly scaling the mountain. He's getting a better perspective on the valley from whence he came, but he still has no idea how much further it is to the summit.

**Phase V**

Suddenly, the believer steps out onto Psalm 40. It's the moment of answered prayer. It's the summit. In an instant, he bursts forth from the trees and finds himself at a mountaintop experience. Psalm 40 bursts forth from his lips:

> I waited patiently for the LORD; and He inclined to me, and heard my cry. He also brought me up out of a horrible pit, out of the miry clay, and set my feet upon a rock, and established my steps. He has put a new song in my mouth — praise to our God; many will see it and fear, and will trust in the LORD (Psalm 40:1-3).

The ultimate song of the summit is to be found in Psalm 18. The psalm's title says it succinctly: "A Psalm of David the servant of the LORD, who spoke to the LORD the words of this song on the day that the LORD delivered him from the hand of all his enemies and from the hand of Saul." Psalm 18 is a glorious celebration of answered prayer.

If you have a Bible nearby, open up to Psalm 18. The first three verses are an exultant expression of praise. In verses 4-5, David describes his fall into the valley. Verse 6 is his cry to God for help. In this psalm David doesn't point to the delay period, but it took many years of praying before he could write Psalm 18. Writing from the mountaintop, Psalm 18 sounds like David's prayers were answered by God quite promptly. A study of his life, however, reveals many years of waiting before God answered.

Verses 7-19 of Psalm 18 contain the Bible's most graphic depiction of what happens when God answers our prayers. See with what indignation God rises up to vindicate His beloved ones! Oh, just go ahead and celebrate your way through the entire Psalm. Thank God for answered prayer!

## Double-Minded?

In the thick of my own personal darkness, when it seemed that God wasn't hearing any of my prayers, I really struggled to find any sort of faith in my heart for deliverance. As I considered my lack of faith, there was one passage in the Book of James that really disturbed me:

> But let him ask in faith, with no doubting, for he who doubts is like a wave of the sea driven and tossed by the wind. For let not that man suppose that he will receive anything from the Lord; he is a double-minded man, unstable in all his ways (James 1:6-8).

I thought to myself, "Oh no! I'm an unbelieving believer. Does that make me double-minded? If so, I won't ever receive anything from God. Which means I'm doomed!" I experienced considerable distress over this until the Lord helped my understanding.

The Lord helped me to see that others who experienced times of darkness also appeared to be double-minded. For example, during his darkness David wrote, "How long will You hide Your face from me? How long shall I take counsel in my soul, having sorrow in my heart daily? ...I will sing to the Lord, because He has dealt bountifully with me" (Psalm 13:1-2,6). Sounds to me like David can't make up his mind. Has God hidden His face from him, or has God dealt bountifully with him? Is David sorrowful, or singing? That could appear on the surface to be double-mindedness.

When you look at the writings of Job and some of the Psalms, there are such mood swings as to give the impression the person is almost schizophrenic.

The psalmist says, "In the multitude of my anxieties within me, Your comforts delight my soul" (Psalm 94:19). He's filled with anxieties, and the comforts of God are delighting his soul. This too I have known. My question was, if I experience the same dichotomy of thoughts and emotions, am I double-minded?

I've discovered that the key to being single-minded in the face of great anxieties is this: to stay focused on God alone. Just don't turn from His face, which is unbelief. Our anxieties want us to divert our eyes and expectations to some human source of help or relief. At that point we're double-minded. As long as you look to Jesus as your complete source, you're single-minded in faith.

> **I've discovered that the key to being single-minded in the face of great anxieties is this: to stay focused on God alone.**

## Assurances For Those In Darkness

If you're presently in a place of spiritual darkness, and you can't see or understand anything that's going on right now, let me dedicate the final thoughts of this chapter to you. You may not feel very hope-filled right now, but receive these assurances as prophetic declarations over your life.

Here's a promise I held to my heart when I read it: "Even in darkness light dawns for the upright, for the gracious and compassionate and righteous man" (Psalm 112:4). The only thing I need to give myself to, according to this verse, is righteousness and gracious compassion. The dawn will inevitably come.

The Lord knows the time when He will visit you. The Scriptures urge us to "keep this commandment without spot, blameless until our Lord Jesus Christ's appearing, which He will manifest **in His own time**" (1 Timothy 6:14-15). As you devote yourself to keeping His commandments blamelessly, He will appear to you, and His light will shine upon you — "in His own time."

The best advice I know to give is, immerse yourself in the word of God. 2 Peter 1:19 says, "And so we have the prophetic word confirmed, which you do well to heed as a light that shines in a dark place, until the day dawns and the morning star rises in your hearts." Peter is referring to the written Scriptures. When you're in need of illumination, the Scriptures will bring you light — if you search them diligently and devotionally. You, too, will discover that His word is a lamp to your feet in the time of darkness (Psalm 119:105).

Give yourself to prayer and the word until God speaks to you. The thing we long for, breathe for, pant for, wait for, is a word that proceeds from the mouth of God. When a word proceeds from God's mouth, it will always accomplish the purpose for which God sends it (Isaiah 55:10-11) because it is the most powerful entity in and beyond the entire uni-

verse. It created the universe. When God speaks, your faith or coopera-
tion or resistance are irrelevant. When God speaks, everything changes.
It is impossible for a word to

> **When God speaks, everything changes.**

come from God's mouth and
then be inhibited by any other
factor, be it demonic resistance,
human carnality or unbelief, the laws of nature, etc. This word is un-
stoppable. Either you submit to it or are crushed by it. There is only one
reason why evil prevails on our planet and why the forces of darkness
appear to have the upper hand: Jesus is keeping His mouth shut. We're
seeing sparks of revival in certain places of the world because Jesus let a
tiny syllable slip from His mouth. Heaven and hell do not realize how
totally unprepared they are for the sword that proceeds from the mouth
of the rider on the white horse. All of human history will be wrapped up
as a napkin, simply by the force of the words of His mouth. The inter-
cessory church waits with longing upon the mouth of the Lord Jesus
Christ. "Say it, Lord!" The same power that initiated human history
will also consummate human history. The mouth that said, "Let there be
light," will once again speak to the darkness of the human predicament
with the same words, and darkness will be vanquished.

## Morning Light

There are two Scriptures that specifically link the idea of physical
healing with the breaking of the morning light. If your darkness is re-
lated to sickness or physical infirmity, then look at these wonderful verses:

> Then your light shall break forth like the morning, your heal-
> ing shall spring forth speedily, and your righteousness shall
> go before you; the glory of the LORD shall be your rear guard
> (Isaiah 58:8).
> But to you who fear My name the Sun of Righteousness shall
> arise with healing in His wings; and you shall go out and grow
> fat like stall-fed calves (Malachi 4:2).

The passages that surround those verses are tremendous and worthy
of contemplation. I declare this to you who are sick, afflicted, handi-
capped, or infirm: The Lord Jesus shall arise on your darkness like the
dawning of a new day, and as He arises in your heart He will come with
healing in His wings. Your Healer comes to you on the wings of the
morning. Can't you just see yourself as a stall-fed calf? Hallelujah!

> Do not gloat over me, my enemy! Though I have fallen, I will
> rise. Though I sit in darkness, the LORD will be my light
> (Micah 7:8).

# JESUS' TEACHINGS ON DELAY

*"My master is delaying his coming"* (Matthew 24:48).

I believe that the final authority on any issue is the Lord Jesus Christ Himself, and so if a truth is scriptural, I like to find it somehow in the life and ministry of Jesus. So let's ask the question, "Do Jesus' teachings reinforce the idea that God delays His answers in order to refine our lives?" As it turns out, Jesus has a lot to say about delay.

Somebody might argue, "I don't think you can substantiate this idea of delayed answers in the life of Jesus. There was no delay when Jesus ministered on earth. He healed people without delay. Whenever He prayed for something He got it right away. You can't find delay in the ministry of Jesus." Absolutely not true — there was a 400-year delay! For 400 agonizing years, there was no prophetic voice in the land. John the Baptist was the voice that broke the silence, preparing the people for God's visitation. Then came Jesus, in the glory and beauty of fulfilled promises. The wait was agonizing, but when Jesus finally came, the visitation was glorious.

## Delay During Jesus' Ministry

There were times during Jesus' ministry when He was delayed from intervening immediately, and at other times He purposely stalled when it was time to move out. As we look for "delayed answers" in the life and ministry of Jesus, let's start with the raising of Jairus's daughter. Allow me to reproduce the story here in full:

> Mark 5:21 Now when Jesus had crossed over again by boat to the other side, a great multitude gathered to Him; and He was

by the sea.  22 And behold, one of the rulers of the synagogue came, Jairus by name. And when he saw Him, he fell at His feet  23 and begged Him earnestly, saying, "My little daughter lies at the point of death. Come and lay Your hands on her, that she may be healed, and she will live."  24 So Jesus went with him, and a great multitude followed Him and thronged Him.  25 Now a certain woman had a flow of blood for twelve years,  26 and had suffered many things from many physicians. She had spent all that she had and was no better, but rather grew worse.  27 When she heard about Jesus, she came behind Him in the crowd and touched His garment.  28 For she said, "If only I may touch His clothes, I shall be made well."  29 Immediately the fountain of her blood was dried up, and she felt in her body that she was healed of the affliction.  30 And Jesus, immediately knowing in Himself that power had gone out of Him, turned around in the crowd and said, "Who touched My clothes?"  31 But His disciples said to Him, "You see the multitude thronging You, and You say, Who touched Me?'"  32 And He looked around to see her who had done this thing.  33 But the woman, fearing and trembling, knowing what had happened to her, came and fell down before Him and told Him the whole truth.  34 And He said to her, 'Daughter, your faith has made you well. Go in peace, and be healed of your affliction."  35 While He was still speaking, some came from the ruler of the synagogue's house who said, "Your daughter is dead. Why trouble the Teacher any further?"  36 As soon as Jesus heard the word that was spoken, He said to the ruler of the synagogue, 'Do not be afraid; only believe."  37 And He permitted no one to follow Him except Peter, James, and John the brother of James.  38 Then He came to the house of the ruler of the synagogue, and saw a tumult and those who wept and wailed loudly.  39 When He came in, He said to them, "Why make this commotion and weep? The child is not dead, but sleeping."  40 And they ridiculed Him. But when He had put them all outside, He took the father and the mother of the child, and those who were with Him, and entered where the child was lying.  41 Then He took the child by the hand, and said to her, 'Talitha, cumi,"which is translated, 'Little girl, I say to you, arise."  42 Immediately the girl arose and walked, for she was twelve years of age. And they were overcome with great amazement.  43 But He commanded them strictly that no one should know it, and said that something should be given her to eat.

One of the first things you may notice from this passage is that Jesus' ministry to this sick little girl was delayed. Every symptom was crying out, "Hurry, we've got to deal with this fast. Get Jesus over here right now!" Jairus was watching his daughter's health deteriorate rapidly, and he knew she didn't have much time unless Jesus came quickly. So Jairus tried to communicate to Jesus the urgency of the moment: "My little daughter lies at the point of death" (verse 23). He was basically saying, "Please don't procrastinate or get side-tracked, Lord. If You don't get to my daughter soon, she's going to die!"

Jesus doesn't seem to pay much attention to Jairus's distress level, however. He loved the people too much to ignore their needs during the walk to Jairus's house. So while on the road to this very sick girl, He slowed the pace down so He could minister to the crowds who thronged Him.

There's one situation in particular that slows Jesus down. It's a woman with a hemorrage who had been losing blood for twelve years. No doubt she was quite feeble because of her anemia, but she had such faith in the Lord Jesus that she forced herself to press through the crowd in order to touch Jesus' garment. She is gloriously healed, but in the process of acknowledging her healing and comforting her, the Lord experiences a significant time delay in the journey.

The slow pace of the throng, together with the delay over this woman's healing, ended up making Jesus too late. The little girl couldn't hang on any longer, and she died. Jairus's prayer was not answered because Jesus was delayed with someone else's need. As an application for us, let me suggest there are certain unique situations when our prayers aren't answered because Jesus is delayed with other dynamics in the body of Christ.

> **There are certain unique situations when our prayers aren't answered because Jesus is delayed with other dynamics in the body of Christ.**

He may not want to heal someone until He first puts something else in order in the body. If this is true, then we see the interactive and inter-dependent nature of the body of Christ.

When they told Jairus of his daughter's passing, they spoke the word of doubt. "Your daughter is dead. Why trouble the Teacher any further?" Immediately Jesus spoke to Jairus's heart with the word of faith: "Do not be afraid; only believe." Those are two extremely challenging words: "Only believe." The Lord commands us to do nothing else but believe. True faith doesn't have a contingency plan. Faith only does one thing: It only believes.

Jesus is not rattled by the ridicule of the mourners (v.40). He quietly just gets rid of them. Then He takes the parents, Peter, James, and John with Him into the house and raises the daughter from the dead. I've wondered, why did Jesus allow only three of His disciples to enjoy the glory of that moment? The answer is to be found in His teaching that to those who have, more will be given. Of the Twelve, Peter, James, and John were the most diligent to follow hard after the Lord Jesus. Their diligence qualified them for this fantastic experience. God doesn't show favoritism, but He has His favorites — He reserves the highest encounters for those who diligently seek Him and walk in abandoned obedience.

## Lazarus

One of the most dramatic and soul-stirring stories in the entire earthly ministry of Jesus is the raising of Lazarus (John 11). That miracle was so gloriously spectacular that it was the proverbial "straw that broke the camel's back" for the Jewish leaders. Lazarus's resurrection from the dead sealed the determination of the Jewish leaders to kill Jesus. He simply had to be stopped.

Such power, such authority, such glory — I daresay there is no greater miracle recorded in Scripture. And let me remind you that it was preceded by one of Jesus' purposeful delays. "So, when He heard that he was sick, He stayed two more days in the place where He was. Then after this He said to the disciples, 'Let us go to Judea again'" (John 11:6-7). Jesus planned a delay in order to show His glory. "This

> **Jesus planned a delay in order to show His glory.**

sickness is not unto death, but for the glory of God, that the Son of God may be glorified through it" (John 11:4).

Jesus raised Jairus's daughter from the dead after a delay; Jesus raised Lazarus after a delay. Mark it: Jesus' delays are a harbinger of greater glory. Is He delaying His coming to you? Get ready, there's incredible glory on the way!

> Then He came to Simon Peter. And Peter said to Him, "Lord, are You washing my feet?" Jesus answered and said to him, "What I am doing you do not understand now, but you will know after this." Peter said to Him, "You shall never wash my feet!" Jesus answered him, "If I do not wash you, you have no part with Me." Simon Peter said to Him, "Lord, not my feet only, but also my hands and my head!" (John 13:6-9).

Peter didn't understand why Jesus wanted to wash His feet. When Peter asked him why He was doing this, Jesus simply answered, "What I am doing you do not understand now, but you will know after this." Well, that wasn't enough of an answer for Peter. Since he didn't understand it right now, he wasn't going to cooperate with the thing.

This is so typical of what happens during delayed answers. We're saying, "What's going on here, Lord? You've got to explain this to me. Why haven't You answered my prayer yet?" And the Lord is simply saying, "What I am doing you do not understand now, but you will know after this."

Unless we choose to walk with the Lord in the thing, we will miss His purposes. Jesus is basically saying, "If you don't allow me to work in dimensions you presently don't understand, then you have no part with Me."

> **Jesus is basically saying, "If you don't allow me to work in dimensions you presently don't understand, then you have no part with Me."**

## Jesus' Teachings On Delay

There were times of delay in Jesus' ministry, but even more significantly, Jesus taught very pointedly on the principle of delay in the kingdom. Let's start with His teaching in the following parable:

> Luke 11:5 And He said to them, "Which of you shall have a friend, and go to him at midnight and say to him, 'Friend, lend me three loaves; 6 for a friend of mine has come to me on his journey, and I have nothing to set before him'; 7 and he will answer from within and say, 'Do not trouble me; the door is now shut, and my children are with me in bed; I cannot rise and give to you'? 8 I say to you, though he will not rise and give to him because he is his friend, yet because of his persistence he will rise and give him as many as he needs. 9 So I say to you, ask, and it will be given to you; seek, and you will find; knock, and it will be opened to you. 10 For everyone who asks receives, and he who seeks finds, and to him who knocks it will be opened."

The friend in this parable hesitates to get out of bed and get three loaves for his neighbor. He tries to deny his neighbor, but since he will not relent but persistently keeps hammering at the door, finally the friend gets out of bed and supplies his request. The net effect, however, is a delayed answer.

So in verses 9-10, Jesus teaches us about delayed answers and what to do when the answer to our prayers is not immediately forthcoming. Notice that He doesn't tell us to cool our jets and learn to rest in the Lord. No, He tells us to ask, to seek, and to knock. The verb tense could be translated like this: "Ask, and keep on asking; seek, and keep on seeking; knock, and keep on knocking." Here Jesus commends persistence and importunity.

> **Jesus teaches us about delayed answers and what to do when the answer to our prayers is not immediately forthcoming.**

**Ask**: Ask Him for the thing you want. Is it a deliverance? A healing? A provision? A miracle? "It will be given to you." Some have incorrectly taught that we should not seek God's hand, but rather seek His face only. Both, in actuality, are scriptural. "Behold, as the eyes of servants look to the hand of their masters, as the eyes of a maid to the hand of her mistress, so our eyes look to the LORD our God, until He has mercy on us" (Psalm 123:2). God's hand represents His provisions and blessings. Jesus affirms this principle of seeking God's hand by encouraging us to ask for divine gifts.

**Seek**: Seek His face. This is not simply the seeking of relief but the seeking of a living relationship with Him. Seek to know Him better. Seek to understand His purposes in the present hour. When you gain Christ, you gain everything! Do you seek the Spirit of wisdom and revelation to know Him better? "You will find."

**Knock**: A door in the New Testament usually refers to the opening of God's will for the individual. Knock until you discover God's will. Knock until the next step opens up before you. Do you long to know which threshold God has for you to cross at this time? Don't quit knocking because "It will be opened to you."

## To Be Found Watching

As you read the following teaching of Jesus on delay, it's obvious that Jesus is referring primarily to His second coming. But I would like to apply it (as a secondary application) to waiting for delayed answers:

> Luke 12:35, "Let your waist be girded and your lamps burning; 36 and you yourselves be like men who wait for their master, when he will return from the wedding, that when he comes and knocks they may open to him immediately. 37 Blessed are those servants whom the master, when he comes, will find watching. Assuredly, I say to you that he will gird himself and have them sit down to eat, and will come and

serve them. 38 And if he should come in the second watch, or come in the third watch, and find them so, blessed are those servants. 39 But know this, that if the master of the house had known what hour the thief would come, he would have watched and not allowed his house to be broken into. 40 Therefore you also be ready, for the Son of Man is coming at an hour you do not expect."

As already stated, this teaching refers primarily to Christ's second coming. But I'm suggesting it can also be instructive for the one who is waiting for Jesus to come to him in deliverance power, and Christ's coming is delayed. Jesus is going to come and answer our prayers, but we just don't know when His coming will be. The promise is, "the Son of Man is coming," and we hold dearly to that assurance of answered prayer. But He's coming "at an hour you do not expect."

While we're waiting for Jesus to show up, what should we do? Jesus instructs us to give ourselves to vigilant watchfulness. Verse 37 pronounces a marvelous blessing upon the one who is found watching and waiting when the Lord comes to him: "Blessed are those servants whom the master, when he comes, will find watching." This speaks of intense, prayerful alertness in the Spirit.

What is the blessing of vigilant watchfulness? Jesus tells us: "Assuredly, I say to you that he will gird himself and have them sit down to eat, and will come and serve them." Imagine having Jesus come to you and serve you at His table! The assurance is that Jesus Himself will spread a table for that beloved saint, and He Himself will feed and serve him.

## The Unjust Judge

Luke records another parable of Christ's that is intriguingly similar to Luke 11:5-8 which is quoted above. It's the parable of the unjust judge, and it's intended to teach the need for persistence in prayer when the answer is not instantaneous:

Luke 18:1, Then He spoke a parable to them, that men always ought to pray and not lose heart, 2 saying: "There was in a certain city a judge who did not fear God nor regard man. 3 Now there was a widow in that city; and she came to him, saying, 'Get justice for me from my adversary.' 4 And he would not for a while; but afterward he said within himself, 'Though I do not fear God nor regard man, 5 yet because this widow troubles me I will avenge her, lest by her continual coming she weary me.'" 6 Then the Lord said, "Hear what the unjust judge said. 7 And shall God not avenge His own elect who cry out day and night to Him, though He bears long with them? 8 I tell you that He will avenge them speedily. Nevertheless, when the Son of Man comes, will He really find faith on the earth?"

Jesus is explicitly addressing the matter of delayed answers in this parable. He is affirming that there are times when God designs a delay in order to produce a specific work in us through the pain of unresolved suffering. His purpose is that we maintain our persistence and intensity of cry until His work is complete in us. It's the crying out to God day and night that qualifies God's elect to enter into His fuller purposes. To quit is to forfeit.

When Jesus says that God "bears long with them," He is describing the season of delay. When Jesus says, "He will avenge them speedily," He is describing the provision. Even though God delays His answers at times, He never waits too long.

> He waits as long as is necessary, but when the season of delay is complete and the intended work in our hearts is perfected, He acts most swiftly and sends His answer "speedily."

He waits as long as is necessary, but when the season of delay is complete and the intended work in our hearts is perfected, He acts most swiftly and sends His answer "speedily." Perhaps you've been waiting for a long time, but when God finally moves on your behalf, you may well be shocked at how suddenly everything changes for you.

In the face of delayed answers, it takes great faith to persevere in seeking only the face of God — to "cry out day and night to Him." Because your mind will imagine all kinds of other possible sources of relief you could conceivably pursue. Your creativity will spring to life, and it will in fact militate against your faith. There are many who give up the pursuit of God at this point, their faith collapses, and they seek out another source of help. It is in the context of addressing that kind of discouragement that Jesus asks, "Nevertheless, when the Son of Man comes, will He really find faith on the earth?" The question is not, will He find saving faith, but will He find the kind of faith that insists on seeking only God in the face of delayed answers?

During the crisis period of waiting, when everything screams at you, "You must do something **now**!", it takes great faith to keep your expectation on God alone. Will this caliber of faith be found among the saints at Christ's return?

## Parable Of The Ten Virgins

The parable of the ten virgins (Matthew 25:1-13) is one of the most controversial parables of Jesus' ministry, particularly because its typology is not explained. It's left up to interpreters to figure out what Jesus meant, and so we have a wide variety of interpretations on the parable.

I've got two reasons for not trying to interpret this parable: 1) I don't want to broadcast my ignorance; 2) I have this hunch that we won't fully understand this parable until we're living in the day which it specifically describes.

But I will point out that the entire parable is couched against the backdrop of "the great delay." We are living in that period, in the day when Christ's return is delayed. This is how Jesus put it in the parable: "But while the bridegroom was delayed, they all slumbered and slept" (Matthew 25:5).

During this hour of Christ's delayed return, it is so tempting for believers to fall asleep from grief and weariness. Jesus concludes the parable by warning us, "Watch therefore, for you know neither the day nor the hour in which the Son of Man is coming" (Matthew 25:13). Understanding that His coming is delayed, Christ urges us to attentive watchfulness. We must not allow the delay to dampen our fervency.

> **During this hour of Christ's delayed return, it is so tempting for believers to fall asleep from grief and weariness.**

## Wise Servant/Evil Servant

I would like us to look at one final parable of Christ's, which also deals with His delayed return. Delay seems to characterize everything about this present church age. See how this delay affects each of us today:

> Matthew 24:45, "Who then is a faithful and wise servant, whom his master made ruler over his household, to give them food in due season? 46 Blessed is that servant whom his master, when he comes, will find so doing. 47 Assuredly, I say to you that he will make him ruler over all his goods. 48 But if that evil servant says in his heart, 'My master is delaying his coming,' 49 and begins to beat his fellow servants, and to eat and drink with the drunkards, 50 the master of that servant will come on a day when he is not looking for him and at an hour that he is not aware of, 51 and will cut him in two and appoint him his portion with the hypocrites. There shall be weeping and gnashing of teeth."

Verse 45 describes the role of many pastors today. Pastors are called to rule in the fear of God and to feed the flock of God. Verse 46 pronounces a great blessing upon the faithful servants of God who persevere during this present hour while Christ's coming is delayed.

This parable refers primarily to the delay of Christ's return, but there is a secondary application here to the fire of delayed answers. When we're seeking God for His intervention into our crisis, and the answer is delayed, our souls come into great testing. Will we lose heart, or will we continue to be faithful to our responsibilities and feed those entrusted to our spiritual care? "Blessed is that servant whom his master, when he comes, will find so doing." Blessed is that servant who is found faithful at the moment of God's visitation. When God comes to you in order to answer your prayers and wipe away your tears, how blessed you will be if He finds you standing faithfully at your post.

"Assuredly, I say to you that he will make him ruler over all his goods" — He will honor you, lift you up, restore your song, and entrust you with greater responsibility in the kingdom.

Jesus then goes on to describe the evil response — the evil servant who says, "My master is delaying his coming." These are words of bitterness and cynicism. Notice that the evil servant loses two things during the season of delay: He loses his heart for the household, and he surrenders his self-control.

> **Notice that the evil servant loses two things during the season of delay: He loses his heart for the household, and he surrenders his self-control.**

In other words, he gets an attitude about the church, and he succumbs to sinful temptation.

I want to suggest that the evil servant didn't begin to beat his fellow servants and turn to profligacy because he thought, "Maybe I can get away with this." Rather, he became bitter toward and disillusioned with the Master. The evil servant is complaining, "What's the use of serving Him, anyways? Where has it gotten me to stay true to Him all this time? As far as I'm concerned, His return is long overdue. I can't handle this time delay any longer. How can He say He cares for us when He stays away so long? There's no point in serving Him; I'll probably die before He answers my prayers — if He answers them at all. I may as well quit this living for the future, and enjoy today." It's the attitude of 1 Corinthians 15:32, "Let us eat and drink, for tomorrow we die!"

My heart is sobered, lest, during the season of delay, I take on the disillusionment of the evil servant.

How do I guard my heart against that kind of bitter disillusionment?

The answer is in 2 Timothy 4:8, "Finally, there is laid up for me the crown of righteousness, which the Lord, the righteous Judge, will give to me on that Day, and not to me only but also to all who have loved His appearing." The key is in continually giving my heart fervently and passionately to my Master, and setting the affections of my heart upon His return. If I'm longing for Him, and loving Him, He will appear to me and crown me with His righteous goodness.

# COMFORT FOR
# THE AFFLICTED

*"I have tested you in the furnace of affliction"* (Isaiah 48:10).

I used to believe that God never used physical affliction and infirmity to do a spiritual work in the hearts of His people. I was taught that God has many means at His disposal to deepen our love and purify our faith, such as persecution and daily trials, and sickness and infirmity were not among those tools. Affliction and illness always come from the hand of the enemy, I was told, and Christ would never send those things our way because He died to deliver us from all those works of the enemy. So sickness is never God's will for the saint, and if it lingers then there's something wrong. These were things I believed and preached — until infirmity hit me.

Before I go further, let me clarify that I believe it is God's will to heal today. Period. But the Lord has adjusted my theology in this area and has specifically helped me to see how that affliction and infirmity are useful tools in His hand to refine His servants.

## There Must Be More

Infirmity came to me at a time when I was feeling spiritually dry. I felt like I was bumping my head on a ceiling, spiritually speaking. I knew there was more in God than what I had experienced, but I couldn't seem to touch it. I was dissatisfied with my walk with God and longed for a greater dimension of kingdom relationship and living. I was doing everything I knew to do, and I had no idea how to move into the deeper things of God. At that time, a deep cry rose up in my heart, and I sought the Lord fervently for a fuller experience in Him. In restrospect, I realize that that cry was placed in my heart by God. He put the cry there, and

He destined an answer to that cry.

God's answer for me was to lead me into a great spiritual wilderness, launched through physical infirmity. Suddenly I found myself in a place of crisis. God had allowed me to be physically handicapped with an infirmity, the doctors said there was nothing more they could do, everything I had ever lived for and

> **Everything I had ever lived for and worked toward was at jeopardy.**

worked toward was at jeopardy, and I had absolutely no clue why this devastation and debilitation was hitting my life.

I went through many many months of great darkness, as I wrestled with God and pressed into Him to try to understand what He was doing in my life. Understanding started to come gradually, and I wrote about those early insights in my previous book, <u>In His Face</u>. Actually, that book was written from the valley, from the place of emotional distress. Many people who address issues related to depression do so from a place of strength, but the Lord led me to write from the place of weakness and crisis. I have nothing to lose, so I have chosen in my writings to be as sincere and honest as I know to be.

Now, as I write this book, I am still under the same physical constraints of this infirmity (I'm not healed yet as this book goes to publication), but the Lord has lifted me out of the depths of the emotional valley. It's almost four years since I was injured, and I am now coming to a place of emotional equilibrium in the grace of God. Nevertheless, my distress continues to be very real, and I cry out to God daily for His purposes to be fulfilled in my life.

## Precious Insight

As I have pressed into the heart of God, the Lord has slowly unfolded an understanding of His purposes in allowing physical affliction to build character in us. Now, I am not saying that all sickness and infirmity is intended by God to produce character in us. Far from it. A lot of sickness is downright devilish, accomplishing nothing but destruction in us, and in such instances God desires that we appropriate the provision of Calvary for divine healing. There are times, however, when God will give Satan permission to touch us (Job is an example), and He will not bring an immediate solution because He intends for the crisis to produce something deep in our hearts. Again, I had no room for that in my theology until my experience forced me to re-examine what I believed.

Following are some of the insights the Lord gave me as I sought Him for answers. These insights did not come to me by doing word studies or by preparing sermons. These insights came to me as my daily bread, food from heaven that literally kept me alive in my season of crisis. There were times when I felt like I would have gone insane had it not been for the word of God! "Unless Your law had been my delight, I would then have perished in my affliction" (Psalm 119:92). These truths kept me alive, and I pray that they will minister life to you as well.

## Sometimes God Uses Affliction To Bring Us Back To Obedience

Although it is not the focus of this book, it's true that the Lord uses affliction at times to correct disobedience. When God spanks His way-ward children, He often uses affliction. God does not discipline us simply to punish us for wrong behavior, but rather to restore us to right behavior. "Before I was afflicted I went astray, but now I keep Your word" (Psalm 119:67).

> God does not discipline us simply to punish us for wrong behavior, but rather to restore us to right behavior.

We must come to the place where we realize that God's discipline is always for the good. "It is good for me that I have been afflicted, that I may learn Your statutes" (Psalm 119:71).

When affliction strikes, it's wise to let your first response be one of broken repentance. Ask the Holy Spirit to search your heart and reveal any way in which your life may be out of order. But do not assume, as many do, that the presence of affliction automatically means that you need to repent of something. That was the wrong assumption Job's three friends made, and they incurred God's anger because of it. Although it does come to us very often because of our disobedience, affliction can come for other reasons as well.

Paul told the Corinthians that some of them were weak and sick, even to the point of death, because they were eating and drinking of the Lord's table "in an unworthy manner" (1 Corinthians 11:27).

> 1 Corinthians 11:27, Therefore whoever eats this bread or drinks this cup of the Lord in an unworthy manner will be guilty of the body and blood of the Lord. 28 But let a man examine himself, and so let him eat of the bread and drink of the cup. 29 For he who eats and drinks in an unworthy manner eats and drinks judgment to himself, not discerning the Lord's body. 30 For this reason many are weak and sick among you, and many sleep. 31 For if we would judge ourselves, we would not be judged. 32 But when we are judged, we are

chastened by the Lord, that we may not be condemned with
the world.

This passage bears out four important principles:
1) As a result of their sin, they were being judged or chastened
   by the Lord (v.32).
2) The Lord's chastening was coming in the form of physical
   infirmity (verse 30).
3) The Lord's purpose in this affliction, however, was to stimu-
   late them toward self-examination and repentance (verse 28).
4) God doesn't afflict in order to condemn us (verse 32), but in
   order that we might be saved.

The Scriptures testify, "For he who has suffered in the flesh has
ceased from sin, that he no longer should live the rest of his time in the
flesh for the lusts of men, but for the will of God" (1 Peter 4:1-2). Physi-
cal affliction (suffering in the flesh) is instrumental in the hands of God
to help us cease from sin. Pain can be an effective motivator toward
obedience.

## Sometimes God Uses Affliction To Bring Us To A Greater Knowledge Of Christ

Affliction naturally produces desperation within us. Some people
respond by trying to survive. Others respond by lashing out at every-
thing within reach. Others collapse and live in a state of depression.
God purposes, however, that we channel that desperation toward a fer-
vent pursuit of His face.

Jesus modelled this for us: "And being in agony, He prayed more
earnestly" (Luke 22:44). How
did Jesus respond when the pain
increased? He sought God more
earnestly. This is what God
wants you to do. If you're re-
ally hurting, not only is this the safe response, it's the response that Jesus
demonstrated.

> **How did Jesus respond when the pain increased? He sought God more earnestly.**

If you allow your desperation to push you into Christ, you will come
to know Him in a profoundly new and intimate way. The apostle Paul
experienced this, writing of it during his second imprisonment in this
way: "For this reason I also suffer these things; nevertheless I am not
ashamed, for I know whom I have believed and am persuaded that He is
able to keep what I have committed to Him until that Day" (2 Timothy
1:12). Because of his sufferings, he is able to say, "I know whom I have
believed." First he believed, then he came to know. It's interesting to

note that during his first imprisonment he describes the knowing of Christ as still a personal goal (see Philippians 3:8-14); but here in his second imprisonment he speaks of it as an attainment (see 2 Timothy 1:12 above). Paul has come to the place where he can say, "I know Him." He is incarcerated, demeaned, shackled, subject to ignominious circumstances in a dungeon, exposed to ridicule and scorn, but there is one thing that causes him to be not ashamed: He knows Jesus!

To know Christ is the greatest of all attainments. Allow affliction, like Paul did, to press you into the face of Christ.

Peter addresses this at length in his first epistle, and most notably in the opening verses of that book: "In this you greatly rejoice, though now for a little while, if need be, you have been grieved by various trials, that the genuineness of your faith, being much more precious than gold that perishes, though it is tested by fire, may be found to praise, honor, and glory at the revelation of Jesus Christ" (1 Peter 1:6-7). Affliction turns up the heat on our faith, Peter says, so that our faith will come through the fire purified and strengthened.

When the Lord rebukes and disciplines us for our unbelief, our first inclination is to despair over our hardness of heart. "Oh Lord, I'm such a mess! I'm such a failure! Is there any hope for my unbelieving heart?" As the Lord has turned up the heat in my life, and brought to the surface the impurities in my heart I had never seen before, I have often found myself responding with despair. "Am I a lost cause, Lord? The more I'm with You, the more glaring my shortcomings become!" The Lord had to remind me of Hebrews 12:5, "Nor be discouraged when you are rebuked by Him." The Lord doesn't rebuke or chasten me in order to cause me to despair but to purify my faith. I must believe that somehow in the rebuke and discipline the Lord is accomplishing in me what I cannot do for myself.

Jesus gave us this wonderful promise, "Behold, I give you the authority to trample on serpents and scorpions, and over all the power of the enemy, and nothing shall by any means hurt you" (Luke 10:19). The young believer picks that verse up, steps forward into the battle with great zeal — and gets knocked out! "I thought Jesus said nothing would hurt me!" the wounded believer cries. He has yet to learn that Jesus didn't promise us immunity from battle scars. We will get wounded in the battle, but our wounds will never truly hurt us. Instead of harming us, those wounds (afflictions) will season us and turn us into veteran soldiers. Stephen got stoned, but he wasn't really

> **Instead of harming us, those wounds (afflictions) will season us and turn us into veteran soldiers.**

hurt. The stoning ushered him into the marvelous privilege of martyr-
dom and eternal glory. Paul suffered lashings, muggings, harassment,
and deprivation, but none of those things really hurt him in the final
analysis. Instead, they qualified him for greater glory.

When moving out against the powers of darkness, we have to be-
lieve that the promise of Jesus still stands: There is no pain or suffering
sustained in the battle which actually hurts us. It takes great faith to
fully embrace this, and this dimension of faith is gained only after we've
sustained battle wounds and come out the better for it.

## Sometimes God Uses Affliction To Bring Us To Greater Spiritual Maturity

God did not create pain and sickness in order to cultivate maturity
in His people. Sickness and pain are products of sin and the curse. God
is the Master Redeemer, however, and He redeems evil circumstances,
causing them to further His purposes. When pain hits us, God designs
that we allow it to propel us into His face. Calamity can thus become a
catalyst for accelerated spiritual growth. God's intention is not to keep
us interminably in the crisis but to use it to establish His kingdom rule in
our lives here on earth, even as it is in heaven (there is no sickness or
pain in heaven).

Satan is always seeking to afflict the people of God. Most of the
time God does not allow him to touch us. Occasionally, however, God
gives him permission. Satan's goal is to disorient and derail us, but
God's goal is to perfect us. It's a gamble for Satan, but he is always a
willing accomplice to afflict God's people. Many will become discour-
aged and immobilized with severe affliction, and in this he celebrates
gleefully. A few, however, will respond by seeking after God. In such cases, affliction back-fires horribly on the enemy, for it thus becomes a catalyst for great growth and maturity in the heart of the saint, equipping him to become a most lethal weapon in the hand of God.

In such cases, affliction back-
fires horribly on the enemy, for
it thus becomes a catalyst for
great growth and maturity in
the heart of the saint, equipping
him to become a most lethal
weapon in the hand of God.

Three New Testament epistles describe this process of maturity (fruit-
fulness) in such a succinct way that they give us a bird's-eye view of how
this process looks. I will quote each passage, and then below the pas-
sage I will put a diagram that outlines the process clearly. Each of these
diagrams is a self-contained sermon.

And not only that, but we also glory in tribulations, knowing that tribulation produces perseverance; and perseverance, character; and character, hope (Romans 5:3-4).

**tribulations ➔ perseverance ➔ character (maturity) ➔ hope**

My brethren, count it all joy when you fall into various trials, knowing that the testing of your faith produces patience. But let patience have its perfect work, that you may be perfect [mature] and complete, lacking nothing (James 1:2-4).

**fall into trials ➔ testing of faith ➔ perseverance ➔ maturity**

But also for this very reason, giving all diligence, add to your faith virtue, to virtue knowledge, to knowledge self-control, to self-control perseverance, to perseverance godliness, to godliness brotherly kindness, and to brotherly kindness love. For if these things are yours and abound, you will be neither barren nor unfruitful in the knowledge of our Lord Jesus Christ (2 Peter 1:5-8).

> **faith**
> **+ virtue**
> **+ knowledge**
> **+ self-control**
> **+ perseverance**
> **+ godliness**
> **+ brotherly kindness**
> _____
> **+ love**
> **= fruitfulness**
> **(maturity)**

Notice that perseverance is a vital ingredient in all three diagrams. There is no pathway to spiritual maturity apart from perseverance. And there is no perseverance without pressures. Fruitfulness is found only as we endure through crisis and hardship.

In speaking of this kind of affliction that produces maturity, Lamentations 3:27 says, "It is good for a man to bear the yoke in his youth." "The yoke" is a reference to the chafing restriction that the Lord will place on the neck of those who are harnessed to Him in order that they

> **It is a good thing when God puts a headlock on a man while he is still young, bringing him into great restriction contrary to his will, so that he can enter into a maturity that exceeds his years, and thus have many years of fruitful ministry.**

might learn to come in step with the Lord Jesus and thus grow into greater fruitfulness. Not only is it good when this yoke is embraced, but it is good when it is embraced in one's youth. In other words, "It is a good thing when God puts a headlock on a man while he is still young, bringing him into great restriction contrary to his will, so that he can enter into a maturity that exceeds his years, and thus have many years of fruitful ministry."

Psalm 102 is a marvelous psalm for meditation by the afflicted. The writer of Psalm 102 describes what he's about to write with the following title: "A Prayer of the afflicted, when he is overwhelmed and pours out his complaint before the Lord." In this psalm, the writer describes an experience very similar to that of Lamentations 3:27 in the above paragraph. He writes, "He weakened my strength in the way; He shortened my days. O my God, do not take me away in the midst of my days" (verses 23-24). He's basically praying the cry of Hezekiah, "Lord, you're taking me away in the prime of my life! I'm too young for this." And yet in verse 28 the psalmist concludes with a declaration that God will bring fruitfulness out of seeming death: "The children of Your servants will continue. And their descendants will be established before You." This is the Lord's assurance to us, that no matter how devastating the affliction seems to be, God has a destiny of fruitfulness prepared for us.

I have discovered that Jesus never imposes this painful process upon us. Instead, He cultivates within us a great dissatisfaction and a deep cry for something higher and greater than we've ever experienced. Then, He answers that prayer. We have no idea how the answer will come, but bottom line, we ask for it. If He answers that prayer, it is because somehow He has found us worthy of this great mercy.

## Sometimes God Uses Affliction To Bring Us To A Place Of Greater Dependence And Brokenness

One morning, while I was feeling particularly crushed by the Lord, my thoughts were directed to Psalm 16:8 and Isaiah 53:10. Isaiah 53:10 describes the suffering Savior with these words, "Yet it pleased the Lord to bruise Him; He has put Him to grief." I was surprised to discover that the margin reading for "bruise" is "crush." "It pleased the Lord to crush Him." That statement does not mean God gained personal satisfaction from crushing His Son — far from it — that crushing was absolutely agonizing to the Father. And yet, it was the Father's pleasure to crush His Son because of what that crushing would produce. When Jesus hurt, the Father hurt. In the same way, God identifies with us in our pain — "In all their affliction He was afflicted" (Isaiah 63:9). The Father doesn't enjoy the process of afflicting us, but He is pleased with the product. Just as Jesus surrendered to the Father's crushing, so we should submit as well. When you're in that place of crushing, you feel like absolutely everything has been stripped away from you. And yet look at the assurance of Psalm 16:8, "I have set the Lord always before me; because He is at my right hand I shall not be moved." I might be broken and crushed, but I won't be moved. If I set the Lord always before me, I'll come through the breaking and will still be standing.

God wants to annihilate our inbred tendency to depend upon our own innate strengths. This is no small task and requires great breaking in our lives. We naturally think far too highly of ourselves. The Scripture says, "to God who alone is wise" (1 Timothy 1:17). So where does that put the rest of us? In the dumb camp. I have viewed myself as getting wiser the more I mature in God, but it's just not true. The only wisdom I have is that which I receive, day by day, moment by moment. Jesus has been made our wisdom, and we have wisdom only to the degree that Christ possesses us. Real wisdom is realizing our continual dependence upon God to give us His wisdom moment by moment.

> **I have viewed myself as getting wiser the more I mature in God, but it's just not true. The only wisdom I have is that which I receive, day by day, moment by moment.**

The sooner I realize that I know nothing, the better. Prayer is not convincing heaven of my agenda but of submitting to heaven's agenda. Prayer has no advance agenda. The purpose of prayer is to hear the heart purposes of God, lend intercession toward that purpose, and make oneself available to the Master's purposes.

Prayer is the means by which the sincere disciple makes sure he's tracking with Jesus. In prayer we're asking, "Are You still doing what I saw You doing yesterday, Lord? Has Your direction changed over the course of this day? Are You holding back, or are You on the move?" Prayer is the self-calibration of the saint, the self-evaluation by which he determines whether he's still in step with Jesus.

We will explore this theme of brokenness further in Chapter Eight.

## Sometimes God Uses Affliction To Catapult Us Into Another Dimension In God

The greatest kindness shown Samson was not the gift of being raised by such godly parents; it was not his divine calling and anointing; it was not the power of the Spirit that flowed through him. The greatest

> **The greatest kindness shown Samson was the plucking out of his eyes.**

kindness shown Samson was the plucking out of his eyes. It wasn't until he lost his eyes that Samson truly began to see. That trauma forced him to really look into the realm of the Spirit. Samson's affliction helped usher him into the greatest exploit of his ministry.

## Sometimes God Uses Affliction To Reveal His Love For Us

If you are willing to receive it, God wants to use your season of affliction to reveal His love to you. Hebrews 12:6 tells us very clearly that chastening comes to us only because the Lord loves us so much. Job once complained, "Neither is the rod of God upon [the wicked]" (Job 21:9). "God's rod is upon the righteous," Job is saying, "but He leaves the wicked alone." Job's right. God's discipline comes to us because of His great love for us. The fact that He leaves the wicked alone is part of their judgment. His correction truly is an expression of His love.

Not only does he want you to feel His love for you at this difficult time; He also wants to perfect your love for Him. If you'll seek His face, you'll find yourself coming to the place where you're saying, "I'm hurting more than I've ever hurt, Lord, but I love You more than ever!"

"I know, O Lord, that Your judgments are right, and that in faithfulness You have afflicted me" (Psalm 119:75).

## Sometimes God Uses Affliction To Give Us A Greater Sense Of Compassion For Others

This was one of the first things I saw the Lord doing through my affliction. I found myself with a new-found compassion for the handicapped and the infirm. My pain has sensitized me to the pain of the world. My attitude toward depressed people was basically, "Snap out of it" — until I went through my own valley of depression.

Because of the pain I've known, I'm discovering that many people are finding it easier to relate to me. Not only do I understand them better, but they understand me better. People naturally identify with vulnerability.

A cry has been birthed deep in my heart for the Lord to minister His healing power through me to afflicted people. When you've been there, you want to touch others. This is the marvelous principle of 2 Corinthians 1:4, "who comforts us in all our tribulation, that we may be able to comfort those who are in any trouble, with the comfort with which we ourselves are comforted by God." When you've gone through something and received the grace of God for that situation, you naturally find your-self wanting to help others in similar circumstances enter into that same comfort.

I believe God wants to raise up ministers in this hour through whom He can release His healing power, but He wants to do it in such a way that His ministers aren't destroyed in the process. No normal human being can handle the accolades and attention that the masses will auto-matically give to someone with a healing ministry. As humble a profile as someone with that ministry might try to maintain, they will be given instant fame and notoriety. If such a servant

> **If such a servant is not to self-destruct, God must first do a great breaking and emptying in his heart.**

is not to self-destruct, God must first do a great breaking and emptying in his heart.

I see some very intriguing dynamics in Jesus' healing ministry. In the first place, you never see Him rejoicing when somebody gets healed. His response to people who are healed is almost diffident. His demeanor seems to say, "So you're healed — no big deal. What I'm interested in knowing is, will you do the will of the Father?" He healed the sick and then taught them to get to know the Father. Secondly, He never taught the people about divine healing, and how to get healed. He just taught them about relationship with the Father. This is where I think some healing ministries have worked against themselves. The Lord is want-ing to raise up healing ministries in this hour whose message will not be healing but the knowledge of Jesus. People will be healed, but the mes-sage they hear will be the kingdom of God. Instead of hearing, "how to get what you want from God," people will be healed and then pointed to the infinite joys of an expanding love relationship with the Lord of the universe.

## Sometimes God Uses Affliction To Encourage Others

In Colossians 1:24 Paul wrote, "I now rejoice in my sufferings for you, and fill up in my flesh what is lacking in the afflictions of Christ, for the sake of His body, which is the church." I don't think Paul was referring exclusively to his thorn in the flesh with these words, but his thorn was part of the affliction he suffered. Paul was saying, "I'm suf-fering affliction for the sake of the church." He's not suffering affliction simply for the sake of staying humble, or of being further purified in God's grace. He's found a purpose in suffering that surpasses his own little world and realizes that his suffering is for the purpose of benefitting the body of Christ. It's one thing to suffer if you see that God is changing you because of it. It's another thing to suffer when it's accomplishing nothing but pain in you but is, nevertheless, accomplishing life in the body of Christ. This is Paul's description of the ministry: "Death in me, life in you." Paul's suffering benefitted the church in several ways:

- He had extra time to write, producing his epistles which became his most significant contribution to the kingdom of God.
- His suffering made him relatable — he wasn't speaking from a vantage point of being untouched but from a place with which others in pain could identify.
- His suffering gave others courage to suffer.
- His suffering kept others from putting him on a pedestal, so that Christ was glorified in his life and not Paul.

## Sometimes God Uses Affliction To Remove Judgmentalism

There's no one quite as insensitive to the poor as the one who has always enjoyed wealth. There's no one quite as insensitive to the sick as someone who has always enjoyed relatively good health. There's no one quite as insensitive to the feeble as the one who has always been strong.

I never thought I was judgmental — until infirmity hit. Then the Lord began to show me how I had carried little attitudes toward weak people. When counseling people in crisis I would ask myself, "Now, what would I do in this situation?" Then I would tell them the course of action I would take if I were in their shoes. And I didn't even see my arrogance.

My underlying attitude was, "If people handled themselves the way I do, they would get out of their mess." I was so insensitive to the fact some people are caught up in trauma and crisis in which they have no control, for which they have no solution, and over which they have no power. They needed divine power and wisdom, and I was doling out my natural wisdom.

The Lord has removed from me the impulsive assumption, "I wonder what they did wrong." When someone was in crisis, my first inclination was always to discover where they had blown it. That judgmental attitude has been removed by the purifying fires of affliction in my own life.

"Mercy triumphs over judgment." God wants to produce a merciful heart within us that embraces the hurting and is totally free to touch them with the power and grace of God.

## Sometimes God Uses Affliction To Restore Real Christianity

Most believers have never experienced authentic, full-bodied Christianity. Myself included. I see it in the New Testament, but I've never yet experienced it first hand in its fullness. Christianity is designed to function under full-throttled revival. Anything less and Christianity becomes ritualistic and powerless (2 Timothy 3:5).

> **True Christianity is seen only under intense pressure.**

The book Lilies Amongst Thorns has moved me deeply. It chronicles eye-witness accounts of the revival that has been igniting the house churches of China in the past couple decades. As I read story after story of believers being imprisoned, tortured, harassed, and beaten for the name of Christ, and yet coming out gloriously victorious, I began to realize that true Christianity is seen only under intense pressure. If the New Testament had not been written during a time of great persecution, today's Chinese believers wouldn't be able to relate to it.

Real Christianity is lost when the pressures subside. Today America has only traces of real Christianity because we have been so coddled in our modern luxuries, conveniences, and ease. Our prayers are without tears; our worship is a ritual; our study of the word is done at convenience; our evangelistic efforts are embarrassing. But where there is little or no persecution, God has other ways of applying pressure to His jewels-in-the-making. I'm referring to the pressure of delayed answers.

Where there is great persecution, there is only one category of Christian: disciples (Acts 19:30). Where there is no persecution, there are two categories — believers and disciples. The westernized world has many believers and few disciples. It's sick. God be merciful to us that believers might become disciples.

One reason God sends or allows financial, physical, and family distress is because He wants the fire of delayed answers to ignite and rekindle our zeal for the Lord. Where there is no distress, Christianity mutates. It is main-

> **The purity of the early church was maintained by the fire that burned against her.**

tained in its pristine purity only under enflamed resistance. The purity of the early church was maintained by the fire that burned against her.

Jesus said to the believers in Laodicea, "'So then, because you are lukewarm, and neither cold nor hot, I will vomit you out of My mouth'" (Revelation 3:16). The church in Laodicea knew very little persecution. The climate of Laodicea was that of religious tolerance. The challenge for the Laodiceans was to serve Christ in the midst of a very permissive, hedonistic society. The Laodicean church had become lukewarm because the fires of resistance had burned low. Things became easy, their zeal became lukewarm, and their Christianity mutated.

So Jesus comes to them and says, "I counsel you to buy from Me gold refined in the fire, that you may be rich" (Revelation 3:18). He is inviting them to embrace the refining fire of delayed answers so that they might be restored to the richness of true Christianity.

The Holy Spirit wants to baptize us with fire (Matthew 3:11). One way He does that is in the fiery furnace of affliction. His purpose is to ignite within us a zeal and fervency for the Lord that will restore to us red-hot Christianity.

## Sometimes God Uses Affliction To Produce An Appetite For Heaven

The Lord wants our minds to be preoccupied with heavenly things (Colossians 3:2). Very few of us are "so heavenly minded that we're no earthly good." The majority of Christians seem to be so earthly minded that they're no heavenly good. Jesus is returning for a bride that is gazing longingly into heaven for her Bridegroom. He wants our affections to lift off the ephemeral things of this life and be placed fully on the certainty of the return of our beloved Lord Jesus.

The fires of revival that are igniting the people of China today are being fueled, interestingly enough, by an emphasis on three Bible doctrines. Could you guess which three they might be? These three doctrines are inciting the fury of the Chinese government because this message is bringing a "Kingdom revolution" to the nation. They are: the baptism of the Holy Spirit, the imminent return of Christ, and eternal judgment. Many of the Chinese believers, imprisoned for their faith, live under the urgent expectation that they will not get out of prison before Jesus returns, even though their sentence may be less than ten years. They live with heaven in their hearts, and the fruit of their focus is creating an international stir.

> **When you're living in hellish circumstances, you gain a renewed passion for heaven.**

The Lord uses affliction and adversity to renew our gaze on heaven, where it ought to be. When you're living in hellish circumstances, you gain a renewed passion for heaven. This is God's intention, and Peter talks about it in his epistle:

> 1 Peter 1:7, that the genuineness of your faith, being much more precious than gold that perishes, though it is tested by

fire, may be found to praise, honor, and glory at the revelation of Jesus Christ, 8 whom having not seen you love. Though now you do not see Him, yet believing, you rejoice with joy inexpressible and full of glory, 9 receiving the end of your faith — the salvation of your souls.

The purpose of suffering, Peter says, is so that we might gain praise, honor, and glory at the revelation of Jesus Christ (v.7), that we might be perfected in love for Jesus (v.8), and that we might gain eternal life (v.9). The purpose of affliction is not just to equip us for ministry in this life but that it might cause us to set our affections on the final product of our salvation — the salvation of our souls.

A couple chapters later, Peter once again points sufferers toward the glories of their eternal inheritance: "Beloved, do not think it strange concerning the fiery trial which is to try you, as though some strange thing happened to you; but rejoice to the extent that you partake of Christ's sufferings, that when His glory is revealed, you may also be glad with exceeding joy" (1 Peter 4:12-13).

## Sometimes God Uses Affliction To Establish A Sign Of Kingdom Visitation

In some instances of affliction, the affliction is itself a sign that points to something God is doing. This was true of Job; this was true of Paul's thorn in the flesh; and it was true of Zecharias, who was struck mute until his son John the Baptist was born. Zecharias's affliction was a sign that pointed very poignantly to the fact that God was visiting the nation.

I spent many months wrestling over what happened to me personally, wondering how I could be struck by Satan with an affliction while I was extolling God in His house. This seeming contradiction continued to haunt me until one day a personal friend of mine, Paul Stern, while talking about Zecharias made this statement: "When Zecharias came out of the presence of the Lord he was mute."

I have always taught, "The answer is in His presence. Just get into God's presence, and everything will come into proper order." Now I'm adjusting that to include this statement: "Get into the presence of God, and you may get more than you bargained for." Zecharias was rendered mute after his encounter with God, as was Ezekiel; Saul of Tarsus came away from Jesus' presence blind; Miriam got leprosy in the presence of God, as

> **Get into the presence of God, and you may get more than you bargained for.**

did Uzziah. And we could mention many others, who discovered first-hand that our God truly is a consuming fire.

Paul realized that his affliction was serving as a sign to his genera-tion of God's ways, for he wrote, "Now if we are afflicted, it is for your consolation and salvation" (2 Corinthians 1:6). Paul also wrote of his life in this way: "To the present hour we both hunger and thirst, and we are poorly clothed, and beaten, and homeless" (1 Corinthians 4:11). These words grip my soul because I find myself asking God, "Lord, why does my life not resemble Paul's in any fashion? What am I doing wrong? What am I missing?" After describing his life, Paul then adds, "There-fore I urge you, imitate me" (1 Corinthians 4:16). Paul's afflictions were a sign of what true servanthood was all about.

There will be leaders in this hour who will suffer affliction for a season, and their affliction will be a sign to the body of Christ. Their bodies and lives will be a living message. Let's be alert to the possibility of God's speaking to us in this way.

## Sometimes God Uses Affliction To Birth In Us A Radical Willingness To Obey

There was a time in Israel's history when God needed a very spe-cific kind of prophet. He needed a man who would fulfill a very unique role in the history of redemption. He would be the last of the judges and the first of the prophets. He would oversee the transition from the era of the judges to the era of the prophets.

For a prophet to move in this kind of anointing in the strategies of God, he would have to live under a highly unusual consecration. So God had to prepare the way by preparing the parents who would bring this child into the world.

How did God prepare this man's parents? By afflicting the mother. The mother's name was Hannah, and she was afflicted with barrenness. Her soul was grieved as years came and went, and she bore no children. Finally, she came to a place of such utter desperation that she made a most astounding vow before God: "Then she made a vow and said, 'O LORD of hosts, if You will indeed look on the affliction of Your maidser-vant and remember me, and not forget Your maidservant, but will give Your maidservant a male child, then I will give him to the LORD all the days of his life, and no razor shall come upon his head'" (1 Samuel 1:11).

This prayer violated every natural instinct that God had placed within Hannah as a woman. Hannah's motherly desire to nurture was overpow-ering in her soul, but she was so distraught over her barrenness that she was even willing to forego that natural human desire. She was willing to give her child over completely to God — if only He would remove from her the stigma of barrenness.

This was precisely the degree of desperation to which God wanted Hannah to come. To help bring Hannah to the end of her rope, he even incited her rival, Peninnah, to mock and taunt her for her barrenness. But it was all because God wanted a Samuel who could be raised in the Temple and could be taught from a young age in the ways of the Lord. In order to have a Samuel, though, God needed a mother who would be brought, through affliction, to a place of absolute abandonment — she would obey God no matter what the cost.

> **In order to have a Samuel, God needed a mother who would be brought, through affliction, to a place of absolute abandonment — she would obey God no matter what the cost.**

Nothing works better than affliction for bringing the devout to this kind of radical obedience.

## Sometimes God Uses Affliction To Reveal His Glory

The disciples asked Jesus why a certain man was born blind — they thought that perhaps he or his parents had sinned. But Jesus said he was born blind, "that the works of God should be revealed in him" (John 9:3). Jesus then proceeded to reveal His glory by healing the man.

For reasons we don't fully understand, there are times when the forces of evil are allowed to gain the upper hand over God's people. Daniel points to this: "I was watching; and the same horn was making war against the saints, and prevailing against them" (Daniel 7:21). The Book of Revelation also talks about this: "It was granted to him to make war with the saints and to overcome them" (Revelation 13:7). Notice that this power is "granted" to the evil one, and he can make no headway against the saints without God's approval.

I cut off Daniel 7:21 above in mid-sentence. The verse goes on to say, "The same horn was making war against the saints, and prevailing against them, until the Ancient of Days came, and a judgment was made in favor of the saints of the Most High, and the time came for the saints to possess the kingdom" (Daniel 7:21-22). When God renders a judgment on behalf of the saints, everything changes! This is the answer for which we wait.

The Book of Revelation also testifies, "The angel whom I saw standing on the sea and on the land raised up his hand to heaven and swore by Him who lives forever and ever...that there should be delay no longer" (Revelation 10:5-6). What a wonderful moment! There is coming a day, O afflicted soul, when the Lord will declare, "There shall be delay no longer."

This is the moment of God's manifest glory.

Well, we have looked at many reasons for affliction and have considered God's purposes in allowing affliction to hurt us. Chances are that some of you reading this book are presently experiencing great affliction and testing. If that's you, then I don't want to end this chapter without emphasizing this final truth: God **will** complete the work He is doing in you! "Being confident of this very thing, that He who has begun a good work in you will complete it until the day of Jesus Christ" (Philippians 1:6).

## The Certainty Of God's Work Being Completed

I have heard the following thought taught or preached in a variety of ways: "Satan killed Jesus, thinking that would give him the upper hand, not realizing that it would backfire on him and be the very cause for his downfall." Upon examination, however, I don't think that's really true.

Consider this: Jesus predicted his death and resurrection many times over, giving His disciples specific details of how it would happen. "From that time Jesus began to show to His disciples that He must go to Jerusalem, and suffer many things from the elders and chief priests and scribes, and be killed, and be raised the third day" (Matthew 16:21). His disciples weren't the only ones listening; Satan was listening, too.

Not only did Christ's disciples have advance notice of His impending crucifixion, Satan did, too. Now Satan's not stupid. He understood the plan. In fact, when Jesus first mentioned His death in Matthew 16, Satan stirred up Peter to try to rebuke Jesus away from the cross. "Then Peter took Him aside and began to rebuke Him, saying, 'Far be it from You, Lord; this shall not happen to You!' But He turned and said to Peter, 'Get behind Me, Satan! You are an offense to Me, for you are not mindful of the things of God, but the things of men'" (Matthew 16:22-23).

Clearly, Satan was trying to dissuade Jesus from Calvary.

But it didn't work. Because when God purposes to do something, it doesn't matter what the devil tries to do, **God is going to fulfill His purposes**. Somebody stand up and shout hallelujah! God may even give the devil specific advance details of what He's doing to do, but it still doesn't matter. God just goes right ahead and does what He wants to do. Satan can't do anything to stop God's purposes, even with advance notice of the specifics of the plan!

> **When God purposes to do something, it doesn't matter what the devil tries to do, God is going to fulfill His purposes.**

"May Your kingdom come, Lord. Bring Your kingdom purposes to fulfillment in our midst. And help us to know and understand Your purposes and walk with You in them. Your kingdom come!"

Take heart, afflicted one. His purposes shall be accomplished!

# BROKENNESS

*"The sacrifices of God are a broken spirit, a broken and a contrite heart — these, O God, You will not despise"* (Psalm 51:17).

God wants to break us of our self-reliance and produce in us a deep humility and profound dependence upon Him. In a word, it's called brokenness.

Brokenness has been the theme of many a great sermon. It's one thing to preach or teach about brokenness; it's another thing to be broken. It's amazing how your appreciation of a biblical truth changes once you experience it.

I can truthfully say that I have been broken by God. The work is certainly not complete in my life, but God has broken me in my season of affliction in ways I had never known before. In this chapter I will share with you some of the things God has done in me personally and some of the insights that have enabled me to understand God's purposes in breaking us.

## Weeping

The most common denominator in the breaking process is tears. When the answers to our prayers are delayed, and our circumstances reach emergency proportions, God uses the crisis to break us open, to empty us of everything that is not of Him, and to soften the soil of our hearts with tears.

> **When the answers to our prayers are delayed, and our circumstances reach emergency proportions, God uses the crisis to break us open, to empty us of everything that is not of Him, and to soften the soil of our hearts with tears.**

I have wept more in the past four years than I ever expected to weep in my entire lifetime. Psalm 42:3 used to be just a Bible verse to me — "My tears have been my food day and night, while they continually say to me, 'Where is your God?'" Now, that verse speaks volumes to me for it has been my personal experience.

In fact, when you're being broken, the Psalms become your mainstay. Before my breaking, I couldn't relate to a lot of the passages in the Psalms. Now, I find myself identifying most intimately with the distressed cries of the psalmists.

To make this personal, I will quote just one entry from my journal that I made during a time of breaking and weeping:

> Journal Entry
> I do not know how to help myself, or what to do. The only thing I know to do is stay in God's face, and even then sometimes I feel like that is accomplishing nothing. I can identify with people who struggle emotionally, and have no idea what to do to extricate themselves from their valley. No matter what counsel comes to them, nothing seems to ignite within them. I think of the standard answers: "Just praise"; "Confess the word"; "Declare what God says about you"; "Get your eyes off your circumstances and onto the Lord"; "Resist the devil." I've done all of these things at various times, and yet there is no break in the valley.

When you're being broken by God, you don't understand what's happening to you. No amount of promise claiming changes anything because God isn't about to relent until the breaking is complete. He is the Potter, and He knows just what it takes to break down each vessel so that it can be reshaped and remade according to His desired purpose.

## Emptying

About three years ago, the Lord gave a word to one of the elders in our local church that has rung in our ears ever since: "We must be emptied before we can be filled." How we long for the fullness of the Holy Spirit, but are we willing to be broken and emptied of everything but Christ Himself? The emptying process requires great blocks of time in His presence, and God is calling His people to that in this hour.

I recall a time when I was at a men's retreat, I was feeling very weak and incapable, and I was clinging to the Lord in my heart. As I considered how helpless I felt to fulfill my ministry calling, I sensed the Spirit of God saying to me, "For the rest of your life, I will be requiring things of you that are beyond your ability to fulfill." (See 2 Corinthians 3:5.) So in other words, get used to it. I saw that God is not trying to increase our giftings and abilities to the point where we're equal to the task, but He's emptying and crippling us until we realize our absolute inability to

> **God is not trying to increase our giftings and abilities to the point where we're equal to the task, but He's emptying and crippling us until we realize our absolute inability to fulfill what He's asking of us.**

fulfill what He's asking of us. Then, when the task is accomplished, our personal ambitions aren't fed, but God receives all the glory. When a broken man or woman, in conjunction with the Spirit's enabling, participates in a work that is totally beyond his or her abilities, the glory becomes God's alone. God doesn't lift our abilities to the challenge, but He lifts the challenge beyond our abilities.

Sometimes we think, "Boy, it sure would have been great to have been one of the twelve apostles and to have walked with Jesus during His earthly ministry!" But we forget what it was like to be one of His disciples. He was constantly in the process of breaking and emptying them. Take for example the time that Peter walks on water.

> And Peter answered Him and said, "Lord, if it is You, command me to come to You on the water." So He said, "Come." And when Peter had come down out of the boat, he walked on the water to go to Jesus. But when he saw that the wind was boisterous, he was afraid; and beginning to sink he cried out, saying, "Lord, save me!" And immediately Jesus stretched out His hand and caught him, and said to him, "O you of little faith, why did you doubt?" (Matthew 14:28-31).

You can't knock it, folks. Peter walked on water. None of the other disciples did. Only Peter had the faith to swing his legs over the side and step out onto the water. And yet, after Jesus catches the sinking Peter, He lands a rebuke on him: "O you of little faith, why did you doubt?"

I'm thinking, "Lord, a little commendation here would be nice. Why not encourage Peter a little bit? After all, he did walk on water. Why don't you build up his faith with some positive reinforcement?"

His ways are nothing like ours.

By rebuking Peter for his unbelief, Jesus wasn't saying, "Come on, Peter, you should have more faith by now!" Instead, Jesus was reflecting back to Peter how small his faith really was.

How easily Peter could have become cocky. "Hey, guys, don't for-

> Peter would have come away from the experience thinking he was a real man of God but Jesus wanted him to come away from the experience realizing how unbelieving he really was.

get which one of us twelve walked on water, now." Peter would have come away from the experience thinking he was a real man of God but Jesus wanted him to come away from the experience realizing how unbelieving he really was. Jesus' rebuke wasn't intended to fill Peter with faith but to empty him of himself. It was only when Peter was completely emptied that the Lord would be able to fill him with mountain-moving faith.

## How Jesus Cultivates Brokenness

God has a proven method for reducing our self-reliance — He chops us off at the knees. One of the best illustrations for this is Jesus' relationship with His disciples. For three years Jesus incessantly decimated His disciples. Look how he talked to them. "You don't know what spirit you are of." "How long will I put up with you?" "Do you still not understand?" "Oh you of little faith!" Being a disciple of Jesus was real tough on the ego.

Many times I've wondered why Jesus was so hard and abrupt with His disciples. I used to think it was because He got upset with them. But then I realized He expected next to nothing of them, so it wasn't a matter of them falling short of His expectations. Jesus didn't choose the Twelve so that He could glean their best ideas in brainstorming sessions. He made it clear that He didn't want any of their innovative ideas, but He simply wanted them to be with Him and to keep their ears open.

"So Lord, why were You so tough on Your disciples?" The answer, I'm convinced, is in that they were so full of themselves. They were ready to drink His cup and be baptized with His baptism; they were

> They were so pleased with themselves that it took three years of Jesus' rebukes to cut them down to size.

ready to follow Him to the death; they were ready to sit on His right and left hand in the kingdom of God. They were watching people get healed and delivered under their ministry and were really beginning to think they were something special. They were so pleased with themselves that it took three years of Jesus' rebukes to cut them down to size. Jesus wanted them to see how unbelieving they really were. He wanted them to realize their complete bankruptcy apart from Him.

Peter was probably the toughest nut of the Twelve to crack. To the very end he maintained his self-confidence. When the final test came, Jesus announced to them, "You're all going to flunk tonight." Peter insisted, "Not me, Lord. Maybe the rest of these losers will flunk, but I'll never fail you, Lord." To that Jesus responded, "Simon, you're going to flunk **three** times tonight!" (See Mark 14:27-31.)

I couldn't help but wonder, "Lord, why were you so hard on Peter?" And then I saw it. Unless Peter had been totally emptied of himself, he could have never been used on the Day of Pentecost as he was. If he hadn't been broken, the Day of Pentecost would have turned Peter into a monster. He would have assumed that the harvest of that day had some kind of connection to his powerful preaching. Just imagine how the logo of his business cards might have read: "Three thousand converted at first sermon!"

God was able to use him, however, in such a powerful way because he had come to the end of himself and finally realized the utter emptiness of his own resources. God reserves the greatest victories for the vessels that have known the greatest brokenness.

> **God reserves the greatest victories for the vessels that have known the greatest brokenness.**

## The Testings Of God

"I tested you at the waters of Meribah" (Psalm 81:7). I will tell you why God tests us: So that we will fail. I used to think God tested us, hoping we'd get it right. Now I see that the purpose of testing is not that we pass but that we learn. God doesn't test us to procure information but to reveal ourselves to ourselves.

The Lord will purposefully bring us to a place of complete personal failure. He will allow us to see that our best efforts are useless. He will test us, knowing that we'll fail the test. That's what He did with Philip in John 6:6.

> Then Jesus lifted up His eyes, and seeing a great multitude coming toward Him, He said to Philip, "Where shall we buy bread, that these may eat?" But this He said to test him, for He Himself knew what He would do. Philip answered Him, "Two hundred denarii worth of bread is not sufficient for them, that every one of them may have a little" (John 6:5-7).

So Jesus is testing Philip. "Where shall we buy bread, that these may eat?" The correct answer is, "Lord, just have the multitude sit down

in groups of fifty, multiply some loaves and fish, and feed everybody!"
Would Philip guess the right answer and pass the test? Nope.

> **Jesus leads us to an awareness of complete personal failure, so that any success that might flow from our lives is attributed only to Him.**

Jesus **expected** Philip to fail the test. Jesus wasn't disappointed at Philip's failure; He was wanting to bring Philip to a place of brokenness and emptiness. Jesus leads us to an awareness of complete personal failure, so that any success that might flow from our lives is attributed only to Him.

Look at this interesting statement of Christ's: "Indeed the hour is coming, yes, has now come, that you will be scattered, each to his own, and will leave Me alone. And yet I am not alone, because the Father is with Me. These things I have spoken to you, that in Me you may have peace" (John 16:32-33). Jesus is saying, "You're all going to fail, and I'm telling you this so that in Me you may have peace."

I don't get it, Lord. How is that kind of pronouncement supposed to give anybody peace? **Jesus wanted them to learn that their peace will not be based upon their ability to stand but upon their relationship to Him.** For them to truly embrace this peace, they would have to first of all collapse. "Only after you've been totally emptied of your self-reliance," Jesus is telling them, "will you then discover what it means to find your peace, not in yourself, but **in Me**."

But even in testing us, Jesus is gracious and redemptive. I saw something in John's account of Peter's testing that encouraged my heart. To see it, you've got to remove the chapter break between John 13 & 14.

> John 13:38, Jesus answered him, "Will you lay down your life for My sake? Most assuredly, I say to you, the rooster shall not crow till you have denied Me three times.
> John 14:1, "Let not your heart be troubled; you believe in God, believe also in Me."

Although there's a chapter break between these two verses, I believe the Holy Spirit put them back-to-back without so much as a pause. Jesus is saying, "You're going to fail, Peter, but don't let your heart be troubled; just believe in Me. Your peace is not predicated upon your ability to stand, but upon your faith in Me."

Our eyes are on You, Lord Jesus.

## The Prodigal's Older Brother

Let me remind you about the elder son in Jesus' parable of the prodigal son (see Luke 15:11-32). When the younger brother had gotten sick of worldly living, he returned home, begging to be made as one of his father's servants. His father, however, welcomed him home and prepared a great feast to celebrate his youngest son's return. When the older brother came home from working in the fields and learned that his father had thrown a feast for his younger brother, he was angry and wouldn't join the party. I'll pick up the story at the point where the father comes outside to reason with his firstborn son.

> "So he answered and said to his father, 'Lo, these many years I have been serving you; I never transgressed your commandment at any time; and yet you never gave me a young goat, that I might make merry with my friends. But as soon as this son of yours came, who has devoured your livelihood with harlots, you killed the fatted calf for him.' And he said to him, 'Son, you are always with me, and all that I have is yours. It was right that we should make merry and be glad, for your brother was dead and is alive again, and was lost and is found'" (Luke 15:29-32).

Now, we all know that the older son's attitude stank. And that we would never be like that. Right? In my case at least, wrong.

I was shocked a short while ago by the "elder son" thought that went through my mind. My eye had fallen on a Christian magazine cover, and I noticed the first headline: "A Pastor's Confession: 'How I Broke Free From Sex Addiction.'" Here's the ugly thought that actually went through my head: "If you blow it, they'll put you on the front cover of their magazine. But for those of us who keep our noses clean, we'll get nothing."

As soon as I thought that, I immediately realized that's the sort of thinking the elder son had toward his prodigal brother who had returned home. He was offended at the fuss the father made over the lost son. The elder son should have rejoiced, if not over his returned brother, then certainly over the fact that his father's heart was fulfilled. To see his father's face beaming

> **The product of brokenness and the quality of heart that God is forming in those He is preparing for spiritual fatherhood is this: To rejoice when the Father's heart is satisfied, regardless of the personal diminishment it may involve.**

with delight should have been enough to satisfy the older son. But he was not broken, so he still placed his own concerns above those of his father.

The product of brokenness and the quality of heart that God is forming in those He is preparing for spiritual fatherhood is this: To rejoice when the Father's heart is satisfied, regardless of the personal diminishment it may involve.

## Unbroken Strength

We are told in the Scriptures to be strong in the Lord, but our first response is to just be strong. We're strong, and we're in the Lord, so we figure we must be strong in the Lord. We don't realize, however, that our strength is self-inspired rather than received. The only way God can teach us to genuinely find our strength in Him is by breaking our own personal strength. The psalmist put it this way, "He weakened my strength in the way" (Psalm 102:23).

This is how God graduates spiritual "young men" into spiritual "fathers" (1 John 2:14). The young men "are strong," but they'll never become fathers until their strength is weakened in the way. The weakness is intended to help them truly come to know "Him who is from the beginning" (1 John 2:14).

Proverbs 20:29 says, "The glory of young men is their strength, and the splendor of old men is their gray head." Young men in the Lord are strong, and that's their glory. When God weakens their strength in the way, they are shattered because their glory is removed. God wants them to gain their glory from something other than their strength, however. Gray hair represents experience, pain, one who has lived through life's difficulties. After removing his glory, the Lord will take the young man through difficulties and traumas, turning his hair gray so that that will now become his glory. He has seen the faithfulness of God through great pressures, and he now has a testimony. It is not the strong but the gray who are fruitful.

> It is not the strong but the gray who are fruitful.

The masses like unbroken strength. It's confident; it's visionary; it's bold; it's aggressive; it pushes against the gates of hell. It's fun to follow young strength because it appears to be accomplishing the most for the kingdom. This is Goliath-killing strength, and the Lord honors it. The Philistines are sent scattering, and the people rally excitedly around their young, strong leader. Everything changes, however, if this strong leader is weakened in the way. The dynamism and charisma and leadership skills that bonded the crowds are gone, and suddenly there's confusion and perplexity. In the evaluation process, we start to see how we've moved in much carnal momentum. We thought we made a great team with God, but we were doing most of the work.

## The Lord's Mercy

I am by natural giftings a strong and stable person. I was raised in a solid Christian family and had many benefits and advantages in my favor as a result. I was never moody; I was never depressed; I was always cheerful and joyful in the Lord and optimistic in my outlook on life. I've always enjoyed relatively good health and a strong frame. The Lord has been good and gracious to me, beyond measure. It's always been easy for me to be strong.

Then the Lord weakened my strength in the way. In my case, I was made to stumble and collapse. I was pastoring a well-established local church at the time, and was rendered incapable of functioning in ministry. I was forced to take a sabbatical. I had the sensation of someone who was hanging from a bar, and whose grip was slowly giving way. I was losing it, and no amount of time in God's face was seeming to help. Eventually, I fell.

When I say I fell, I do not mean that I fell into sin. I mean that all my ability and strength to stand was totally spent, and I collapsed. **But here's the wonder of God's mercy: When my fingers gave out and I fell, the arms of Jesus caught me.**

For the first time in my life my heart had failed. The psalmist cried, "My flesh and my heart fail; but God is the strength of my heart and my portion forever" (Psalm 73:26). I discovered that we don't really know what it's like for God to be the strength of our heart until our heart and flesh have failed.

> I discovered that we don't really know what it's like for God to be the strength of our heart until our heart and flesh have failed.

As I said, I was raised in a godly home and can't even remember the day I accepted Christ into my life. From my earliest words I have always affirmed that I loved Jesus. I had many glorious encounters with Christ in my childhood years. But when my strength failed, for the first time in my life I felt lost. I was pursuing God with all my heart, but I felt lost. Suddenly I realized, "This is what it feels like. This is what the lost feel like." And then God visited me in His mercy. He picked me up and carried me when I couldn't walk on my own. I felt like I got saved all over again. His mercy wrapped around me, and He carried me.

To this day I don't understand the how and why fully, but I never fell away from God. His mercy saved me. Instead of getting angry and bitter and accusing God of wrong, I ended up falling more in love with Him than ever.

I learned in a personal way that being a Jesus-follower is a supernatural walk. I cannot walk like Jesus unless He takes one arm, the Holy Spirit takes the other arm, and they walk me one step at a time.

> **Jesus walks on water; to follow Him, you've got to walk on water. It's a completely supernatural walk.**

Without God's help for every step, I cannot possibly walk a single step in the way of Jesus (even as Peter could not walk on water a single step without Jesus). Jesus walks on water; to follow Him, you've got to walk on water. It's a completely supernatural walk. There's only one way to do it, and that is through moment-by-moment crying out to Him for help. Jesus isn't looking for people who have such a deposit of strength in their hearts that they can follow Him; He's looking for people who are so weak that they recognize they cannot take the next step without the immediate help of the Holy Spirit.

"By You I have been upheld from birth; You are He who took me out of my mother's womb" (Psalm 71:6). I didn't survive my birth because of any effort or strength on my part; I was completely at the mercy of God. And somehow He wants me to live in that continual awareness — to carry a childlikeness about me that is continually dependent upon Him for every breath, for everything. I deceive myself into thinking that my own strength can carry me. We all start off totally helpless as we come into this world, but then we grow to trust in ourselves more and more. It's deception. Some of us say, "Lord, strengthen me," because we want God to make us so strong that we don't need Him anymore.

> **When we compare ourselves to the God of eternity, the oldest silver-haired seniors in our midst are infants before God.**

One day I was listening to a worship tape led by Kent Henry, in which he was likening God's relationship with us to the way he related to his 6-month old daughter. He said he just likes to kiss her little itty-bitty face, and then he said that's what God wants to do with us. I'll admit that initially I recoiled a little at the idea. I didn't want God to think of me as a 6-month old infant — I'm more mature than that! But when I began to think about it, when we compare ourselves to the God of eternity, the oldest silver-haired seniors in our midst are infants before God. Next to Him, we're all little babes. But in our arrogance we like to think of ourselves as mature. When Jesus told us to be childlike, He wasn't telling us to condescend or put on ways that are below our maturity level. He was saying to be ourselves — to realize that we're but little children. If we can carry the humility and simplicity of a child with us at all times rather than the refinements of the maturity we think we have, we'd learn to enter the kingdom.

So many of our declarations of strength are but a blustery fluffing of our feathers and strutting around each other. We pound our chests and boast of our spiritual victories. We sing about "making war in the heavenlies" but are basically just flailing into the air. No wonder God has to pull the rug out from under some of us. If instead we'd acknowledge our weakness and place our gaze upon Him, we would find the true secret of tapping into His strength in the time of need.

In the passage where he talks about his thorn in the flesh, Paul talks about the weakness God brought him to:

> 2 Corinthians 12:7, And lest I should be exalted above measure by the abundance of the revelations, a thorn in the flesh was given to me, a messenger of Satan to buffet me, lest I be exalted above measure. 8 Concerning this thing I pleaded with the Lord three times that it might depart from me. 9 And He said to me, "My grace is sufficient for you, for My strength is made perfect in weakness." Therefore most gladly I will rather boast in my infirmities, that the power of Christ may rest upon me. 10 Therefore I take pleasure in infirmities, in reproaches, in needs, in persecutions, in distresses, for Christ's sake. For when I am weak, then I am strong.

The word "thorn" is a visual picture of the kind of discomfort Paul was experiencing. We don't know exactly what the discomfort was, but it was in his flesh, and it was demonically incited. It was more than a sliver; it was a thorn that hurt with every movement. It didn't totally stop his ability to function, but it hassled him at every turn. The discomfort was significant enough that he literally pled with the Lord to remove it. Those with a physical infirmity understand just how such a thorn can feel.

Paul said the thorn came, "lest I should be exalted above measure by the abundance of the revelations." That statement has three possible meanings, and I think all three apply to some degree:

1. He was given the thorn lest he be lifted up in pride and think too highly of himself. Even the great apostle Paul was not

beyond the potential of pride.

2. He was given the thorn lest he depend upon the deposit of what God had imparted to him, and lean upon that rather than upon the power of the indwelling Spirit in the immediacy of the moment. It's easy for a preacher to relax a little and think, "I've preached this before; I can do it again." The thorn caused him to feel a great dependence upon God.

3. He was given the thorn lest he become exalted above measure in the eyes of others, and they think too highly of him. Considering the great revelations Paul had, it would be tempting for people to really fuss and fawn over him, but it's hard to be overly impressed with the feeble sight Paul made. The verse immediately prior (verse 6) supports this meaning: "lest anyone should think of me above what he sees me to be or hears from me."

There is no indication in the text that the infirmity was permanent, but it's obvious that Paul came to the place of being able to embrace it as part of God's will and purpose for his life at that time. More about that later.

> **Paul so completely appreciated the purposes of God in his fiery afflictions that he actually took pleasure in them!**

Verse 10 is the ultimate statement, and something toward which I am straining: "Therefore I take pleasure in infirmities... For when I am weak, then I am strong." To actually take pleasure in infirmities — this is an incredible attainment indeed. Paul so completely appreciated the purposes of God in his fiery afflictions that he actually took pleasure in them!

Let me clarify that last quote in this way: "For when I am weak [in the flesh], then I am strong [in grace]." We misunderstand Paul's exhortation to Timothy, "You therefore, my son, be strong in the grace that is in Christ Jesus" (2 Timothy 2:1). We see that as somehow meaning that we should rise up in a strength that is evident to others so that others can see that we're strong in God. Paul, however, doesn't say "be strong in yourself" but "be strong in grace." Grace is the enabling of God that totally supersedes all our human inadequacies. So Paul is saying, "In the midst of your weaknesses, and in the midst of your feelings of inadequacy, allow the grace of God to flow through you like a river, and minister life through you despite the weakness of your vessel." In fact, Paul learned that more of God's life can flow through a vessel that is fully self-aware of personal weakness and inadequacy. Such a vessel is truly broken before God.

Paul is not saying that we should rejoice in every infirmity that comes to our lives. But when it comes from God, it is to be received as God's gift in order to bring us to a place of greater brokenness and in order that we might learn the secret of God's strength being perfected in our weakness.

## Man's Strength Constricts

Any minister whose strength is not born out of weakness is still functioning to a limited degree in the flesh. Unbroken strength can't sustain and remain pure. It is only that strength which is rooted in a profound weakness through the breaking of God that will have the potential to remain pure in its outworking. The reason so many displays of strength raise a check in one's spirit is because it's a strength that apprehends the word and promises of God without the soul being broken and rendered bankrupt. If you haven't been

> **The brokenness of which we speak here cannot be contrived or self-induced or embraced through choice.**

utterly broken, you cannot embrace and walk in the provision of the promises of God without your flesh picking up some kind of arrogance and self-delight. The brokenness of which we speak here cannot be contrived or self-induced or embraced through choice. It is the Potter who must break the clay.

Man's strength constricts God's freedom to work through us as He desires. Our strength gets in His way and actually works against His purposes. When we are strong, we diminish our usefulness to the Master and restrict the flow of God's power. The more we understand our weakness, the greater our candidacy to be channels of divine life and blessing.

There is a difference between being talented and being fruitful. Young men work off the strength of their natural talents, and they're being faithful stewards, but they're not necessarily being very fruitful. Talents (public ministry) can look like fruitfulness to man, but only God can measure true fruitfulness. Fruitfulness is the amount of harvest that God is able to enjoy from our labors. We will be rewarded only for those things that touched the Father's heart. A one-talent person moving in 100-fold fruitfulness will accomplish more for the kingdom than a ten-talent person working at 30-fold fruitfulness. God's intention, regardless of the talents we possess, is to bring all of us into 100-fold fruitfulness. To do this, He must prune (break) His branches (John 15:2).

## Strengthen Your Brethren

When Jesus prophesied Peter's breaking, He made an interesting statement: "And the Lord said, 'Simon, Simon! Indeed, Satan has asked for you, that he may sift you as wheat. But I have prayed for you, that your faith should not fail; and when you have returned to Me, strengthen your brethren'" (Luke 22:31-32). Peter was the strong one of the twelve, and he was the one that Satan asked for. Jesus allowed Satan to sift Peter, but for His own purposes. Peter would be weakened and would lose his confidence in his natural strengths.

His strength was broken, but his faith didn't fail. The final product, Jesus assured him, would be that he would strengthen others. Jesus was saying to him, "After your strength fails, and you learn how to find your source of strength in Me alone, then go and strengthen your brethren." When you're strong yourself, you're convinced that you're imparting strength to others. You don't even realize how little you strengthen others. But when weakened and sifted, and when we come through with our faith

> The choice is to be one who is strong, or one who strengthens others.

intact because of Jesus' intercession, then we have something from which to strengthen others. The choice is to be one who is strong, or one who strengthens others. If you're being broken by God, be encouraged — when you have returned, you will strengthen your brethren.

# CHAPTER 9

# DESPERATE DEPENDENCE & HEART ENLARGEMENT

*"I will run the course of Your commandments, for You shall enlarge my heart"* (Psalm 119:32).

God is presently taking many of His servants through great personal distress, referred to in Scripture (among many other metaphors) as the spiritual "wilderness." God has a very clear purpose in mind. When the wilderness has completed its work in us, we will be broken, humble, weepy, and soft — with a new fire kindled in our eyes! It will be a fiery love for the One who led us through the wilderness, our beloved Lord and Bridegroom, Jesus Christ.

"Who is this coming up from the wilderness, leaning upon her beloved?" (Song of Solomon 8:5). It is the believer who has allowed the wilderness to produce within her an abandoned obedience, a matured love, and a selfless servanthood. The wilderness represents the difficulties of this present world — our struggles with the flesh and temptation; affliction, tribulation, and hassles; dry seasons in God. "Coming up from the wilderness," she is on the other side of the desert, and notice her most striking characteristic: She is "leaning on her beloved."

The bride in the Song of Solomon represents the pathway of all fervent believers as God brings us into fruitful spiritual maturity. By the time she gets to Chapter Eight, she represents the believer whose love is fully matured. We would expect the fully mature believer to be a spiritual giant, a veritable pillar, standing head and shoulders above others. But no, she can hardly even stand up. She has been so broken by the wilderness that she depends upon her Beloved for virtually every step. **This** is the true scriptural depiction of spiritual maturity.

Maturity in Christ is measured by how much we've come to depend on Him. The greater the dependence, the greater the maturity. God is looking for brokenness, help-lessness, weakness, and absolute dependence upon Him.

> **The greater the dependence, the greater the maturity.**

## Four Kinds Of Dependence

I see four different levels of dependence:

- We all start out at "total independence." This is the natural state of every unbeliever. Those outside Christ rely exclusively upon their own resources to survive.

- Second, there is "claimed dependence." When we first come to Christ we eagerly say, "Lord, I depend completely upon You!" But we're oblivious to the fact that we don't know the first thing yet about dependence. We continue to rely upon the personal support systems we naturally built before we came to Christ. The Lord loves us so much, though, that He will begin to help us see our self-reliant independence.

- Then there's "realized dependence." This is what happens when the Lord shows us how utterly dependent we are upon Him, and we embrace the truth that we can do nothing apart from Him (John 15:5). At this level the believer sincerely cries out to God for help in every area of life.

- Finally, there is what I choose to call "desperate dependence." This level of dependence, illustrated in Song of Solomon 8:5, is achieved only through the purposeful formation of the Holy Spirit. He leads us into a wilderness experience that He creates specifically and personally for just us. By the time He's finished with us, we hopefully will have learned this ultimate expression of dependence. One indicator that you've come to a place of desperate dependence is this: Time spent with Jesus in prayer is no longer a discipline, nor is it merely a delight; prayer (relationship with God) has become for you a matter of sheer survival.

> **Time spent with Jesus is no longer a discipline, nor is it merely a delight; prayer has become for you a matter of sheer survival.**

## King Hezekiah

To see how the Lord produces this desperate dependence within us, we will turn to one of the most colorful Bible illustrations of this truth

— the story of Hezekiah, king of Judah. Hezekiah was a powerful, godly king (he was discipled by the mighty prophet Isaiah). He purged the land of idolatry, repaired the Temple, and restored proper Temple worship. Then he observed the Passover — nothing like it had happened since the days of Solomon. The priests were once again supported by tithes.

Not only did Hezekiah lead the nation in spiritual reform, but he was also a powerful military leader. Because of his devotion to the Lord, Hezekiah saw one of the greatest deliverances of the entire Bible — 185,000 Assyrian enemies were killed overnight by a destroying angel. Hezekiah stands out as one of the most godly kings the nation of Judah had.

I want to show how Hezekiah illustrates for us the processes God uses to bring His servants into greater dependence. And I wish I could say that in Hezekiah's case it worked. But it didn't. Hezekiah is an example of a man who was unwilling to embrace the "desperate dependence" God tried to produce in his heart. Sometimes

> **It's possible to remain loyal in our love for the Lord but still miss His highest purposes for our life.**

we learn best through negative examples. Personally, all too often I learn best from mistakes. So when we see how Hezekiah blew it, perhaps it will help us to learn a valuable lesson.

As we review Hezekiah's story, I'd like you to be on the lookout for this sobering truth: It's possible to remain loyal in our love for the Lord but still miss His highest purposes for our life.

The segment of Hezekiah's life we're going to examine is recorded in Isaiah 38 and 39, but before we look at those portions, let me paint their historical backdrop. During Hezekiah's reign, Assyria was the foremost world power. Assyria had captured Samaria, and exiled the Israelites in the northern kingdom back to Nineveh. And now Assyria was knocking on the door of the southern kingdom, the nation of Judah where Hezekiah was king, with the intention of conquering Judah as well.

The chapters of Isaiah 36 and 37 record the Assyrian offensive against Judah. In the crisis of the Assyrian siege Hezekiah came to a place of true "realized dependence." He was fully convinced that God was his only hope, and he cried out to God in desperation for His intervention. Isaiah 37:36 tells how that 185,000 dead Assyrians were discovered the next morning, and the remainder of the

> **"So now I'm going to bring you to the greatest test of all."**

enemy's army had returned for Nineveh. It was a glorious deliverance!

But as we come to the next chapter, Isaiah 38, I can hear God saying, "Okay, Hezekiah, you're doing good. You've realized your absolute dependence upon me. You've stayed true to Me in your heart, and you really love Me. So now I'm going to bring you to the greatest test of all. I'm going to see if you're willing to embrace the ultimate level of dependence — desperate dependence."

In Isaiah 38 the ultimate test is introduced:

> Isaiah 38:1, In those days Hezekiah was sick and near death. And Isaiah the prophet, the son of Amoz, went to him and said to him, "Thus says the LORD: 'Set your house in order, for you shall die and not live.'" 2 Then Hezekiah turned his face toward the wall, and prayed to the LORD, 3 and said, "Remember now, O LORD, I pray, how I have walked before You in truth and with a loyal heart, and have done what is good in Your sight." And Hezekiah wept bitterly. 4 And the word of the LORD came to Isaiah, saying, 5 "Go and tell Hezekiah, Thus says the LORD, the God of David your father: 'I have heard your prayer, I have seen your tears; surely I will add to your days fifteen years.'"

## The Furnace Of Affliction

This test is introduced to Hezekiah by means of a life-threatening affliction. As we have said, God sometimes uses physical affliction as one of His ways to produce a greater godliness within us. This is the means by which God chose to work in Hezekiah.

The nature of the test was this: "Will your season of affliction change you, Hezekiah? Will it produce a greater dependence upon Me? Will you allow this affliction to complete its intended work in your heart?"

Physical affliction is intensely stressful. The crisis that affliction precipitates provides a context where God can reveal the depths of our hearts and produce a desperation within us that can cause us to seek God with greater fervency. Hezekiah was no exception. The intensity of his trial produced great anxiety of heart and mind, and Isaiah 38:3 says he "wept bitterly." He mourned the loss of the best years of his life (see verse 10). He was about to die in his prime, and so he cried out to God with all his heart.

> Hezekiah recognized that God wanted to work something within him through the affliction but, as we'll see, the attempt was unsuccessful.

The Lord heard his prayer and added fifteen years to his life (verse 5). After his recovery, he realized that his "great bitterness" was intended by God for his own benefit (see Isaiah 38:17). Hezekiah recognized that God wanted to work something within him through the affliction but, as we'll see, the attempt was unsuccessful.

## Here Comes The Test

After Hezekiah's recovery, it's as though God says, "All right, Hezekiah, you've come through this fiery trial, and now let's see if it's produced in you the desperate dependence I'm looking for." (After removing the fire from your life, God always tests the gold to see how pure it is.) This test comes in the form of envoys from Babylon (Isaiah 39). The previous test came in the form of an invading Assyrian army, and Hezekiah passed that test. But now this second test comes in the form of smiling ambassadors, and Hezekiah isn't ready for the test to come in such a friendly fashion.

> Isaiah 39:1, At that time Merodach-Baladan the son of Baladan, king of Babylon, sent letters and a present to Hezekiah, for he heard that he had been sick and had recovered. 2 And Hezekiah was pleased with them, and showed them the house of his treasures — the silver and gold, the spices and precious ointment, and all his armory — all that was found among his treasures. There was nothing in his house or in all his dominion that Hezekiah did not show them.

Babylon was a pretty powerful nation, and it was quite an honor for such a mighty nation to give Hezekiah this kind of attention. The fact is, Babylon was trying to pull together a political alliance in order to throw off the Assyrian yoke. When Babylon had heard that 185,000 Assyrians had been killed and that now Hezekiah had recovered from his sickness and was going to be continuing at the helm of the nation of Judah, Babylon sent some ambassadors to strengthen their political ties.

Hezekiah was unable to handle the acclaim that would come to him upon his restoration. I can just imagine God's frustration at this moment. It's as though God were thinking, "I really do want to bless you. I want to answer

> **Hezekiah was unable to handle the acclaim that would come to him upon his restoration.**

your prayers. I want to heal you. But then when I do, you get weird. It goes to your head, and you start to act as though you deserved it or something." God delays healings today for much the same reason. Sometimes He's waiting for us to get to the place where our souls will be able to steward the attention that God's healing touch precipitates.

The ambassadors' fawning attention went to Hezekiah's head. He thought to himself, "I can't believe it, the king of Babylon thinks I'm a force to be reckoned with. He sees me as a world power. I am being courted by the real movers and shakers. I'm really starting to play with the big boys."

God was looking for desperate dependence, but instead, pride began to manifest in Hezekiah's heart. He lost perspective on how the victory over Assyria was an act of God from beginning to end and how that his recovery of health was only God's merciful kindness toward him. Hezekiah thought he had mastered this area of dependence upon God, but the right circumstances were used of God to surface the pride of his heart. God knew Hezekiah's heart better than Hezekiah did.

## Knowing The Heart

2 Chronicles 32:31 provides a fascinating commentary on this story: "However, regarding the ambassadors of the princes of Babylon, whom they sent to him to inquire about the wonder that was done in the land, God withdrew from him, in order to test him, that He might know all that was in his heart."

The translators of the New King James Version capitalize the word "He" in the above phrase, "that He might know all that was in his heart." But it could just as easily be translated "he," meaning "that Hezekiah might know all that was in his heart." God knew what was in Hezekiah's heart all along, but the test came in order that Hezekiah might be able to see it as well.

If he had learned desperate dependence, Hezekiah would not have been seduced by the smiling ambassadors. He would have said, "You guys don't understand, I had nothing to do with all this. It was all of God!" Instead, he said, "Let me show you around; I'd like you to see the wealth and power of my kingdom." And God's heart sank, for Hezekiah was still impressed with his natural resources — the arm of flesh. Hezekiah had failed the test, indicating that the fiery furnace of affliction did not complete the intended work in Hezekiah's heart. He had not gained the ultimate level of dependence.

The smiling ambassadors got him. When he was under siege by a vast army, it was easy to be dependent upon God. But when his high-powered friends began to fuss over him, the true state of his heart was revealed. The greatest tests of our hearts don't come to us in the face of our enemies but in the presence of our friends.

> **The greatest tests of our hearts don't come to us in the face of our enemies but in the presence of our friends.**

## Spiritual Pride

As seen in Hezekiah's story, the main symptom of spiritual pride is sincere decisionmaking without consulting God. We sincerely want to do what's right and what's pleasing to God, but in a moment when our defenses are

> **The main symptom of spiritual pride is sincere decisionmaking without consulting God.**

lowered we make a decision based upon common sense. The issues seem rather insignificant to us, so we go ahead and use our "good judgment." Hezekiah wasn't refusing to consult God about showing his kingdom to the Babylonians. It was just an oversight — he didn't think it mattered. It wasn't a big deal at all to Hezekiah. But it was to God. And Hezekiah no doubt began to see the truth that God is pressing into many of His saints in this hour, that there is nothing good about our own "good judgment." God wants us to lose our confidence in our common sense and rely on Him implicitly for every area of decision in our lives.

What we have said so far in this chapter is that God attempted to use the distress of a physical infirmity to produce a "desperate dependence" within Hezekiah. Hezekiah's wilderness experience did not produce in him the response God desired which is evidenced by the fact that he still retained a certain amount of confidence in his wealth and power. The sobering lesson of Hezekiah's life is this: It's possible to love the Lord sincerely but fall short of His highest purposes.

## A Second Dynamic: An Enlarged Heart

But there was a second dynamic in this situation that God was trying to accomplish in Hezekiah: God's design in the trauma of his sickness was not only to produce a desperate dependence, but also to enlarge Hezekiah's heart.

The Scriptures make it clear that God wants to enlarge our hearts. Psalm 119:32, "I will run the course of Your commandments, for You shall enlarge my heart." Before we apply this to Hezekiah's life, let me state some principles regarding the enlarging of our hearts.

## What Is An Enlarged Heart?

Let's begin by defining "an enlarged heart." An enlarged heart is a heart that has been expanded by God to carry the concerns of others. It has a passion for reaching beyond the concerns and issues that affect our own personal life, to embrace the needs of others.

We can see Paul's enlarged heart in his statement of 2 Corinthians 7:3, "you are in our hearts, to die together and to live together." The church at Corinth was only one of many churches Paul had planted, but he relates to them in this passage as though they were the most important church in the whole world. Those believers were so much a part of his heart that he felt like his living or dying was inextricably connected to their living or dying. We can be certain that Paul felt that way about all the churches he planted. Truly he had an enlarged heart!

> **An enlarged heart is a heart for the world.**

An enlarged heart is a heart for the world. "For God so loved the world." It is a heart that beats with the passions and concerns of God Himself. What's amazing in Paul's case was his passion, not only for the churches he had planted, but also for his nation, the Jews. In Romans 9:1-3 he makes the absolutely sincere claim that he could wish himself cut off from Christ if it would mean the salvation of his fellow countrymen. That kind of big-heartedness is absolutely mind-boggling to me. Paul carried a passion for both the Gentiles and the Jews. Truly he was a "world Christian."

An enlarged heart has been given a greater capacity to channel God's love to others. When Paul said to the Philippians, "For God is my witness, how greatly I long for you all with the affection of Jesus Christ" (Philippians 1:8), he was basically saying, "The love Jesus has for you fills my heart and flows through me toward you."

To illustrate this, let me bring up the problem I have with watering my garden. We have a small garden plot in our backyard, and watering it with the sprinkler ought not to be much of a job at all. The problem is, the pipes in our basement are old and corroded on the inside, which reduces the water pressure to my garden hose significantly. To water my garden in the heat of summer should only take about twenty minutes or so, but instead it consumes the better part of an evening. What I need is some new plumbing in our basement, with some pipes that have a greater capacity to conduct the flow of water. In a similar way, our hearts often only give out a little dripping of the love of God. The problem is not with the supply of God's love but with the constriction of our hearts.

God wants to expand our hearts beyond the limited interests of our own sphere of influence. Is my heart heavy when a nearby gospel-preaching church is suffering a loss of members, even when part of me wants to rejoice that those members are now coming to my local church? An enlarged heart finds its interests much broader than the confines of its own ministry involvements. It freely delights in seeing the blessings of God abound elsewhere, even when that blessing is not presently touching its own immediate sphere. It is free of all jealousy, competition, and comparison.

## How God Enlarges Our Hearts

God uses trauma and crisis to enlarge our hearts. Our hearts resist God's stretching processes, and usually it takes something very traumatic to work a permanent enlargement of our hearts. David cried out, "The troubles of my heart have enlarged; bring me out of my distresses!" (Psalm 25:17). David was learning that God enlarges the troubles of our heart — to enlarge our heart. This is clearly seen in David's life, because although David felt ready to lead the nation after killing Goliath, God knew that he needed several years in "the wilderness" to properly enlarge his heart for the great dynasty God had in store for him.

Even our physical hearts get constricted. This is what causes heart attacks. Veins and arteries around the heart become clogged with cholesterol and plaque, and the flow of blood to the body is restricted. A commonplace surgical procedure in our day for rectifying that is called "angioplasty." A balloon is inserted in an artery somewhere near the hip, and it is directed up to the heart, put in place where the blockage is, and then the balloon is blown up. The clogged artery is stretched open, and proper blood flow can resume. This is a marvelous illustration for how trials, pressures, afflictions, and crises

> **This is a marvelous illustration for how trials, pressures, afflictions, and crises are instruments of "God's angioplasty," to enlarge our hearts with His passions.**

are instruments of "God's angioplasty," to enlarge our hearts with His passions.

I am not suggesting that troubles are the only device God uses to enlarge our hearts. Psalm 119:32 makes it clear that radical obedience also contributes to heart enlargement. But crisis is particularly useful in God's hands for stretching us out of our comfort zones. It's no small thing to take a constricted, self-centered, self-absorbed Christian and turn him into a world Christian. At this point some readers are probably thinking, "So that's why God's been stre-e-etching me lately!"

## Some Principles Regarding Heart Enlargement

1) We are absolutely incapable of enlarging our own heart.

It must be done by the heavenly Surgeon. 1 Kings 4:29 says that "<u>God</u> gave Solomon wisdom and...largeness of heart." God does this to leaders because leaders need it. The needs within God's flock are so diverse that His leaders need this enlarging work done in their hearts.

2) One of the distinguishing earmarks of an enlarged heart is weeping and tears.

Now, I know some people that are naturally "weepy" — because of their personality they weep very readily. That's not what I'm talking about. I'm talking about a brokenness that is not native to your personality.

A great example of this is the prophet Jeremiah. The Spirit had warned the people through Jeremiah that their sin would bring God's judgment. But the people of Israel said his words weren't from God. They struck him; they imprisoned him; they put him in a muddy pit where he almost died; and then they abducted him against his will to Egypt. But when the city of Jerusalem finally fell according to Jeremiah's words, did he say, "I told you so"? No. He said, "My eyes overflow with rivers of water for the destruction of...my people" (Lamentations 3:48). Even after his prophecies of destruction were fulfilled, his enlarged heart won out. Instead of pointing the finger, all he could do was weep. Truly he carried his nation in his heart!

That Paul's heart was enlarged is manifest by the tears that flowed routinely from his eyes as he cared for the flock —

> **The enlarged heart will inevitably produce tears.**

"Therefore watch, and remember that for three years I did not cease to warn everyone night and day with tears" (Acts 20:31). The enlarged heart will inevitably produce tears.

We see the largeness of Jesus' heart as He wept over Jerusalem. His words over that great city were, in essence, as follows: "My heart is large enough to gather all of you under My wing, but you would not." The ultimate illustration of an enlarged heart, of course, is the cross. In His crucifixion, Jesus demonstrated that the enlarged heart does not just love those who receive it, but it pours out its life for those who are killing it.

3) An enlarged heart tastes of divine pleasures.

Yes, the enlarging of our hearts is a painful process, but in the end it brings a harvest of great glory. An enlarged heart is expanded in its ability to embrace the height and width and length and breadth of Christ's love. And there is **nothing** like receiving a revelation of Christ's love for you! The enlarged heart shares in the delight of the Master as 100-fold fruitfulness springs forth from your life. In the most profound and sublime sense, the enlarged heart has more fun.

## Back To Hezekiah

Now that we've seen what an enlarged heart is, and how God produces that within us, let's take this concept and plug it into the story of Hezekiah. As we're about to see, Hezekiah was a sincere and godly man whose heart God tried to enlarge, but it didn't work.

> **Hezekiah was a sincere and godly man whose heart God tried to enlarge, but it didn't work.**

As a reminder, Isaiah chapters 36 & 37 chronicle the story of the Assyrian invasion of Judah and how God brought Hezekiah to a place of real dependence on Him. Because Hezekiah relied upon God alone, He brought a tremendous victory over the Assyrians. In the next chapter (Isaiah 38) it's as though God were saying, "Okay, Hezekiah, when your own skin was on the line, you really cried out to Me and saw Me as your only source of help. I'm glad that you seek My face when your life is in the balance. But how about when the lives of others are in the balance? Will you cry out to me with the same passionate concern for others when their lives are on the line, but yours isn't? This is what I want to work in you, Hezekiah, I want to enlarge your heart for the concerns of others." This was God's foremost purpose in allowing Hezekiah to become sick.

God designed Hezekiah's sickness to enlarge his heart. And then after healing him, God visited him again to test him and to see if his heart had truly become enlarged through his affliction. The nature of this test is given for us in Isaiah 39, and it's necessary for the purposes of this teaching for us to look at the entire chapter:

> Isaiah 39:1 At that time Merodach-Baladan the son of Baladan, king of Babylon, sent letters and a present to Hezekiah, for he heard that he had been sick and had recovered. 2 And Hezekiah was pleased with them, and showed them the house of his treasures — the silver and gold, the spices and precious ointment, and all his armory — all that was found among his treasures. There was nothing in his house or in all his dominion that Hezekiah did not show them. 3 Then Isaiah the prophet went to King Hezekiah, and said to him, "What did these men

say, and from where did they come to you?" So Hezekiah said, "They came to me from a far country, from Babylon." 4 And he said, "What have they seen in your house?" So Hezekiah answered, "They have seen all that is in my house; there is nothing among my treasures that I have not shown them." 5 Then Isaiah said to Hezekiah, "Hear the word of the LORD of hosts: 6 'Behold, the days are coming when all that is in your house, and what your fathers have accumulated until this day, shall be carried to Babylon; nothing shall be left,' says the LORD. 7 'And they shall take away some of your sons who will descend from you, whom you will beget; and they shall be eunuchs in the palace of the king of Babylon.'" 8 So Hezekiah said to Isaiah, "The word of the LORD which you have spoken is good!" For he said, "At least there will be peace and truth in my days."

I want you to see, as we examine these verses, how that Hezekiah failed the test. The test established that Hezekiah's heart had not been enlarged through his crisis but rather had remained constricted and self-centered.

At this point someone might argue with me, "How can you say that Hezekiah didn't have a large heart? He rooted out idolatry; he re-established Temple worship according to Moses' pattern; through his submission he saw 185,000 Assyrians killed in one night! He did a **lot** for his generation!"

That's precisely the point. He did a lot — **for his generation.** Look again at verses 7-8 above, and you will see that Hezekiah didn't have a heart for the generations that would follow. When it involved the interests of his own generation, and when it involved his status before his peers, Hezekiah's heart was huge. He cared deeply and dearly for those of his generation. But he lacked a heart for the next generation. He had myopic vision; he had a small heart.

> **He cared deeply and dearly for those of his generation. But he lacked a heart for the next generation.**

## A Heart For The Next Generation

Earlier on, God had spoken a most forceful word to Hezekiah through the prophet Isaiah: "In those days Hezekiah was sick and near death. And Isaiah the prophet, the son of Amoz, went to him and said to him, 'Thus says the LORD: "Set your house in order, for you shall die and not live"'" (Isaiah 38:1). What was Hezekiah's response to that powerful word of judgment from God? He cried out to God for mercy! God responded to his desperate cry, healed him, and gave him fifteen more years to live.

Now, God comes to Hezekiah a second time with a forceful word of judgment via the prophet Isaiah: "'And they shall take away some of your sons who will descend from you, whom you will beget; and they shall be eunuchs in the palace of the king of Babylon'" (Isaiah 39:7). What does Hezekiah do in response to this word? Does he cry out for mercy, like he did when it involved his own life? No. The shallowness of what was accomplished in Hezekiah's heart is now manifest. His feeble response is seen in verse 8: "So Hezekiah said to Isaiah, 'The word of the LORD which you have spoken is good!' For he said, 'At least there will be peace and truth in my days.'"

He doesn't cry out at all. There's no intercession. There are no tears from Hezekiah. God's judgment involved the generations to come, so Hezekiah takes on a passive stance. His response sounds pious, but in actuality it's very lazy. He basically says, "Well, that's the judgment of God, and who can change God's mind? Since that's what He's spoken, that's what's going to happen. God's going to do what God's going to do." Inside his constricted heart he was actually saying, "At least there will be peace and truth in my days."

I can imagine God's disappointment being expressed in thoughts something like these: "Oh Hezekiah, you missed it! I sent an affliction to you, so that you could experience a kind of pain you never knew. Your life was so insulated that you couldn't really empathize with the hurts of others. So I brought sickness and pain into your life, to sensitize your heart to the pain

> **"Your life was so insulated that you couldn't really empathize with the hurts of others."**

of others. I wanted this affliction to empty you of yourself so that you could embrace a compassion for the heartache of others. But now, when you have the opportunity to be broken over the distress of future generations, you are smug and self-content. You have failed the test, Hezekiah. I see that your heart has not been enlarged by your personal affliction."

You've got to see the heartbreak of God at this point. He had performed "divine angioplasty" on Hezekiah, but the procedure was unsuccessful. God was hoping to raise up an intercessor who would cry out to Him for the generations yet to be born, but Hezekiah just didn't get it.

## Why The Angioplasty Was Unsuccessful

You might ask, "Why didn't it 'take'? Why didn't Hezekiah's affliction enlarge his heart?" I am convinced the answer lies in this: He was healed too soon. The period of his illness was comparatively short, and then Hezekiah was healed graciously by God. The affliction was intended to stretch Hezekiah's heart because the distress of physical affliction will always force us to press beyond the boundaries of our present attainments in God. We're forced to cry out to Him. We're compelled to find His heart in our distress. We're pressed into the face of God like never before. Our fervency and passion to find God is heightened, and we become desperate to understand His purposes in our pain. In Hezekiah's case, God removed the heat (i.e., God healed him) before the gold was completely purified. Hezekiah's healing appears to be an act of God's mercy, but in actuality it left Hezekiah an unchanged man because the duration of the stretching was too short.

This illustrates a profound truth about the ways of God. When God brings distress, pain, affliction, and suffering into our lives, He does so for a purpose. He wants to enlarge our hearts. But our hearts are resistant to change. In order for the enlargement to be complete, the period of pain must be long enough in duration to complete the work. We don't know how long that is, only God does.

> **In order for the enlargement to be complete, the period of pain must be long enough in duration to complete the work.**

And that's why God often responds to our cries for deliverance with the words, "Not yet." All we want is for the pain to stop; but He wants something far more valuable. God's going for the gold. He wants the gold of a refined character, of an enlarged heart. He wants the crucible to make us more like Christ. And He's committed to sustaining the heat until the work is complete.

## Manasseh

One symptom of Hezekiah's constricted heart was that he fathered the most ungodly king of Judah's entire history — Manasseh. One reason Hezekiah cried so bitterly when God told him he would die was because Hezekiah had no heir. After God extended Hezekiah's life by fifteen years, Manasseh was conceived. On the surface, it would appear that Hezekiah's passion to have an heir reflected a deep concern for the generations that would follow. But Hezekiah's apathy toward discipling his own son revealed that he wanted a son largely for selfish reasons — to carry on his name. God had said to Hezekiah, "Put your house in order"

> **He was successful in bringing spiritual revival to the entire nation, but he lost his own boy. And in so doing, he lost the nation.**

(Isaiah 38:1), but Hezekiah wimped out on that directive. He was successful in bringing spiritual revival to the entire nation, but he lost his own boy. And in so doing, he lost the nation.

This appears to be the pivotal point of Judah's history. The nation plummeted, in the final analysis, because Hezekiah did not establish proper spiritual order in his house. His son Manasseh precipitated the downfall of the nation.

Perhaps Hezekiah was too busy with kingdom business to commit himself vigorously to imparting a passion for godliness to his son. Whatever the reason, when Manasseh inherited the throne, he gave himself perversely to the lowest levels of idolatry, even to the point of sacrificing his own son in the fire. He practiced sorcery, consulted mediums, and filled Jerusalem with innocent blood (2 Kings 21:6; 24:4). It's amazing that a godly man like Hezekiah would raise such a rebel. The reason is somehow connected to the fact that Hezekiah did not carry a compelling concern for what would be the welfare of the nation after his decease.

I want you to notice how God talks about Manasseh. Many years later, God is still outraged over Manasseh's wickedness. Notice what God says to Jeremiah a couple generations later: "Even if Moses and Samuel stood before Me, My mind would not be favorable toward this people...I will hand them over to trouble...**because of Manasseh the son of Hezekiah, king of Judah, for what he did in Jerusalem**" (Jeremiah 15:1,4). Even though the nation of Judah had a couple spiritual awakenings after Manasseh, especially during the reign of Josiah, God had determined judgment for the nation. Although the nation had repented, God could not dismiss Manasseh's abominations.

Who fathered Manasseh? The godly king with the constricted heart.

## Persevering To Completion

Let me repeat, for emphasis, that Hezekiah represents the sincere believer who loves the Lord but misses God's highest purposes. Hezekiah embodies a fearful spiritual truth: It's possible to be sincere, have good intentions, with a heart to please God, and be disqualified from God's best for our lives.

> **It's possible to be sincere, have good intentions, with a heart to please God, and be disqualified from God's best for our lives.**

What spiritual lesson must we learn from Hezekiah in order to find the desperate dependence and heart enlargement that he missed? Here's the lesson: When God sends crisis and pressure our way, in an attempt to lift us to a higher spiritual plane, let us persevere in patience and love until His work within us is complete.

Perhaps your life has been hit recently with something traumatic. Take some time praying over this question, "Is God wanting to use this crisis to enlarge my heart?" If so, it's very likely that your pain will sensitize you to the pain of others. You will weep over things you never wept over before. You will feel yourself being stretched. And like Hezekiah, one day God will deliver you. But will you be any different when the release comes? It's possible for the potter's vessel to be removed too soon from the fire. Even though it's extremely difficult, we must eventually come to the place where we can sincerely offer this prayer: "Lord, I'm asking for an immediate deliverance. But even more than that, I'm asking that You not deliver me until my heart has been fully fashioned according to Your purpose for this season."

Oh, how painful when God delays His answers to our prayers! How we long for an immediate reprieve. And yet the testimony of countless saints, beginning with that of Job, affirms that God uses the periods of delay as some of the most productive seasons of our lives, because of the depth of spirituality they produce within us.

And my, how we American Christians need enlargement of heart! If ever there was a self-absorbed generation, it's 20th-century America. All that many Americans care about is this generation and this nation. The leaven of our culture has infiltrated the attitudes of the church. Just one symptom is the constant struggle so many churches face in trying to recruit teachers to teach children's classes. We carry a greater passion for our personal comfort and convenience than for raising up today's children into tomorrow's prophets.

If it's the sincere cry of your heart, then go ahead and pray it: "Dear heavenly Father, bring me to a desperate dependence, and enlarge my heart." The pathway will not be comfortable, but if you will constantly abide in Him and persevere by His grace to the end, He'll make you into a world Christian.

# Part Two

# Quietness
# and
# Confidence
# (Isaiah 30:15)

# CHAPTER 10

# THE ASSYRIANS ARE COMING!

*"For thus says the Lord GOD, the Holy One of Israel: 'In return-
ing and rest you shall be saved; in quietness and confidence shall
be your strength.' But you would not"* (Isaiah 30:15).

The writings of Isaiah are among the most sublime of the entire Old
Testament, and this statement is one of the most compelling declara-
tions that the Holy Spirit speaks through Isaiah: "In quietness and con-
fidence shall be your strength." This is one of the pinnacle truths of
God's word, and we will give these chapters of Part 2 to expounding this
verse.

## Background To Isaiah 30:15

The thirtieth chapter of Isaiah is made so much more meaningful
when we understand its historical context. The best estimates place the
writing of this chapter in the proximity of the conquest of the Northern
Kingdom of Israel. The nation of Israel is divided into two separate
kingdoms at the time, the Northern Kingdom of Israel based in the capi-
tal city of Samaria, and the Southern Kingdom of Judah based in the
capital city of Jerusalem.

Assyria is the foremost world power and is making imperialistic
crusades into outlying nations. Her goal is to conquer the civilized world.
King Hezekiah is sitting on the throne of Judah in Jerusalem, and he is
watching the Assyrian army roll toward him like an unstoppable sunami,
gobbling up everything in its path.

War is always ugly, but the Assyrians were particularly ruthless.
Their national god was called "Ashur," and their military expeditions
were intended to establish not only Assyrian political power but also

Assyrian religion. So theirs were literally "holy wars" as their greed for supremacy was fueled by a religious zeal to impose the worship of Ashur upon other peoples. Those who resisted faced horrifying consequences.

So on purely human terms, Hezekiah and the people of Judah had good reason to fear the Assyrian hordes. The cry throughout the land was, "The Assyrians are coming!" But God always expects His people to rise above the natural plane and dwell, by His grace, in a supernatural dimension. As Assyria advanced, God challenged Hezekiah to believe

Him for the impossible. Ulti-

> **Hezekiah was intimidated into seeking help from other sources.**

mately, Hezekiah was intimidated into seeking help from other sources. Fear overwhelmed his faith, and he turned for help to Egypt.

## Looking To Egypt

Judah and Egypt were both being threatened by Assyria's advances, and as happens frequently with political alliances, Judah and Egypt became friends because of the common enemy they faced. Hezekiah was a good king who loved God, but instead of looking to God as his exclusive resource, Hezekiah thought he would explore all his options. He cried out to God for help, but he also solicited the help of Egypt.

Isaiah 30 gives us a peak into four ways that Judah was looking for help from Egypt:

1. They looked to Egypt for counsel.

> Isaiah 30:1, "Woe to the rebellious children," says the LORD, "who take counsel, but not of Me, and who devise plans, but not of My Spirit, that they may add sin to sin; 2 Who walk to go down to Egypt, and have not asked My advice, to strengthen themselves in the strength of Pharaoh, and to trust in the shadow of Egypt! 3 Therefore the strength of Pharaoh shall be your shame, and trust in the shadow of Egypt shall be your humiliation. 4 For his princes were at Zoan, and his ambassadors came to Hanes."

Zoan was the place where Egypt's sages and Pharaoh's chief advisors lived (Isaiah 19:11). Hezekiah sent a delegation of nobles to Zoan to confer with Egypt's top minds. Egypt had a long-time record of military prowess, and Hezekiah probably wanted to glean from their battle experience.

How easily we also, like Hezekiah, grieve the Lord's heart by turning to the wisdom of the world. Have you noticed that when you're in crisis, everybody becomes an expert? Your friends and coworkers start doling out the advice. There can be incredible pressure to follow the advice of your worldly coworkers or family. When you tell them what the Bible has to say about your situation, they look at you like you're from Mars. As it was for Hezekiah, it can be so tempting to cave in to the counsel of well-intentioned but ungodly people. And when we do, God says that we "add sin to sin." Following worldly counsel only compounds our problems.

2. They looked to Egypt for commercial trade.

As the Assyrians came nearer, their approach was cutting off the trade routes that had fed the economy of Judah, so Judah was looking for Egypt to accelerate their trade of goods. And so the Lord spoke through Isaiah, "The burden against the beasts of the South. Through a land of trouble and anguish, from which came the lioness and lion, the viper and fiery flying serpent, they will carry their riches on the backs of young donkeys, and their treasures on the humps of camels, to a people who shall not profit" (Isaiah 30:6). The Lord is basically saying to Judah, "You're looking for Egypt to bolster your economy, and they're going to export their treasures up to you, but it will not profit you in the least."

Judah saw Egypt as its source of supply, and it's easy for us to do something similar today. What is your source of supply? When we see our job as the source of our supply, we'll start making all kinds of compromises. For example, we might accept the wrong promotion and end up working so much overtime that we're useless in the kingdom of God.

Some Christians have been intimidated into working on the Lord's Day because they've viewed their job, rather than God, as their source. God has ordained that we take a day each week for rest and worshipful meditation, but some believers work that day fearful that they'll lose their job if they don't. Or maybe they won't be able to pay the bills. And because of their compromise, they don't enter into the full liberty of kingdom living provided for them in Christ.

Christians should be among the most valued of employees because everything we do is unto the Lord. When we're on the job, we give 101% of ourselves because we do it as to the Lord. But we also draw our boundaries. Our job is permitted to require only so much of our time, and then it must bow to the other priorities God has called us to.

   3. They looked to Egypt for war horses.

   The Assyrians used horses in battle, and Hezekiah figured that if they were to have a fighting chance, they'd need horses, too. So we see in verse 16 that they turned to Egypt to supply them with horses: "And you said, 'No, for we will flee on horses' — Therefore you shall flee! And, 'We will ride on swift horses' — Therefore those who pursue you shall be swift!" (Isaiah 30:16).

   Make no mistake, Christians have battles. (As though that's news to anybody!) When the battles come, however, it can be so tempting to turn to the war horses of the world. Take pecuniary problems. When financial pressures invade, one of the world's war horses is that trusty credit card. Before I talk about credit card abuse, I want to clarify that credit cards can be okay to use as a convenience mechanism, when you have the money in the bank, and you can pay the balance in its entirety when it's due. It's understandably easier to use a piece of plastic rather than carrying a wad of cash with you. So I'm not maligning the controlled usage of credit cards when we have the money in the bank to cover our purchases.

   The world uses credit cards, however, as a means of salvation in times of crisis. When the crunch is on, the world just says, "Charge it!" So they spend money they don't have (see Romans 13:8). When the financial pressure is on, some Christians pray about it, but then when they don't see an immediate provision they say, "Thank God for MasterCard!" They don't realize that the delay of the provision is part of God's design for this particular season, and they actually short-circuit God's purposes by turning to Egypt.

> **They don't realize that the delay of the provision is part of God's design for this particular season, and they actually short-circuit God's purposes by turning to Egypt.**

They would have known a deepened maturity and would have gained a wonderful testimony, but instead they choose the "immediate deliverance" the credit card seems to afford and become impoverished spiritually for it.

   I can imagine God gesturing from His throne and exclaiming, "You never gave Me a chance!"

   "Yes I did, Lord. I gave you a week!"

   Selah.

   At the moment of crisis, we often face tremendous pressure to make a quick decision. Our family looks at us and says, "Well, you need to do **something**!" So we act impetuously, without waiting for God's provision, and bring heartache upon ourselves.

Let me mention yet another of the world's favorite war horses: that unassuming little health insurance card. We feel a crick in the neck or a pain in the tummy, so right away we say, "I'm going to the doctor." Why? Because it's covered! It can be so tempting for Christians, at the first sign of pain, to head for the hospital or for the doctor's office because they know their health insurance provider will pick up the tab. Again, let me clarify myself because I want to emphasize that I thank God for doctors and hospitals. In my opinion, they represent some of the most caring people in our land today. There are times when they are a tremendous blessing to us.

Here's where the rub is: when going to the doctor becomes our first recourse. Some Christians, in the face of a health need, will pray and ask the Lord for His provision, but when the answer doesn't appear immediately,

> **Here's where the rub is: when going to the doctor becomes our first recourse.**

they're off right away to the doctor. The Lord has spoken so clearly to us in His word, "**I'm** your Healer! I want to be the one who heals you. Look to Me!"

"Well, Lord, You know that I did come to you first with my health problems, but when You didn't answer my prayer right away, I had to do something."

How often we fail to recognize that the delay is part of God's provision for us! God is saying, "I'm going to heal you, but I'm also going to delay the healing for a season. That's going to put you under a lot of heat and pressure. But if you'll persevere and maintain your confidence in Me, you will come through this thing and in the end not only be healed, but greatly enlarged in your heart as well."

Is it possible that we don't see more healings today because we don't give God a chance? Smith Wigglesworth, when asked his opinion on doctors, thought it was better to die trusting than to live doubting. A testimony of healing in which God, doctors, operations, and medicines shared the credit always failed to find his full approval.

Now, I'm not saying it's wrong or sinful to consult a doctor. I'm saying it's wrong to consult a human doctor first before consulting Dr. Jesus. Ask Him what He wants you to do. If He gives you the nod to go to a physician, then go. And if He puts it within your heart to stand in faith for a divine healing, then stand and believe. This latter option carries the greater potential for blessing because as you

> **The greater the delay, the deeper the work.**

prepare yourself to wait for God's timing you know this: The greater the delay, the deeper the work.

As Smith Wigglesworth said, "Great faith is the product of great fights; great testimonies are the outcome of great tests; great triumphs can only come out of great trials."

Let's get back to the context of Isaiah 30.


4. They looked to Egypt for armed warriors.


Hezekiah was hoping he could sweet-talk Egypt into sending some warriors up to help them. We don't have to guess what the Lord thought about that: "Woe to those who go down to Egypt for help, and rely on horses, who trust in chariots because they are many, and in horsemen because they are very strong, but who do not look to the Holy One of Israel, nor seek the LORD!" (Isaiah 31:1).

Notice that when we turn to worldly resources for help in areas in which God wants to be our provider, we don't just miss out on the blessing of God's provision. We also incur a curse over our lives.

Hear the heart of your Father: "Don't look to the world for counsel, or for help, or for resources. Look to Me! I want to be your Everything!"

## Quietness And Confidence

The nation of Judah couldn't see that God was for them; all they could see was that Assyria was against them. It was during this period when the nation was under fear and dread of the Assyrians that the prophet Isaiah penned these words from the Lord: "For thus says the Lord GOD, the Holy One of Israel: 'In returning and rest you shall be saved; in quietness and confidence shall be your strength.' But you would not" (Isaiah 30:15).

These are gripping words, particularly in light of the fact that Assyria was breathing down the neck of the nation of Judah. Let's take the verse apart:

"in returning" — The Lord is calling them to return from pursuing other solutions. Returning is an act of repentance (see Hosea 6:1). The Lord is saying to them, "Come on back from Egypt, come home, and put your faith completely upon Me. Return your eyes to Me alone, press into Me, be reminded of My good intentions toward you, and let your expectation be entirely on Me."

"and rest" — In calling them to rest, God was basically saying, "Chill out. Relax. Stop all your frenetic activity, and learn to wait for Me to act."

"Uh...the problem, though, is that we've got an advancing army here, Lord.  I mean, we've got to do **something**, God!"

And the Lord's simply saying, "Do nothing."

The prophet then repeats these two themes (commonly called a "Hebrew parallelism").

"In quietness" — The word "quietness" corresponds thematically to the earlier word "rest," but it's a colorful word in itself.  It's the same word that is used in Scripture to describe wine that "settles" on its lees (Jeremiah 48:11).  As wine is being prepared, there is a process whereby it is placed on a shelf in total stillness so that the tiny

> **So God is literally saying to them, "Settle down."**

particles of sediment can settle to the bottom.  So God is literally saying to them, "Settle down."

"and confidence" — This word corresponds thematically with "returning," and it's as though the Lord were saying, "You need to recover the certainty that I will take care of you.  Unbelief and fear have robbed you of your confidence, and it's time to return and renew your stand of faith in who I am, and in what I have promised you in My word."

## Torn Between The Two

There can be a very real tension when trying to walk out the balance between "quietness" and "confidence."  It's very much like a paradox. In calling us to quietness and confidence simultaneously, God is basically saying, "Get your focus back on Me, seek Me with all your heart, renew your confidence that I will deliver you — and sit down, button up your lip, and do nothing."

The confused believer asks God for clarity: "Okay, Lord, do You want me to rise up in faith and confidence or settle down into a place of restful quietness?  Which one, Lord?  Rise up, or settle down?"

The Lord's answer is, "Yes."  He's wanting us to do both.

God is a God of paradox.  A similar tension is expressed in Hebrews 4:11, "Let us therefore be diligent to enter that rest, lest anyone fall according to the same example of disobedience."  An expanded paraphrase of Hebrews 4:11 might read like this: "Let us therefore give ourselves energetically and intensely, rising up with diligent resolve and earnest application, working and laboring assiduously — in order to kick back, chill out, settle down, shut up, sit down, relax, and rest peacefully."

The ways and thoughts of God are confusing to the natural mind.

What's more, they are very frustrating to the natural mind. No matter how hard he might try, the natural man simply cannot fulfill the righteous life that God requires.

I'll use the following example to try to illustrate the ways of God. You're running late for the airport, so you inhale a bowl of cereal, dash out the door, careen down the highway, veer into the airport, sprint down the corridor to the ticket counter — only to discover your airplane is delayed two hours. God does that kind of thing with us. Sometimes with God it's "hurry up to slow down."

And then, sometimes God does it the totally opposite way. Sometimes He'll keep you waiting for what seems like an eternity, so you can go ballistic. Just when you're getting used to doing nothing, everything explodes, and you hardly have time to breathe you're so busy.

## God Can Wait

Sometimes God seems to take forever. You wait and wait and wait. But when He finally moves, He does more in one hour than you could accomplish in a lifetime. So it's your choice: be busily consumed with your paltry attempts or wait on God until He moves in the fullness of His glory and purposes. God's sense of timing is like this: He waits forever and then moves suddenly and instantaneously. There's only one way to even begin to tune into God's sense of timing, and that is through waiting. Waiting transports us out of the temporal, out of our time-zone, and into His time-zone.

> So it's your choice: be busily consumed with your paltry attempts or wait on God until He moves in the fullness of His glory and purposes.

God can out-wait anybody. He just waits and waits, while the crisis looms larger and larger, and He waits some more. He waits until the crisis becomes an impossible predicament. And then He waits some more! Finally, when the remotest chance of escape is completely gone, God intervenes suddenly and miraculously. A good example of this is Abraham.

God promised Abraham a son when he was 75 years old, even though Sarah was barren. And then God waits five years, ten years, fifteen years, twenty years. By now it's too late. Even if Sarah were not barren, she is now too old, and so is Abraham. Twenty-five years. Count them. Twenty-five interminable years. Finally, when all natural hope was exhausted, God provided supernaturally, and Sarah became pregnant! God is the King of wait.

Even Jesus experienced the pain of waiting for the Father's timing.

Jesus had to wait thirty years before moving out into public ministry. If you look at the ratio of His life, for every year of public ministry He had to wait ten years. That's a 10-to-1 ratio. Try suggesting that as a preparation-to-ministry ratio for pastoral candidates today! At one level, Jesus was ready at age twelve. Already He had the knowledge to confound the sharpest scholars of His day. He could have been "The Prodigy Prophet." But instead the Father said He had to wait. For thirty years Jesus walked in the balance of quietness and confidence — quieting His soul daily as He waited on the Father's timing, and yet confident that His day of manifestation was most assuredly coming.

I am writing about this because to walk in the tension of quietness and confidence has become the greatest challenge of my life. I am not writing because I've mastered it but because I'm after it. There are pinnacles in the kingdom that are higher, but I know of none that are steeper.

> **To walk in the tension of quietness and confidence has become the greatest challenge of my life. I am not writing because I've mastered it but because I'm after it.**

I believe this message is very relevant to the body of Christ right now. It seems that many believers, who up to this point have been fairly stable in their walk with Christ, are suddenly finding themselves facing challenges that they have no idea how to overcome. You may feel a lot like Hezekiah. You've been serving God faithfully, but now stuff (a.k.a. the Assyrians) is coming against you, and you have no understanding why. You've gone through your spiritual checklist, but nothing's changing. You've interceded; you've rebuked; you've repented; you've claimed. You're at the end of your resources, and you don't know what else to do. Something inside wants to panic, "The Assyrians are coming! I've got to do **something**." The Lord wants to bring you to a clearer understanding of finding your strength in quietness and confidence.

## Cease From Anger

One of the first things the Lord wants to touch is our anger. This is seen in Psalm 37, where verses 7 and 8 are written as a pair of parallel verses with repeated themes. Psalm 37:7, "Rest in the LORD, and wait patiently for Him; do not fret because of him who prospers in his way, because of the man who brings wicked schemes to pass. 8 Cease from anger, and forsake wrath; do not fret — it only causes harm." Verse 7 starts with "Rest in the LORD," and the parallel verse starts with "Cease from anger." To rest in the Lord is to cease from anger. The rest and quietness God has for us is found only as we forsake wrath.

God also wants to cure us of impetuous decisions. In Isaiah 28:16 the Lord said, "'Behold, I lay in Zion a stone for a foundation, a tried stone, a precious cornerstone, a sure foundation; whoever believes will not act hastily.'" In its original context, the Lord was actually directing this statement to Hezekiah. God was saying that the person of faith will not act hastily or out of desperation when the crisis is on. Faith means: no frantic decisions in the face of crisis. The man of faith is willing to wait patiently for God's direction, provision, and salvation. The man of faith is unhurried and unflustered, calmed by a confidence in the unstoppable nature of the kingdom. He cannot be flustered into impetuous, snap decisions.

## Discerning The Source

When overwhelming circumstances (the Assyrians) are breathing down our neck, one of the questions we must handle is that of origin. Where did this crisis come from? It's a very important question because the answer will determine what our response must necessarily be.

There are at least four possibilities, or combinations thereof:

1.  Natural causes.

> **Faith means: no frantic decisions in the face of crisis.**

    We live in a fallen world, and accidents happen to good people. In some cases, troubles come to us because we just happened to be at the wrong place at the wrong time. Not every car accident is an attack. Sometimes accidents are just the result of driving fast vehicles in an imperfect world.

2.  Personal sin.
    Some difficulties we experience are either the direct consequences of sinful actions, or they are intended by God to cause us to turn from our sin. If your troubles have come upon you because of disobedience, you need to repent.

3.  Spiritual attack.
    Satan hates God's people, and he will do everything in his power to make our lives miserable, difficult, impaired, and painful. Sometimes the enemy gets angry at our progress in the kingdom and just outright comes against us. In times like this, God will give Satan limited freedom to attack us because He wants us to learn how to do spiritual warfare, to rise up in faith, to learn how to defeat the enemy, and see God's kingdom established. When demons are crawling all over you, oppressing and devouring you, that's not the time to say, "Oh, I'm just waiting on God." God wants you to learn how to

appropriate the provision of Calvary in the face of hell's offensive.

4. Purposed by God.

Sometimes God allows trauma or pressure in our lives to refine and change us so that we might become more like Christ and mature in love. It is this fourth category that is the foremost consideration of this book. In this sense, the devil becomes God's pawn. At times God will use the devil, but He will take the thing the enemy intends for evil and turn it around for good. It is at such a time that we must learn the secret of quietness and confidence.

# 11

# DANCE OF THE TWO CAMPS

*"For thus says the Lord GOD, the Holy One of Israel: 'In return-*
*ing and rest you shall be saved; in quietness and confidence shall*
*be your strength.' But you would not"* (Isaiah 30:15).

In the last chapter I said that to walk in the tension of quietness and confidence has become the greatest challenge of my life. The human tendency is to gravitate toward one or the other. Either it's quietness, or it's confidence. It would be easier on my flesh if I knew that God was saying either "rise up" or "quiet down" because then I could give myself wholeheartedly in just one direction. But when He says to do both, I have no idea how to do that, so I find myself crying out to God for help.

One of the greatest struggles in my own personal dilemma has been the question, "How do I position my soul?" I've wondered, does He want me to go after Him and pursue faith for healing? Or does He want me to back off, chill out, and give myself completely to total relinquishment and absolute surrender? As I agonized over this question month after month, I wrote out my struggles in my personal Journal. At the risk of being misunderstood, I'm going to print here some of my Journal entries during that period. I am opening these entries to you in the hope that they will serve those who find themselves in a similar place.

Please understand that these Journal entries: 1. were written in the privacy of my prayer closet and were never intended originally to be shared publicly; 2. are not statements of theological truth but rather the honest wrestlings of a desperate heart. As you read them, I think you'll be able to detect the struggle between the respective paths of quietness and confidence.

Journal entry:
I continually work under the impression that there's something I must do to come to a place of healing — some dimension of faith to find, or some dimension of surrender, confession, consecration. [Others] challenged me today to strive to enter into God's rest. It's so hard to rest when I feel I should be doing something. When I read testimonies of people who have been healed, it didn't happen by them doing nothing; it happened by pressing into a new level of faith. In all honesty I'm afraid to simply rest — could end up being not much more than wasted time, a postponing of the dimension of faith that I must inevitably find. I don't want to spin my wheels; I want to get on with God.

Journal entry:
I relate to Job 9:27-31 — it doesn't seem to matter what I consider doing, there's always some reason why that isn't the answer, or why it isn't sufficient. If I rest and do nothing, it seems that's exactly what happens, nothing. If I wrestle and seek to press into God, I feel like I'm striving. I'm damned if I do, and damned if I don't.

Journal entry:
I want to come to a place of perfect rest in God in my circumstances, but I cannot do that at the cost of letting go my hold on God's promises. I don't see God's promises as just offers of blessing, but as expressions of His character and person, expressions of who He is and how He has chosen to relate to man. So to let go of God's promises is a denial of who He is; it is a rejection of His character and His intentions toward me. Everything about the revelation of God in Scripture tells me that He is a God who wounds but then heals up. He leads through valleys, but always through, never just into. "God doesn't leave you there," the Scriptures seem to echo over and over to me.

Journal entry:
Is my infirmity making me a bitter person? Is it ruining me? If so, let it be; I will not let go. I will not resign myself to accepting this. I will not say, "If it be Thy will." I will not find a way to cope, to adjust, to live with it. The promises of God are too clear to do that — it would be a repudiation of His character. He is my healer. This infirmity is not His will for my life and ministry. He hasn't wounded me to leave me wounded.

Journal entry:
I've been struggling afresh with the entire thought that I need to find a

place of greater rest in this thing. [Others] have listened to my wrestlings and have told me I need to rest. But I find some of my most rewarding times to come when I go on a fast and press into God with all my might. When I wrestle with God with all my heart. Fancy telling Job he needed to find a place of rest. When you're in a place of physical infirmity, all you can do is pour out your wrestlings to God (which is what the book of Job is). I don't understand just why, but it seems to me that the thing that will unlock my deliverance and precipitate God's visiting me will not be "resting." I think it will be "seeking." Yes, I think it's easy to strive in a carnal, unproductive way in something like this. But I also think it's possible to wrestle with God until dawn comes.

In times of crisis, the balancing of quietness and confidence can become a veritable juggling match. A scriptural term for this is, "the dance of the two camps" (Song of Solomon 6:13). It is the dance of trying to find our balance between two seemingly paradoxical truths.

## Dance Of The Two Camps

The scriptural phrase "dance of the two camps" is a single word in the Hebrew language — "Mahanaim." Mahanaim was the place where Jacob divided his company into two camps so that if Esau would attack one camp, the other would be able to escape (see Genesis 32:9). When Solomon wrote of Mahanaim, chances are he had the more immediate association of the role Mahanaim played in his father's life. When King David, Solomon's father, was fleeing for his life from his own son Absalom, David fled to Mahanaim. Thus, Mahanaim represents the burden of choice the Israelites faced at that time, whether to support Absalom or David. Each one was forced to venture his best guess — would Absalom end up

> **Mahanaim represents the burden of choice the Israelites faced at that time.**

the winner, or David? Those who threw their lot in with David were vindicated because even though it didn't look like it at the time, David was God's anointed and chosen man for the throne.

The context of Mahanaim, "the dance of the two camps" (Song of Solomon 6:13), seems to bear out the idea that it refers to the friction that happens between sincere believers and insincere people who claim the name "Christian." Throughout history, fervent believers have always taken the most heat from institutionalized, religious "Christians." It's the Davids who have always been persecuted by the Sauls. When you get zealous for God, nobody will hate you more than the "Christian" who has no fervency for Jesus.

To give the term a broader application, church history has seen many dances between two camps. Perhaps the most notable would be the tension between the Calvinists and the Armenians. A contemporary dance occurs between "liberal" and "conservative" theologians who wrestle between two aspects of God's character — His justice and His love. Yet another dance is that which we're working with here in this book, the dance between quietness and confidence.

We've got two general schools of thought in the body of Christ today that I am choosing to call the "Quietness Camp," and the "Confidence Camp." The Quietness Camp emphasizes the necessity of surrender to the sovereignty of God, and the Confidence Camp emphasizes the availability of God's promises and power to those who will believe. Before I describe the "dance" that happens between them, we need to survey their respective positions.

> **The Quietness Camp emphasizes the necessity of surrender to the sovereignty of God, and the Confidence Camp emphasizes the availability of God's promises and power to those who will believe.**

## The Quietness Camp

First, let's look at the Quietness Camp. This camp has in its ranks some of the greatest saints of all history: Jeanne Guyon, Francis of Assisi, Fénelon, John of the Cross, Blaise Pascal, Thomas à Kempis, William Law, Ignatius Loyola, Teresa of Avila, and many others. To this list you could add the names of the Desert Fathers, the Puritans, the mystics, and the pietists. The overarching theme of this camp could be, "God's in control — trust Him!" Andrew Murray wrote a book whose title says it succinctly: Absolute Surrender.

There are so many passages that could be quoted, by multiplied hundreds of authors, to reflect the stance of the Quietness Camp. Here's just one quote from Jeanne Guyon as a sampling: "True abandonment holds back nothing. Not life, nor death, nor salvation, nor heaven, nor hell. Throw yourself into the hands of God. Nothing but good can come from it. Your Lord has promised to take care of all those who forsake themselves and abandon themselves to Him alone."

Here are some Scriptures the Quietness Camp might put forward as representing the heart of their position:

- It is good that one should hope and wait quietly for the salvation of the LORD. It is good for a man to bear the yoke in his youth. Let him sit alone and keep silent, because God has laid it on him; Let him put his mouth in the dust — there may yet be hope. Let him give his cheek to the one who strikes him, and be full of reproach. For the Lord will not cast off forever. Though He causes grief, yet He will show compassion according to the multitude of His mercies (Lamentations 3:26-31).

- "Nevertheless, not as I will, but as You will" (Matthew 26:39). [This great statement of our Lord Jesus, as He resigns Himself to the Father's will, is championed as the ultimate expression of faith and trust in the face of calamity and trouble.]

- Though He slay me, yet will I trust Him (Job 13:15).

## Pros And Cons

The Quietness message is a mighty gift to the church. It is a great attainment when we find that place of unquestioning and absolute surrender to His Lordship and goodness. If ever a generation needed to hear this message, it's ours. So many believers today have been weaned on a "take the world for Christ" theology that insidiously stirs up the self-promoting ambitions of sincere preachers who think their motives are pure. Many of today's "visionary leaders" are unbroken steeds, warriors without a limp, ministering from a place of strength instead of weakness. They are very sincere in their desire to build up the kingdom of God, but they are dangerous in that they have not yet come to discern the difference between their visionary campaigns and God's ways. The Quietness Camp specializes in understanding how God shapes a strong, determined vessel into a weak, dependent vessel that is useful in the Master's hands.

> The Quietness Camp specializes in understanding how God shapes a strong, determined vessel into a weak, dependent vessel that is useful in the Master's hands.

Affirming the invaluable contribution of the Quietness Camp, there are points where I struggle personally with the Quietness position. I have struggled with a variety of authors, but to communicate as clearly as possible, I will single out a book that I read recently by Gary Thomas, entitled, In The Face of God. Thomas seems to fall squarely in the Quietness Camp, and in referring to the need for absolute surrender, he says in one passage, "The scrapper in each of us must be retired." He makes that statement in the context of referencing Jacob's night-long wrestling with the angel. Thomas goes on to say, "There will likely be a time in our Christian journeys when, like Jacob, we will wrestle with God all night long. That night may last for months or even years. But there must eventually come a dawn when we say, 'OK, God, You win. You've broken me and I'm Yours. No more fighting. No more complaining. Lead me where You will. Not my will but Thine be done'" (p.84).

I do not agree with this interpretation of Jacob's wrestling. There is nothing in Jacob's story that indicates God was trying to get the fight out of him. To the contrary, it's Jacob's fighter-nature that precipitates the blessing of God in his life. Sometimes I wonder, what would have happened if Jacob had totally surrendered and just let go of the angel? I think he would have foregone the blessing. Jacob finally got the blessing because he wouldn't let go.

Jesus commends this kind of tenacity in His parable of the widow who wouldn't desist in her demand for justice (Luke 18:1-8). Clearly, God has put within man a "fighter instinct" that is His divine provision for us, an inner drive that enables us to press into the face of God in times of great yearning.

On the other side, it's true that we can fight for something in the flesh, and miss God. Like Abraham, it's possible to strive in a carnal way toward a good goal and in the end give birth to an Ishmael. Here's where the pain is. It can become a constant struggle to discern, "Lord, at what point do I cross the line from tenacity into carnal striving?" No book can answer that question for you. Thank God we have the Holy Spirit who abides within to help us!

## Does God Want Us Infirm?

One of the giants of the Quietness Camp was a man by the name of Blaise Pascal, a man of great spirituality who died prematurely of a debilitating infirmity. He had found a place of great surrender to God's will, no matter what might happen to him physically. A remarkable theologian, in time he became too sick to continue his great theological treatise. So he turned toward reaching out to the poor. Author Gary Thomas comments: "He simply found a new way to carry out his desire to serve God. Everything was placed upon the altar, and there was no bitterness at all when God decided to keep it. Pascal just kept serving the Lord. God, make me like that man!"

I am about to incur the disagreement of some of my readers, but I cannot stand with Thomas in his above statement. The human spirit has been created by God to be greatly resilient, and it is no mark of spirituality when a person is able to find ways to redirect his or her energies because of physical limitations. The world has many people who have been injured or impaired in their ability to function in certain ways physically and, as a result, have discovered other ways to give expression to their creativity and talents. To do so is not a sign of spirituality or surrender but simply a common response that is characteristic of man's resilience. Unbelievers have done it, as have believers. But for some reason we'll look at a believer who has embraced physical impairment and redirected their energies into other expressions, and we'll admire their surrender to God's will.

I am writing this during a season of physical impairment. The Quietness Camp would probably offer me counsel something along these lines: "Embrace the fact that God has injured and restricted you, and do something else with your life according to the best of your remaining abilities." For them, that would constitute "absolute surrender." But for me, that's surrendering the integrity of God's promises to be my healer.

Ignatius Loyola is quoted as saying, "We do not for our part wish for health rather than sickness, for wealth rather than poverty, for honor rather than dishonor, for a long life rather than a short one; and so in all other things, desiring and choosing only those which most lead us to the end for which we were created." Such statements are classic to the Quietness Camp, and yet are difficult to reconcile with the prayer of the apostle John, "Beloved, I pray that you may prosper in all things and be in health, just as your soul prospers" (3 John 1:2).

I recently heard a preacher declare, "God's more interested in your character than you getting your miracle." In other words, get your focus off your deliverance and enjoy the character that is being produced in your life. But I find myself asking, "Why can't we have both? Why can't we become more Christlike in our attitudes and also experience the power of His resurrection?" I'm glad Jesus didn't preach that gospel to the crowds who came to Him! Yes, I believe God can work in someone's life through sickness, but the whole purpose is to bring them to a place of healing and renewed fruitfulness.

Clearly then, while I hold great appreciation for the contribution of the Quietness Camp to our understanding of God's ways, I see its message as incomplete and at times imbalanced.

## The Confidence Camp

Now let's take a look at the Confidence Camp. I believe it's reasonable to put men like John Wesley, William Booth, Billy Sunday, and Dwight L. Moody in this camp, but for the purpose of being relatable I will focus on twentieth century leaders. The beginning of the twentieth century saw the witness of some great men and women who pioneered many of the convictions of the Confidence Camp, such as F.F. Bosworth, Smith Wigglesworth, Aimee Semple McPherson, John Lake, and Rees Howells. According to my own personal analysis, this camp gained great strength in the 1940s and 1950s through the ministries of men and women who were commonly known as "healing evangelists." Far from a complete listing, we could mention Oral Roberts, Jack Coe, T.L. Osborn, Kathryn Kuhlman, A. A. Allen, William Branham, as well as many others.

The great cry of these ministries was, "Jesus saves, heals, and delivers! He is the same, yesterday, today, and forever! It was His will to heal when He walked the roads of Galilee, and it's still His will to heal today!" The entire world was impacted with their message and with the displays of supernatural power that attended their crusades as the word of God was preached with signs following. Tulsa, Oklahoma became the headquarters for many of these ministries, and in time people began to call it the "Word of Faith Movement." Many ministries sprang from Tulsa because of the fathering efforts of Oral Roberts and Kenneth Hagin Sr. Some of today's prominent leaders who have been greatly impacted by Tulsa ministries are Kenneth Copeland, Fred Price, John Osteen, Ray McCauley, Marilyn Hickey, and Billy Joe Daugherty — to name just a few.

I mention these names only to try to help my readers get a point of reference. I feel that I personally have profited especially from the ministry of Kenneth Hagin. His writings helped me to see that Jesus didn't die in order for us to get stomped all over by the devil. Some believers are being harassed and assaulted by the enemy, but instead of rising up in the provision of Calvary, they lay back down and prayerfully whimper, "Not my will but Thine be done, O Lord." That's not submission; that's ignorance.

> **Some believers are being harassed and assaulted by the enemy, but instead of rising up in the provision of Calvary, they lay back down and prayerfully whimper, "Not my will but Thine be done, O Lord." That's not submission; that's ignorance.**

## Divine Healing And God's Will

Perhaps more significantly than anything else, this is the truth that was heralded to the church: "It **is** God's will to heal you!" When the leper came to Jesus and said, "Lord, if You are willing, You can make me clean," Jesus responded by saying, "I am willing; be cleansed." And immediately his leprosy was healed! (See Matthew 8:2-3.) When it comes to healing, we no longer have to pray, "If it be Thy will," because we **know** His will! Jesus expressed His will in Matthew 8:2, "I am willing, be healed."

David declares, "Bless the LORD, O my soul, and forget not all His benefits: Who forgives **all** your iniquities, who heals **all** your diseases" (Psalm 103:2-3). Matthew testifies, "And He cast out the spirits with a word, and healed **all** who were sick" (Matthew 8:16). The Confidence Camp has boldly trumpeted their claim that it's God's will to heal all our diseases and provide for all our needs (Philippians 4:19). Opposition from critics has been fierce, but it's difficult to argue with Scripture that is accompanied with tangible manifestations of physical healings and miracles.

The Confidence Camp has done much to edify and strengthen the body of Christ, imparting an understanding of the work of the cross and a boldness to believe God for supernatural intervention. As with the Quietness Camp, their contribution has been wonderful and certainly ordained of God.

## Limited Maturity

Having established the validity of the Confidence Camp, I will go on to say that I have struggled over some of the things I've seen in that camp. I have seen how the "faith message," when not properly balanced with other scriptural truths, has tended to produce self-aware Christians. In extreme cases, Jesus is portrayed almost as my servant, instead of me as His servant. Jesus becomes something like a personal Santa Claus, who delivers all the gifts that I want. He's my Savior, my healer, my deliverer, my provider, my protector, my supply, my my my... Now, all that is true, but when that is the constant message, it can produce a self-absorbed focus. The message becomes, "How to get what you want from God." "How to get your prayers answered." "How to live like a King's kid in this life."

In so doing, many in the Confidence Camp have held their students at a certain level of immaturity. They have done very well at teaching their people "who you are in Christ," but that is a relatively youthful teaching. Consequently, many believers have hung out at the "young adult" level instead of progressing into the deeper truths of "who Christ is in you."

> **In so doing, many in the Confidence Camp have held their students at a certain level of immaturity.**

Some in the Confidence Camp have taught that sickness, infirmity, grief, and heartache have no place in the believer's life. They have taught believers how to take immediate measures to overcome all such distress. I wonder, though, if some of our faith teachings might attempt to short-circuit some of God's dealings, and thus circumvent some of the ways the Lord wants to enlarge our hearts. Is it possible to "claim" our way out of duress that God had designed to produce a deeper maturity in us? The children of Israel demonstated an unwillingness in the wilderness to accept the hunger and thirst that God destined for them. They illustrate that it's possible to get what we want, to our own hurt.

Dr. Fredrick K.C. Price was recently quoted in "Spirit Life Magazine" (Jan/Feb 1996), in reference to Hebrews 11:6, as saying, "Anything that is negative or harmful, God couldn't have anything to do with, because that's not a reward!" But if we have no understanding of the God who brings pain into our lives for His higher purposes, then we may well end up rebuking the devil for something that came to us from God's hand.

The faith message of the Confidence Camp is a great message, but it does not reflect the highest levels of maturity in Christ. Perhaps this is seen best in the following passage:

> 1 John 2:12, I write to you, little children, because your sins are forgiven you for His name's sake. 13 I write to you, fathers, because you have known Him who is from the beginning. I write to you, young men, because you have overcome the wicked one. I write to you, little children, because you have known the Father. 14 I have written to you, fathers, because you have known Him who is from the beginning. I have written to you, young men, because you are strong, and the word of God abides in you, and you have overcome the wicked one.

In these verses, John describes three general levels of spiritual maturity: spiritual childhood, spiritual adolescence or young adulthood, and spiritual fatherhood. The "young men" are the spiritual adolescents, the young adults in Christ. Notice the spiritual attainments of the young men:

- they have overcome the wicked one
- they are strong
- the word of God abides in them

These are very dynamic attainments. These young men are strong in the grace of Christ, they have learned spiritual warfare, they have experienced great spiritual victories, they know the word, they live in the word, and they can teach the word in profound and compelling ways. All of this is incredibly true of the Confidence Camp. The problem is, many have viewed this as the ultimate spiritual attainment when in fact there is yet another dimension of fruitfulness in Christ — fatherhood.

On the whole, the Confidence Camp has fallen short in awakening believers to knowing "Him who is from the beginning." The steppes of spiritual fatherhood are attained only at the price of great personal pain and suffering, and whereas the Confidence Camp has taught how to gain victory **over** pain, they have lacked the ability to teach how to gain victory **through** pain.

## The Dance

So far in this chapter I have endeavored to describe the positions of the Quietness Camp and the Confidence Camp and to express the strengths and potential defects on both sides. With that as a backdrop, let me assure you: The sparks really fly between these two camps! I've seen people in the Quietness Camp express their contempt for certain leaders in the Confidence Camp. And I've heard preach-

> **The sparks really fly between these two camps!**

ers in the Confidence Camp ripping to shreds some of the truths held dear by the Quietness Camp.

To illustrate the passion of the debate, I'd like to tell you about a television program I saw one time, in which a Confidence Camp preacher came against St. Francis of Assisi. This preacher was saying that there is no such thing as "holy poverty." He declared emphatically that poverty is not holy but a curse. From that point he proceeded to teach the people that God has promised to supply all our needs (Philippians 4:19), so believers don't have to live under the curse of poverty any longer. I agree with the point this preacher was trying to make but also realized that he totally misunderstood Francis's call to "holy poverty."

Francis of Assisi lived in the thirteenth century, at a time when the Roman Catholic Church was probably the wealthiest and most influential organization on the planet. Corruption was rampant, and Francis saw how the wealth of the church had contributed to its excessiveness, self-indulgence, and ecclesiastical hypocrisy. The Lord gave Francis a vision of how to present a prophetic witness to a corrupt church, and it involved the voluntary acceptance of a vow of poverty ("holy poverty"). Francis and his followers pledged themselves to a lifestyle of simplicity, trusting God for their daily bread. In this way, God brought renewal to the Roman Church through a band of beggars. Their radical willingness to emulate Jesus' lifestyle (who didn't have a place to rest His head) inspired a profound renewal in their generation, as well as touching subsequent generations with their fervency.

There's a difference between voluntary poverty and involuntary poverty. The first can be embraced in obedience to Jesus; the second is a curse. Perhaps he didn't understand this distinction, but the television preacher I watched put all poverty in one category and came against the whole thing. He called his listeners to break free of all poverty through the grace of Calvary's provision.

In this and a myriad of many other ways, proponents of each camp have clashed and danced and debated most heatedly over the years.

## When God Increases The Pressure

Perhaps you've read all this about the dance of the two camps, and you still don't understand what the fuss is all about. Maybe you find yourself wondering, "What's the big deal? I have no problem with embracing both quietness and confidence at the same time." In actuality, quietness and confidence are **easy** to balance — until the Assyrians invade. Maybe you've experienced this, but it's interesting how we can have victory in a certain area and feel like we've got that area fairly well mastered, and then when mayhem strikes we suddenly find our previous attainment to be woefully inadequate. It's one thing to have faith in times of peace; it's altogether another thing to have faith that survives times of war.

When all hell breaks loose, it's amazing how quickly our quietness and confidence can disappear. It can be an enormous challenge to rebuild both quietness and confidence while the crisis continues to rage about us.

## Embracing Both Camps

Walking through the furnace of affliction, I have asked the Lord whether I should give myself to fervent seeking (confidence) or to restful waiting (quietness). I saw the scriptural validity of both postures but didn't know which way He wanted me to posture my soul. As I sought the Lord on this, asking Him whether to direct my soul toward quietness or toward confidence, I sensed the answer coming from the Lord's heart: "Yes." He was saying, "Give yourself to both." He wanted me to see that the answer is in receiving **both** camps.

God wants you to become fully surrendered to the fullness of His will and purpose for your life (quietness), and He also wants to heal you (confidence). The two seem almost contradictory at times, so let me express

> It's God's will to heal you, to provide your financial needs, and to answer all your prayers that are according to His will, but sometimes He delays the answer in order to work a greater surrender in our hearts.

as clearly as I can my best understanding of God's ways in this arena: **It's God's will to heal you, to provide your financial needs, and to answer all your prayers that are according to His will, but sometimes He delays the answer in order to work a greater surrender in our hearts**.

When the crisis hits, and you feel that you're about to be drowned by an Assyrian army, hear the heart of your Father: "Find a place of quietness in Me by settling your soul and stilling your spirit, and relinquish everything into My hands; and let your heart rise up in confidence in Me, by pressing into My face, devouring My word, claiming My promises, and making the good confession!"

How to do both of those simultaneously may well be one of the greatest spiritual challenges you'll ever face.

## Concluding Journal Entry

I opened this chapter with some excerpts from my Journal. Let me close with yet another excerpt, this one written at a time when the truths of this chapter were starting to crystalize in my understanding. You will see that I was still in process, but the progress is evident:

There has been a new level of quietness and confidence in my heart in the past week, and I'm watching to see if it's permanent, or just another phase. When it's permanent, I'll know God has done something significant in me. There is a renewed confidence that God will heal me — in His time. I'm seeing even clearer how the Lord is lifting me to a higher plane, and the more I see it, the more my confidence grows. My prayer is, complete the work you've started in me, Lord. I am to the point where I am actually grateful that God hasn't healed me yet, because if I had been healed earlier, there are things I have attained in the Spirit that would not have been attained. There is no question that the desperation of my soul has awakened a fervency in me for the knowledge of the Son of God. The greater the pain, the greater the desperation; the greater the desperation, the greater the fervency; the greater the fervency, the greater the potential for depth of relationship. In my case at least, my pain has been the gift of God, His mercy initiated toward me. He has mercy on whom He has mercy. He placed the cry for a higher plane within me, and now He's leading me on His pathway to that higher plane.

# CHAPTER 12

# WAITING FOR
# DELAYED ANSWERS

*"For thus says the Lord GOD, the Holy One of Israel: 'In return-
ing and rest you shall be saved; in quietness and confidence shall
be your strength.' But you would not"* (Isaiah 30:15).

We concluded in the previous chapter that God wants us to receive
from both camps — from both the Quietness Camp and the Confidence
Camp. As I have sought to do that, let me tell you where God has brought
me. The best way I can describe it is with two millstones. Imagine two
millstones coming together and grinding wheat to powder. That's the
picture God brought to my mind to express where He had me.

### The Middle Squish

He didn't have me with one foot in the Confidence Camp and one
foot in the Quietness Camp. He had me right in the vortex of where the
two come together, and He was grinding me to powder in the tension of
where the two rub against each other. God stuck me in that place of
friction and heat and then announced the delay. So this wasn't going to
be a quick pass-through, but the crushing would be ongoing and con-
tinual.

I figured there had to be a way to glean the best from both camps
and be enriched by both, while coming away with a balanced and bibli-
cal perspective that was somewhat different from either. I just didn't
realize there would be so much heat on the pathway to finding it. It's a
blessed heat, however, for it produces an invaluable brokenness in the
heart when we receive God's dealings instead of becoming bitter.

There was one dynamic I didn't figure on, however. I learned that
when you find yourself in the squeeze between both camps, nobody in

either camp likes you. The folks in the Quietness Camp don't think you understand surrender to God's will because you insist that it's God's will to deliver you. The folks in the Confidence Camp don't see anything redemptive in the way you're suffering, and they figure if you were truly walking with God that you'd be healed already.

## Psalm 34:19

The tension between the two is expressed so beautifully in Psalm 34:19, "Many are the afflictions of the righteous, but the Lord delivers him out of them all." When it really comes down to it, folks on the extreme ends of both camps probably don't enjoy this verse very much. The Confidence Camp doesn't like the first phrase, "Many are the afflictions of the righteous." If a person is really walking in righteousness, some of them teach, then he will walk in divine health and divine provision and divine protection. There will be a hedge about his life, and he will not be susceptible to afflictions. If, however, anything does happen to him, then they love the second half of that verse: "but the Lord delivers him out of them all." They will shout a hearty "amen!" to that.

The Quietness Camp feels the totally opposite way about this verse. They embrace with conviction the first phrase, "Many are the afflictions of the righteous." Ah, yes, how well they know those words. These sons of Job understand clearly that God allows affliction in the lives of the righteous in order to purify their lives, and produce a deeper fruitfulness in them. They'll even sing about their many afflictions. But then they stumble over the second half of the verse, "but the Lord delivers him out of them all." I wonder if they might even feel that statements like that can be misleading, giving people false expectations of God's supernatural intervention. Some of them certainly feel that if you put your heart upon being delivered that you're putting your focus on the wrong thing and missing the point of God's dealings altogether. They might say things like, "You're seeking the healing and not the healer."

The good news is, when you seek Jesus, you get everything. You get healing because He's the healer; but you also get maturity because He's the refiner's fire.

> **The good news is, when you seek Jesus, you get everything.**

It's time, friends, for the church to say yes to both sides of Psalm 34:19, "Many are the afflictions of the righteous, but the Lord delivers him out of them all."

## Jesus On Quietness/Confidence

When I think I'm getting fresh insight into a spiritual truth, I always like to find that truth in the life or teachings of our Lord Jesus. If I can see it in Jesus, then I feel especially safe. I believe I see Jesus articulating this very dilemma between quietness and confidence, but He uses two different words: "receive" and "take."

The quietness side of the equation is reflected in Luke 18:17, "Assuredly, I say to you, whoever does not **receive** the kingdom of God as a little child will by no means enter it." Jesus is simply saying that the kingdom must be received. In fact, Jesus is quite emphatic about it. He's basically saying, "There's only **one** way to enter the kingdom, and that is by receiving." In another place He affirms, "It is your Father's good pleasure to **give** you the kingdom" (Luke 12:32). So the message is clear: The Father gives the kingdom, and we receive it as little children — with an open, yielded, simple embracing of all that God chooses to give.

The confidence side of the equation is reflected in Matthew 11:12, "And from the days of John the Baptist until now the kingdom of heaven suffers violence, and the violent **take** it by force." Here Jesus says the kingdom is **taken**. The word "taken" (Greek "harpadzo") means, "to seize, snatch away, catch up, take by force." It suggests the exercise of a sudden force. "So the kingdom," Jesus is saying, "is available only to those who violently take it." The same idea is reinforced in Luke 11:9, "Seek, and you will find."

So which is it?? Do I receive the kingdom, or do I take the kingdom? Do I settle and quiet my heart to receive what He wants to give, or do I rise up in confidence and take my kingdom inheritance by force? Jesus simply answers, "Yes." The Holy Spirit is the only one who can teach us how to walk this out.

> **Do I settle and quiet my heart to receive what He wants to give, or do I rise up in confidence and take my kingdom inheritance by force? Jesus simply answers, "Yes."**

## A Quick Work

In the last chapter I made this statement: "It's God's will to heal you, to provide your financial needs, and to answer all your prayers that are according to His will, but sometimes He delays the answer in order to work a greater surrender in our hearts." God uses delay as one of His chief tools of refining human character.

Those who are attuned to the heartbeat of the Holy Spirit in this hour also recognize that the Spirit is stirring an incredible urgency in the hearts of His people because the hour is so late. The harvest is ripe, and the need for laborers who will minister in the words and works of Jesus is of critical proportions. Jesus is returning so very soon (somebody say hallelujah!), and so God is doing a quick work in His people today. He's preparing us quickly. To do a quick work, God is turning up the heat and pressure everywhere. It's happening the world over. Saints and leaders everywhere are testifying to shakings, fire, distress, persecutions, and affliction. The hour is late, and God's people must be prepared quickly.

Understanding the urgency of the Holy Spirit, this next statement will sound contradictory, but it's very true: To do the quickest work, God waits.

To do the quickest work, God uses the hottest flame. There is no hotter flame, in my opinion, than waiting on God. Nothing purifies us faster than when we have to wait on God.

> **There is no hotter flame, in my opinion, than waiting on God.**

The "Assyrians" invade your life. In other words, a crisis erupts, or an emergency suddenly hits. You're thrown into a tailspin, and you have no idea what to do. So you cry out to the Lord, "God, what should I do? Quickly, Lord, answer me! I'll do anything, just tell me quickly."

The Lord responds, "Wait on Me. Look only to Me. Don't look to Egypt for help. Don't look to other human resources. Fix your eyes on Me, and wait for Me."

Folks, when your world is collapsing, and God just tells you to wait on Him, it doesn't get any hotter than that.

Your friends look with alarm at the crisis in your life, and they ask, "What are you doing about this?"

You say, "Nothing."

"Nothing? Did you say nothing?"

"Yes, nothing. I'm not doing anything about this situation. I'm waiting on God."

Imagine how they're looking at you. They're thinking, "I can't believe this. When is she going to grow up? When is she going to start exercising responsibility for her life?"

Nobody understands you right now. Your life is in shambles, and it appears that you're doing nothing about it except laying there and crying out to God. Nothing is changing, and God is saying to wait. This is how God does a quick work in us.

## How God Prepared Moses

Sometimes we're tempted to pray, "Okay, Lord, I'm willing to wait on You. But why do You make Your servants wait **so long**?" We need to be awakened to this general kingdom principle: The

> **The greater the wait, the greater the work.**

greater the wait, the greater the work.

This principle is seen most graphically in the life of Moses, who perhaps had to wait the longest of anyone in the Bible for God's answers to come to his life. Moses had to wait through forty years of training in the wilderness before God released him to lead His people. We look at forty years and groan, "I'll be **dead** in forty years, Lord!" To wait forty years seems to us today to be the ultimate punishment.

But let me remind you of the glories Moses knew. Perhaps no one had to wait as long as he did, but I dare say that no one else in the Bible (apart from Jesus) knew the glory of God like Moses did either. He saw the burning bush, the rod turned into a serpent, the ten plagues upon Egypt, the parting of the Red Sea, water out of the rock, manna on the ground. Then God appears to him on Mount Sinai — there's thunder and lightnings, a thick cloud, a very loud trumpet blasting, the mountain is on fire, and smoke is billowing off it like a furnace — and God calls Moses to the top of the mountain! He receives the Law, comes down to the golden calf scene, and then goes up the mountain for a second set of forty days. It's at this time that Moses prays, "Please, show me Your glory" (Exodus 33:18).

It's reasonable to think that God could have been upset with Moses' request. "You ungrateful wretch! After all I've done for you, after all the miracles I've displayed before you, after the way I've allowed you to come into My presence, all you can ask for is more?" But instead of being upset with Moses, God seems to be pleased, for He proceeds to reveal to Moses the most that he could handle; He shows His back to Moses. When Moses came down the mountain from this visit, he didn't realize it, but his face actually shone with the glory of God.

Moses had his priorities in proper order. Above all, he longed for the glory of God. One of the holiest hungers we can have is for the glory of God. O, to see His glory! God honored Moses' request and gave to him the most unique view of Himself in all of history. When you consider the incredible glory Moses experienced, it's fascinating to notice this prayer at the end of his life: "You have **begun** to show Your servant Your greatness and Your mighty hand" (Deuteronomy 3:24). Moses is saying, "As great as the revelations of Yourself to me have been, I've only **begun** to see Your greatness and power." Wow! If what Moses experienced was the Alpha, then I'm really anxious to share in the Omega.

Now here's a very difficult question, dear reader. Do you think Moses' forty years in the wilderness were worth all that glory? And are you willing to

> **Do you think Moses' forty years in the wilderness were worth all that glory?**

wait for God in the wilderness for as long as God ordains, joyfully realizing that the longer the wait the greater the glory?

## Connecting Verses 15 & 18

Back to Isaiah 30. Look with me, please at the context of God's call to quietness and confidence:

> Isaiah 30:15, For thus says the Lord GOD, the Holy One of Israel: "In returning and rest you shall be saved; in quietness and confidence shall be your strength." But you would not, 16 And you said, "No, for we will flee on horses" — Therefore you shall flee! And, "We will ride on swift horses" — Therefore those who pursue you shall be swift! 17 One thousand shall flee at the threat of one, at the threat of five you shall flee, till you are left as a pole on top of a mountain and as a banner on a hill. 18 Therefore the LORD will wait, that He may be gracious to you; and therefore He will be exalted, that He may have mercy on you. For the LORD is a God of justice; blessed are all those who wait for Him.

I want you to see the link between verses 15 and 18. In verse 15, the Lord calls the people to quietness and confidence. But they didn't like that message, so in verse 16 we see that they adopt "Plan B." They decide to flee for their lives. So in verse 18 the Lord comes to them and basically says, "You're in a panic right now, and I see that you're running for cover. You can run all you want, but I'm going to wait for you to exhaust all your options. And when you've come to the end of yourself, then I'll be able to bring my salvation to your life."

Fact is, God can wait an awfully long time. Time is one commodity of which He's got plenty extra. Notice, however, the focus He wants us to maintain: "Therefore the LORD will wait, that He may be gracious to you" (v.18a). The Lord is saying, "I want you to keep in mind why I'm waiting so long. I'm waiting for you because I intend to be gracious to you."

| "My grace comes to those who wait." |

In other words, God is saying, "My grace comes to those who wait." If we flee, we forfeit the grace.

## How God Is Exalted

Look now at verse 18b, "And therefore He will be exalted, that He may have mercy on you." God's going to wait until you come to the end of yourself. Then He's going to have mercy on you. Mercy in this context means "undeserved help."

God is not exalted in our lives when we say, "Lord, You know that I've followed you faithfully — I've dotted every 'i' and I've crossed every 't' — and now I'm handling this trial so perfectly that You really ought to answer my prayer." How can God be exalted in that kind of situation? Glory to you, you deserve His blessings.

God is exalted, rather, when we say, "Lord, You know I've blown it. You know that I've been weak and I've failed, but You still answered my prayer, even when my responses weren't perfect. You showed me mercy when I didn't deserve it. You're incredible, Lord!"

That's what verse 18b is saying. God is exalted when we're humbled, and waiting is one of the most humbling things you'll ever do. If God's blessings touch us before we're broken, we'll find a way to accept partial credit. When God's grace touches and transforms a vessel that's been

> **God is exalted when we're humbled, and waiting is one of the most humbling things you'll ever do.**

completely broken, He alone is exalted.

When God calls us to wait on Him, He really needs to shower His mercy on us because when it comes to waiting we all blow it. We all get a bad attitude. We all get impatient. We all get angry. We all have a little pity-party. None of us is capable of handling waiting properly. Waiting pulverizes us and surfaces all the garbage in our hearts that we never even knew existed. By the time God's finished with us, we've blown it so many times that He can finally say, "Okay, now I can reveal my mercy and be exalted in this person." We realize that His redemptive work in us was not because of our right responses, but only because of His mercy. In the end, only He is exalted.

## A God Of Justice

Verse 18c, "For the LORD is a God of justice."

Now this is the part we have such a hard time believing. To say He is a God of justice is to say He always does what is right, He is always true to His word, He is always self-consistent, and He never withholds a blessing that is due the righteous. God's justice may be delayed (delayed answers), but He always comes through for those who persevere in righteousness. When His justice is delayed, however, the human tendency is to accuse God of injustice.

God is a God of justice. That is a declaration of His character and His ways. That's who He is. The saint's shelter, in time of storm, is the very essence of God's personhood. It's the confidence that He is a God of justice that enables us to persevere. That He is a God of justice points to two truths: 1) He was just in allowing the crisis to hit our lives. How easily we can accuse God by saying, "I didn't deserve this." Instead, the Lord wants us to come to the confession of Nehemiah 9:33, "You are just in all that has befallen us." 2) His justice means that He will most assuredly be true to His promises and fulfill His word in our lives.

It's in this setting that we need to look at Isaiah 40:27, "Why do you say, O Jacob, and speak, O Israel: 'My way is hidden from the Lord, and my just claim is passed over by my God'?" The people were accusing God of being less than fully just because He was not supplying their "just claim." They were standing on the promises; they were claiming the word of God; they were asking God to honor His covenant with them. And the answer wasn't coming. So they grew impatient and began to malign the character of God. They said, "God doesn't always fulfill His promises. You can pray, but He doesn't always answer. Sometimes He doesn't even seem to pay you any attention. It's as though your existence is hidden from Him, and He forgets totally about you. Claim the promise if you want, but chances are He'll pass over you, too."

When the Lord showed that verse to me (Isaiah 40:27), it hit me very hard because I realized that's exactly what I had done. I had accused God of bypassing me, of not fulfilling His promise in my case. Then the Lord gently reminded me of the statement just four verses later: "But those who wait on the Lord shall renew their strength" (Isaiah 40:31). The Lord connected the two verses for me and whispered to my heart, "I am a God of justice, and I will fulfill your just claim — if you wait on Me."

> **The Lord connected the two verses for me and whispered to my heart, "I am a God of justice, and I will fulfill your just claim — if you wait on Me."**

When I'm walking in righteousness, the promises of God are my "just claim." When I invoke the promises of God as my just claim, I am not being arrogant; I am not being presumptuous; I am not being audacious or insolent. I am exercising my rightful place in Christ, and I am affirming who God is. I cross over into presumption when I try to tell God when and how to fulfill His promises in my life. Isaiah 30:18 is giving us the key here: God's justice comes to those who wait.

Recently I read the poignant story of a Chinese brother who was imprisoned a few years ago for preaching the gospel. His name is Yun, and he was transferred to a certain prison where the Lord directed him to go on a fast. He fasted from both food and water for 74 consecutive days which in itself was a most remarkable miracle. During his fast, he endured horrendous abuse by the guards and his fellow prisoners. Rewarded by the guards for abusing Yun, his fellow prisoners urinated on his head daily. But Yun held to his fast and prayed incessantly. At the end of his fast, the Spirit of boldness came upon him, he preached the gospel to his cellmates, and all fifteen of them repented and came to the Lord in one afternoon. Yun's story is a compelling illustration that God is a God of justice who rewards those who wait upon Him.

## Succumbing To Unbelief

The first commonly made mistake during the time of delay is, we so often fall into unbelief. We suppose, "God's not doing anything, so I better do something." When we succumb to unbelief, we derail God's purposes for our lives. One of the foremost reasons for unbelief is that many believers don't understand God's purposes in delaying the answer. They don't know God. They assume the delay means God isn't going to intervene, and they sabotage the whole thing by giving up and taking matters into their own hands. Far too many saints miss God's best because they panic and move out in their own wisdom. God watches while His precious ones are destroyed, and He says, "It's all because they don't know Me." (See Hosea 4:6, which says that God's people are destroyed because they don't have a knowledge of God.)

If there's unbelief in our hearts, there's no fire that's better at bringing that to the surface than having to wait. Waiting really is the hottest flame. Jehoram, one of Israel's kings, learned this first-hand. 2 Kings 6 records the story of how the Syrians had besieged Samaria, and King Jehoram was seeking God for a deliverance (seen in the fact that he was wrapped in sackcloth). It seems that Elisha had been encouraging Jehoram to wait upon God for His deliverance, but when Jehoram saw that the people had resorted to cannibalism in order to survive, he decided that he had waited upon God long enough. Waiting wasn't working. He concluded that Elisha had been deluding him with vain hopes of God's intervention, and so he moved into action.

Jehoram said, "God do so to me and more also, if the head of Elisha the son of Shaphat remains on him today" (2 Kings 6:31). He also said, "Why should I wait for the LORD any longer?" (2 Kings 6:33). In other words, Jehoram was saying, "That's it! I've had it! No more waiting on God. Elisha's counsel isn't working, so he's going to meet the fate of a false prophet." So he set out to murder the prophet Elisha.

When there's wickedness in our hearts, God will wait until that wickedness surfaces. He is capable of applying as much heat as it takes to surface the garbage in our hearts, no matter how much we might try to

> He is capable of applying as much heat as it takes to surface the garbage in our hearts, no matter how much we might try to mask our sinfulness with piety.

mask our sinfulness with piety.

One of the strongest temptations in my season of affliction has been, "Just quit. Resign the church, and quit the ministry. God's given you a bum rap. He's rewarded your service with calamity. Crawl into a cocoon, feel sorry for yourself, and fall off the face of the earth. Disappear, because God has wronged you." It's so tempting to give up and say, "That's it, I'm not doing this anymore." But to do so is to forfeit the blessing that comes to those who wait for God.

## Demanding Immediate Relief

The second common error during the time of delayed answers is that some believers, instead of being willing to wait, insist that God provide for them right now. It's the demand of the prodigal son, "Give me my inheritance, **now**!"

The children of Israel did this very thing during their wilderness wanderings:

> Psalm 106:13, They soon forgot His works; they did not wait for His counsel, 14 But lusted exceedingly in the wilderness, and tested God in the desert. 15 And He gave them their request, but sent leanness into their soul.

When it says, "They did not wait for His counsel" (v.13), it means they demanded immediate provision. "We're thirsty and we want water, now!" "We're hungry and we want meat, now!"

Verse 15 reveals the consequences of their impatience: "And He gave them their request, but sent leanness into their soul." They ended up with fat stomachs and skinny souls. It's frightening to consider that we can have our prayers answered but be impoverished for it. As George

> It's frightening to consider that we can have our prayers answered but be impoverished for it.

Veach once shared with me, "We can insist on something to our own hurt."

The children of Israel blew it in the wilderness. But Someone came along to show us how to do it right. When He came to His wilderness, Jesus modelled the godly response. While Jesus was in His wilderness, Satan came to tempt Him, and he hit Him in precisely this same area. Satan prodded Jesus to jump off the pinnacle of the temple, reminding Him of the promise in Psalm 91. Satan said, "'If You are the Son of God, throw Yourself down. For it is written: "He shall give His angels charge over you," and, "In their hands they shall bear you up, lest you dash your foot against a stone"'" (Matthew 4:6). Satan was saying, "Listen, Jesus, the promise of the Father is Yours, it's right there in black and white. Psalm 91 is written for You, Jesus, this is Your promise. Go ahead, claim Your promise, **now!**"

The Scripture records, "Jesus said to him, 'It is written again, "You shall not tempt the LORD your God"'" (Matthew 4:7). In essence Jesus was saying, "You're right, Satan. Psalm 91 is written for Me, that is My promise. But I will not insist on claiming that promise right now. God will fulfill that promise for Me when He chooses to, and I will wait for His timing. To insist that God fulfill that promise right now would be tantamount to tempting the Lord My God." Jesus passed the test because He was willing to wait.

And fulfill that promise the Father did! It was but a matter of a few weeks later when the people of His hometown got so angry with Him that they tried to throw Him off the edge of a precipice (Luke 4). But the Father sent some angels to bear Jesus up, in fulfillment of Psalm 91, and Jesus passed right through the crowd without them even seeing Him. To demand immediate fulfillment of God's promises is deadly; to wait expectantly for Him to fulfill His promises brings life.

## The Blessing: When God Speaks

Isaiah 30:18d, "Blessed are all those who wait for Him." Let's return to this final phrase of Isaiah 30:18, which is our text for this chapter.

This Scripture invokes a blessing upon all who are willing to wait for God. The blessing is simply this: In time, God will speak. Ah, for this we live! When God speaks, everything changes.

There are two words for "word" in the original Greek language of the New Testament, and they are the words "logos" and "rhema." "Logos" is the collection of all the "rhemas" God ever spoke. The Bible is the logos of God, but every logos word at one time was a rhema word. Rhema describes the word as it's coming out of God's mouth (Matthew 4:4). Rhema comes with God's immediate creative power. When Joshua cried, "Sun, stand still!", he spoke under the inspiration of a rhema word, and the sun immediately stopped in the sky. Once that incident was recorded in the Bible it became a logos word. You can speak that logos word over and over, but I'm inclined to guess that the sun will never stand still for you.

We read the logos word of God because we want His life to touch us. The life of God doesn't really touch and feed us, however, until the Holy Spirit breathes upon that logos and makes it a rhema word that is spoken directly to our hearts. You can meditate upon a logos promise for years and years with nothing ever changing. Then suddenly, after reading that verse scores of times, the Holy Spirit can breathe it alive to your heart as a rhema word. In that instant that promise is **yours!**

This is the blessing that comes to those who wait. God will visit you with a rhema word, and your night will shine like the noonday sun! When a rhema word proceeds from God's mouth, it **always** accomplishes the purpose for which God sends it (Isaiah 55:10-11).

We tend to put our focus on the wrong thing. So often we've made faith our quest — "If I can only have enough faith, I know I'll be healed." Instead of seeking faith, seek the face of God. To seek His face is to seek His mouth (because the mouth is part of the face). To seek His face is to seek His voice. To seek His face is to long for the words of His mouth.

"Faith comes by hearing." Once you hear from the mouth of God on your situation, the matter is settled.

> Once you hear from the mouth of God on your situation, the matter is settled.

You don't have to worry about getting faith at that point. When God speaks, faith erupts within us instantaneously and automatically. The focus must not be on getting faith but on hearing Him. God is simply saying, "Wait for Me to speak."

## Two Observations

Let me point out two observations here: 1) You cannot decide **when** God will speak. All you can do is stand, pant, and wait. 2) You cannot decide **what** God will speak. We do not lift out a promise of Scripture and say, "Here, Lord, this is what You are to speak." True humility waits upon God for Him to speak what is in His heart.

Hear the awesome declaration of God's word: There is an incredible blessing in store for the one who, instead of demanding immediate relief, waits for God.

To wait for God does **not** mean:
* to bide your time
* to put it in neutral and just coast
* to kick back and just hang out
* to throw up your hands and say, "whenever"
  To wait for God **does** mean:
* to be in His face
* to gaze and stare at Him

- to press into Him with panting and longing
- to be vigilant and alert

The image that comes to mind is that of a tiger ready to pounce. Every muscle is taut; every nerve poised. The picture the Scripture paints is that of a night watchman who looks intently for the first signs of dawn — "My soul waits for the Lord more than those who watch for the morning — yes, more than those who watch for the morning" (Psalm 130:6). In this way we wait for God. As certain as the breaking of the dawn, so is the certainty that God will visit those who wait for Him.

## Abraham

The Scriptures testify repeatedly to the blessing that comes to those who wait. More than an empty promise, the Bible describes the blessings that actually came to many holy men and women who waited for God. We've already mentioned Moses, so let's talk for a bit about Abraham's 25-year wait. God came to Abraham when he was 75 years old and promised him a son. But Abraham had to wait 25 years before his son was actually born.

I've thought a lot about that and have wondered why God waited until Abraham was 100 years old. Frankly, I think Abraham would have been a better father for Isaac at age 75 because old men don't make the best fathers. The older we get, the harder it is to hear, the less tolerance we have for the noise of children, the more we're disturbed by generational differences, etc. Abraham could have easily fathered Isaac 25 years earlier. So I've wondered why God waited so long.

Then I sensed the Lord dropping the answer in my heart: "25 years earlier Abraham would have been only the father of Isaac; by waiting 25 years and persevering through the many trials of that prolonged delay, he became the father of the faithful." (See Romans 4:16.) All believers of all time and of every nation call Abraham their father because he didn't cast away his confidence. "Blessed are all those who wait for Him." Again let me ask, do you think 25 years of waiting was worth it?

## David

Let me remind you again of David. David was ready to be King after killing Goliath. He had the brains, the braun, the talent, the charisma, the popularity, the anointing, the willingness — everything seemed to be in place. But instead, God sends him into the wilderness for seven to ten years of intense soul training. Again I wondered, why did David have to have those agonizing years of running as a fugitive from Saul? Then the answer became clear: Seven years earlier, he would have simply had an earthly kingdom; by enduring through the years of unfulfilled promises, he was given an everlasting kingdom (Psalm 89). The issue before David was, would he end up with a temporal throne or an eternal throne? Once again the question comes, do you think an eternal throne was worth the wait? "Blessed are all those who wait for Him."

Fast answers produce shallow benefits. Oh how we love fast answers, but speedy deliverances do little to stretch the heart. Delayed answers season the soul and prepare one for usefulness.

> **Fast answers produce shallow benefits.**

To the righteous one who waits for God, the certainty of healing and provision (justice) is beyond all doubt. The length of the wait is entirely unknown, however, and in the hands of God. Personally, I am committed to discovering the blessing of verse 18: "Blessed are all those who wait for Him."

## Learning To Wait

One of the greatest lessons on the road to spiritual maturity is that of waiting on God. 100-fold fruitfulness is available only to those who have learned to wait. The Bible is literally loaded with references to waiting on God, but because we live in an "instant" culture the church has grossly underestimated the significance of this spiritual discipline.

We have instant coffee, instant potatoes, instant milk, and instant meals that you just pop in the microwave. So naturally, we want instant answers to our prayers. "Lord, why don't You just nuke up a little provision for us right now?" Zap, zizzle, pop — done. Wouldn't it be nice...

Then somebody tells us, "No, you have to wait on God." So we figure, okay, we'll hang out and wait for God. The problem is, we totally misunderstand the purpose of waiting. So we mistakenly think: Maybe God needs time to catch up to us. Or maybe God's busy elsewhere, and we've got to take a number and wait our turn. Or maybe God wants to prolong the Church Age, so He's got everything on slow speed. Or maybe God's waiting for some other things to come together in another corner of the kingdom before He can act in our corner. Or maybe God's irritated with our instant society, and He wants to break us of our hyper impatience by forcing us to wait. Or maybe God hasn't figured out yet what He wants to do with us. Or maybe this is a staring contest, and God's going to prove that we'll blink first. Or maybe He wants us to learn to do without awhile. Or maybe God can't stand leaders with go-getter personalities, so He's going to force them to shut down, chill out, and get a life.

Whatever the reason, we figure we've got to wait, so we sit down, put our feet up, and stare at the clock. We have little understanding of why we wait or how to wait.

Why we wait: Because when God finds a man or woman who will truly wait on Him, He is free to act. God has done some of His greatest history-moving while one of His servants simply waited on Him. We're impatient because we have limited resources. God has unlimited resources, so He can wait as long as He wants. God longs to reveal His ways to men, but they can be made known only to those who will agree to wait.

How to wait: Run after Him with all your heart, mind, soul, and strength. Waiting is aggressive repose. Waiting is a stationary pursuit. Waiting is intense stillness. Waiting is vigilant listening.

> **Waiting is a stationary pursuit.**
> **Waiting is intense stillness.**
> **Waiting is vigilant listening.**

## Samuel And Saul

Samuel was a prophet who had learned to wait on God, and because of that, God was able to use him in singular ways. There is one incident in the history of Samuel and Saul that helps us to see how implicitly Samuel had learned to wait.

Saul was king for two years now, and war had erupted with the Philistines. The Philistines gathered together against Israel, and their army was so overwhelmingly massive next to Israel's little troop that the Israelite warriors were fearfully hiding in caves and holes. The only hope was if God would fight for them, and Samuel had given his word that he would come within seven days to offer the burnt offering and bless Israel's armies (1 Samuel 13:8).

The Bible doesn't tell give us Samuel's perspective on this incident, so the scenario I'm about to depict is fictional, but I think it could have happened something like this:

Samuel gets up one morning and thinks to himself, "Well, it's time to get over to Gilgal, to offer up the burnt offering, so Saul can take his troops into the battle." So he gets out his suitcase, and as he starts to pack the Lord speaks to him and says, "Wait a bit. Put the suitcase away. Don't go just yet." So Samuel unpacks.

He gets up the next morning and figures he better get packing when the Lord speaks again, "Wait a minute. Not just yet." So the morning turns into the afternoon, and Samuel starts to get concerned. He realizes how critical his role is in this battle. With God's blessings, the battle is a shoe-in. Without God's blessings, well, they don't have a foot to stand on. So Samuel is anxious to go and perform the sacrifice. The fate of the entire nation literally rests in his hands.

Afternoon turns into evening, and the Lord still isn't speaking.

Samuel gets up early the next morning, and he figures that if he packs and gets on his donkey first thing, he can make it before the seventh day expires. So he jumps out of bed, grabs his suitcase, only to have the Lord come again and say, "Wait."

At this point, I can imagine Samuel venturing to speak a little of his mind. "Lord, this is not my style. I'm always punctual."

"Wait."

"I don't get it, Lord. I'm sitting here doing nothing, and Saul is depending on me to come."

"Wait."

"Lord, if I don't catch the next train out of here, it's going to be too late!"

"Wait."

"Lord, do You realize how devastating this is going to be to the army? They're all counting on me to come. Morale was already low among the men, and if I don't show up, Saul won't have anybody left in his army!"

"Wait."

"Lord, I gave Saul my **word** that I'd come. You're making me out to be a liar!"

"Wait."

Although the conversation didn't happen exactly that way, this had to have been a very difficult thing for Samuel. God is making him wait until it's too late. Don't let anybody kid you, sometimes God does wait till past midnight.

> Don't let anybody kid you, sometimes God does wait till past midnight.

"Well, forget it, it's too late now," I can suppose Samuel thinking. "I guess our nation will just get swallowed up by the Philistines, and I know who they'll blame — me. It'll all be my fault, that's for sure. So much for my career. Oh well, I heard that Greece is nice this time of year..."

Just then God breaks in and says, "Yes, it's too late — now go!"

If Samuel had not known God's ways, he would have argued, "Oh no You don't! I'm not going now. I might be slow, but I'm no fool. I'm not going to walk into that trap. They're all probably ready to stone me. No, Sirreee, I'm not showing my sweet face around that army now. That would be tantamount to committing suicide."

But Samuel knew God's ways. He knew that sometimes God waits till it's too late. He knew that God had a purpose in the delay. So when God told him to show up late, he was willing, ready, and available to obey God. Once Samuel got to Gilgal, he realized why God had him wait. Saul had impetuously gone ahead and offered up the sacrifice himself. Saul, in contrast to Samuel, had not learned about waiting. He saw that the people were scattering from him, so he took matters into his own hands and offered the burnt offering himself.

God had waited so that the true motivations of Saul's heart could be exposed. The only way Saul's true nature would surface would be if Samuel were to arrive too late. God's purpose in the delay was very clear, but there was only one way that God's purposes could have been accomplished: He had to have a man who was willing to wait past midnight. Samuel was such a man.

> God's purpose in the delay was very clear, but there was only one way that God's purposes could have been accomplished: He had to have a man who was willing to wait past midnight.

One of the foundational lessons the prophets had to learn was how to wait on God. Until we learn to wait, God can't use us to the fullest degree (100-fold fruitfulness) to fulfill His purposes.

## Elijah And The Famine

Elijah is another prophet whose life is a wonderful example of the necessity of learning to wait on God. Put yourself in Elijah's shoes at the time when he boldly declared to King Ahab, "As the LORD God of Israel lives, before whom I stand, there shall not be dew nor rain these years, except at my word" (1 Kings 17:1). Then the Lord directed him to go to a certain brook and wait for the next word from God. While there, he was told, the ravens would feed him.

This wasn't a totally comfortable season of waiting. Never mind living on the mountainside, Elijah had to eat what the ravens brought him. Ravens naturally forage on carcasses, but I'm sure the Lord commanded them to bring healthy food to Elijah. Nevertheless, hot meals they were not.

When the brook ran dry due to the drought, the Lord sent Elijah to a Gentile widow in a town called Zarephath, where she had an upper room for him to stay in, and fried dough to eat.

By the way, most people think God visited Israel at Mount Carmel when Elijah prayed over the waterlogged sacrifice and fire fell from heaven, consuming the sacrifice and the altar. But God's visitation had actually happened three and a half years earlier when Elijah appeared before Ahab. God's visitation was the famine. The fire of God consuming Elijah's sacrifice was but the imminent outflow of God's visitation. Sometimes we pray for a visitation from God, expecting for fire to fall.

> **God's visitation was the famine.**

When a famine hits our life, we don't realize God has just answered our prayer. Circumstances suggest that God has forsaken us, but in actuality He has just visited us. Let's not be like the Jews of Jesus' day who came into judgment because they did not know the time of their visitation (Luke 19:44). God's visitation does not always come packaged the way we would have expected. Sometimes His visitation is a famine. The famine is His way of bringing us to desperate dependence and great spiritual thirst. So if you're in an especially dry time spiritually, perhaps it's because God has visited you! Here's a word of encouragement: **If God has visited you with famine, get ready, fire's a-comin'!**

Back to the widow's place. I want us to see that for Elijah this season of waiting was less than pleasant. He's waiting for another word from God, waiting for the time when the famine is to end, but there's no word coming. Only heat, sun, and dust.

He's watching the land suffer, the animals suffer, the children suffer. In every direction, all he sees is deprivation and devastation. Nothing is able to grow in this drought, and it's breaking his heart because he feels responsible. He has no way of knowing how long it will be before the Lord comes to him with another word. He feels totally helpless and out of control.

I think it's safe to suggest that he never expected the drought would last for three and a half years. "A few months without rain is one thing, Lord, but this protracted drought is destroying the land. I can understand Your wanting to get the attention of Your people, but do You have to go to such extreme measures?"

He's no longer eating at the "Roadkill Cafe" (ravens), now he has the joy of eating fried dough for breakfast, for lunch, for supper, and for inbetween-meal-snacks. After all, how many dishes can you prepare with oil and flour?

Besides, he's under house arrest in a widow's home. What else would you call it when you can't afford to let your face be seen by anyone? Ahab is scouring the earth, trying to find him. He can't even go for a walk lest he be discovered. So Elijah just sits in his oven-hot little bedroom, eating fried dough, looking out the window, and waiting. Month in, month out.

"Lord, surely you've got more important things for me to do right now than just sit here and stare at these walls. There's a lot of spiritual potential here in this room, just sitting idle. I could have raised up a whole graduating class at the School Of The Prophets during this three-year period! By now, we could be impacting the nations of the world! But no, I'm sitting in this sauna, discipling no one, and doing nothing for You."

Then there's the loneliness factor. He has no peer companionship. He's got to keep a discreet distance between himself and the single lady who is hosting him. Plus, she's a Gentile, which doesn't leave much room for fellowship. He never gets any faxes. No phone calls, no visitors, no e-mail. He's got no one to give him spiritual confirmation or encouragement. None of the sons of the prophets swing by to tell him he's on the right course.

During the long months of waiting, surely he must have had moments of self-doubting. "It's been over three years now. Maybe I can't hear from God anymore. If He spoke, would I be able to hear Him?"

"Lord, is there anything that might be hindering my hearing? Have I succumbed to arrogance? I may not even realize it, but maybe I've gotten prideful over this thing. Has all this gone to my head — this feeling of power over the elements? Am I caving in to spiritual pride?"

"Maybe my thoughts are displeasing the Lord. I've done my best to act with particular propriety around this widow, but maybe I shouldn't be living in a house with a widow."

"Is God wanting me to use some common sense here? Maybe He's looking for me to use my own good judgment and declare the famine over when I see it's been long enough. After all, He did give me a brain."

"Spiritual warfare — that's what I need to do! The enemy has come against me and is hindering my ability to hear God. Maybe I just need to do some rebuking and resisting."

All this is conjecture, of course, as we try to guess what struggles Elijah might have faced during those 42 long months of waiting on God. It's possible that he might have pled with God from time to time, "Lord, please! Let me go and declare the famine over! It's too hard on me to see all these people suffering so!" We can be assured that Elijah had a great heart for the well-being of God's people.

But bottom line, all Elijah can do is wait. God was able to deliver this prophetic word to Ahab through Elijah because God knew Elijah would wait on Him. Since Elijah was willing to wait on God, God was able to bring an entire nation to repentance at Mount Carmel. Now that's 100-fold fruitfulness!

Waiting on God is one of the highest spiritual disciplines. Again, the highest dimensions of fruitfulness are entered only through this portal called,

> **The highest dimensions of fruitfulness are entered only through this portal called, "Waiting on God."**

"Waiting on God."

> For since the beginning of the world men have not heard nor perceived by the ear, nor has the eye seen any God besides You, who acts for the one who waits for Him (Isaiah 64:4).

# 13

# QUIETED BY HIS LOVE

*"For thus says the Lord GOD, the Holy One of Israel: 'In return-
ing and rest you shall be saved; in quietness and confidence shall
be your strength.' But you would not"* (Isaiah 30:15).

There are at least three temptations that seek to derail the believer
who is waiting for God to speak:
1. The temptation to demand an immediate answer. Those who
   insist on an immediate respite do so because they fail to ap-
   preciate the profound spiritual work that God does in our lives
   through the waiting process.
2. The temptation to give up. This is an even stronger tempta-
   tion than the first. The voices sound something like this:
   "God has forgotten me; He doesn't care what I'm going through
   right now."
   "I'm too much of a mess for God to bother with me. I can
   think of ten reasons right now why God shouldn't bless me."
   "I'm going to wait and wait and wait, and then one day I'm
   going to come to my senses and realize God never intended to
   answer my prayer all along."
   "I didn't do anything to deserve this. God has done wrong
   by me. What benefit is there to serving God anyways?"
   "I've been keeping my nose clean all this time, and it's
   gotten me nowhere. I've had it. I'm gonna hit the town to-
   night and have a good time."
   The voice of unbelief is so compelling because it's so ra-
   tional. And it justifies our self-pity and anger. Succumbing
   to its overtures, however, is one of the fastest ways to find
   ourselves living in opposition to God and forfeiting all the
   ground we've gained in God's grace.

3. Finally, there's the temptation to just "do **something**." Circumstances are screaming for decisiveness. "This is not the time to hesitate or just wait and see. This is the time for action," our logic is telling us. "I should at least do what I'm able to do. As they say, God helps those who help themselves." Many believers have caved in at this point and then later realized that they prolonged God's timetable by muddying the waters with their own initiatives.

To wait quietly upon God is to refuse to save oneself. That's what the three Hebrew children did. They said, "Either God saves us, or we perish in this fiery furnace. But we will not compromise in order to save ourselves."

The psalmist said, "The Lord will perfect [complete] that which concerns me" (Psalm 138:8). It's a great attainment when, in the face of crisis, we gain the conviction that God is going to resolve this thing. We don't have to take matters into our own hands, God is going to perfect this.

Three times Jesus was goaded, while hanging on the cross, to just do something. "Save Yourself," they taunted. The Jewish leaders started it (Luke 23:35), the Roman soldiers picked up the chant (Luke 23:37), and the reviling thief who was crucified with Him spat it out at Him as well (23:39). "Save Yourself!" "Save Yourself!" "Save Yourself!"

This is the great temptation to the one who is suffering in the way of Christ: to do what is in his own power to save himself. Jesus had the power to save Himself, and sometimes God will place us in situations where we

> **This is the great temptation to the one who is suffering in the way of Christ: to do what is in his own power to save himself.**

actually have the power in ourselves to change things. This too is a test. Will the disciple, like his Lord, refuse to utilize the power that is available to him?

## Quietness

In this chapter we're going to explore the first half of the "quietness and confidence" equation. Consider the following principles regarding quietness.

• Quietness is not silence.

"Be anxious for nothing, but in everything by prayer and supplication, with thanksgiving, let your requests be made known to God" (Philippians 4:6). This call to be rid of anxiety is basically a call to quietness. "Let nothing unsettle your heart." But then the invitation comes to "let your requests be made known to God." So the apostle Paul is saying, "Quiet your heart, and then express your requests to God." We are to vocalize our requests but to do so from a heart of quietness. So quietness is not silence, but it is a quiet heart.

• Quietness is not an instant attainment.

We should not be discouraged when we continue to struggle with a disquieted heart. The greater the trauma, the longer it can take to embrace true quietness. That place of quiet rest is most sublime and is to be pursued with the whole heart until it is attained.

• If not constantly nurtured, it's lost.

This quietness is not the sort of thing that once gained is your total possession. Once you find it, it is immediately challenged. I've been amazed at the times that I've gone to bed with a quiet heart, sensing the comfort of the Holy Spirit, strengthened in the assurances of God's word — only to wake up the next morning completely distraught. What happened overnight, I'll never know. But somehow during my sleep that sense of quietness vanished. I would have to return to the word of God and to prayer and establish afresh the quietness of heart that the Spirit imparts.

## He Will Quiet You

The prophet Zephaniah received a revelation of the rejoicing Lord. Zephaniah's was the last Bible book written before the Southern Kingdom of Judah was exiled to Babylon. Zephaniah predicts that judgment was about to fall, but then he added that afterwards they would return in their hearts to the Lord and be restored. Here's what he writes as he describes the restoration that would take place after their captivity:

Sing, O daughter of Zion! Shout, O Israel! Be glad and rejoice with all your heart, O daughter of Jerusalem! The LORD has taken away your judgments, He has cast out your enemy. The King of Israel, the LORD, is in your midst; you shall see disaster no more. In that day it shall be said to Jerusalem: "Do not fear; Zion, let not your hands be weak. The LORD your God in your midst, the Mighty One, will save; He will rejoice over you with gladness, He will quiet you with His love, He will rejoice over you with singing" (Zephaniah 3:14-17).

When the people of Judah were taken away to Babylon, they already had this prophecy in their possession. I can imagine them sitting in Babylon, dejected, feeling abandoned by God. Someone might have piped up and said, "Listen, guys, do you remember the word that God gave to Zephaniah? He said He would restore us to Jerusalem, and make us glad again." At the time that would have seemed like a fantasy or a dream. Considering their present pain and depression, how could they ever be made to rejoice again?

But the Lord saw their future, and He had plans to bless and prosper them (see Jeremiah 29:11). To help the captives settle their hearts in the midst of great distress, the Lord speaks a wonderful spiritual principle through Zephaniah: "He will quiet you with His love" (v.17).

## Quieted With His Love

The "quiet" of Zephaniah 3:17 comes from the same Hebrew root word as the "quietness" of Isaiah 30:15. It means to rest, be quiet, be still. And Zephaniah gives us the key to this quietness: it

> **"He will settle you down with His love."**

is found in His love. "He will settle you down with His love." He's the initiator of this love; we're the recipients.

There are two ways God applies this love to our hearts.

First, He reveals His love to us. It's a sovereign and holy act of God when He comes to us and whispers straight to our spirit, "I love you." There is nothing more precious in all of human existence than that moment when God quickens to us just how much He loves us. It's totally disarming and altogether wonderful. All hell is breaking loose in our lives, but suddenly that doesn't seem to matter, because we realize, **"He loves me!"**

This is what quiets the heart. It's God making known His passionate affection for us. He wants to make Romans 8:37 a reality in our hearts.

Yet in all these things we are more than conquerors through Him who loved us (Romans 8:37).

In what things are we more than conquerors? The context tells us in what things: "...tribulation, or distress, or persecution, or famine, or nakedness, or peril, or sword" (Romans 8:35). We are more than conquerors **in** all these things. How? The answer is, "through Him who loved us." Receiving a revelation of His fathomless love enables us to overcome. It's the revelation of how much He loves us, in the midst of the tribulation and distress, that quiets our hearts. We're at rest in the storm. This Scripture calls us "more than conquerors" because we're tasting of victory ever before the battle's over.

I have to remind myself that God is kind, merciful, and good **all the time** — even when nasty circumstances come my way. He doesn't withhold His mercy for a spell and see if we still trust Him. No, He is incessantly merciful and kind, even when wounding us. "Faithful are the wounds of a friend."

There's a second way in which God quiets us with His love, and that is by enflaming our hearts with love for Him. He says, "Not only am I going to use this crisis to reveal My love to you, but I'm going to use it to perfect your love for Me." God is using your present trauma, dear saint, to perfect your love!

> **"Not only am I going to use this crisis to reveal My love to you, but I'm going to use it to perfect your love for Me."**

## Perfected Love

Oh, can't you see it? Can't you see that He's drawing you forward in the midst of your crisis and placing a fervency within you like you've never known? When you begin to see how He's elevating you to new levels of passion, a deep warmth will begin to settle and quiet your heart. "He's changing me! He's perfecting my love. I really do love Him more than ever!"

> There is no fear in love; but perfect love casts out fear, because fear involves torment. But he who fears has not been made perfect in love (1 John 4:18).

Some have interpreted this verse to mean that when God's love for us (which is perfect) touches our life, that fear is cast out. But the verse is primarily referring to our love for God. When our love for Him is perfected, that's when all fear is cast out. When we love Him with a perfect love, there is no room left for fear. To the degree that I love Him, to that degree fear no longer has room in my soul.

> **To the degree that I love Him, to that degree fear no longer has room in my soul.**

## Offended By God

The Lord asks us, "Do you love Me?"

From the sincerity of our hearts we reply, "Yes, Lord, I really do love You."

"Okay," He says. "Since you love Me, I'm going to offend you. I'm going to allow something to touch your life for which you're totally unprepared."

That's where the Assyrians come in. God allows something to invade our lives, bringing heartache, confusion, desperation, and even anger, fear, and anxiety.

"Would Jesus purposefully offend me?" someone might ask. "He wouldn't do that, would He?" The answer is, yes. He not only would, but He will. If you choose to believe in Jesus, the time will come when you will have opportunity to be offended at Him. It's inevitable.

It happened to John the Baptist, who was the greatest prophet of all time (other than Jesus Himself). He couldn't figure Jesus out because Jesus wasn't fulfilling his expectations. So Jesus relayed this message to John: "And blessed is he who is not offended because of Me" (Matthew 11:6). John had a choice before him — either get offended and turn away from Christ, or remain true even when he didn't understand what was going on.

The reason the opportunity for offence comes is this: Your love will be tested. Do you really love Him? God is wondering, "If I do something contrary to your theology, will you get offended, or will you still love Me?" This is how He tests our love, helping us to see that our love has need of perfection. As we allow Him to quiet our anger with His love, we are ushered into new dimensions of knowing God and His ways.

Someone reading this might be inclined to think, "Oh no, I would never get angry at God!" If that's what you think, then you're deceived. You are deceiving yourself. If you have never been angry at God, it's only because He has graciously spared you that degree of calamity. If the calamity were great enough, you would get angry at Him.

God **expected** Job to get angry at Him. It's part of the process. When first offended by God, we get angry because we don't understand what He's doing. God knew Job would experience some anger, but He didn't expect him to **stay** angry. He expected Job to press in earnestly and find God in his calamity.

When you find the face of God in the midst of your calamity, and you see His incredible love for you, the anger is dealt with. When you get a revelation of His love, fear melts away. His love quiets the soul. If you're still mad at God, it's because you haven't really seen Him yet. You can't behold God's face and stay angry with Him — He's just too beautiful! Even though you may not like what He's doing to you or in you, if you can see His face, you won't be able to stay mad at Him because you'll see His overwhelming goodness.

> When you get a revelation of His love, fear melts away. His love quiets the soul.

Once quieted, the soul can respond in love to God. This is what really touches God's heart — when He sees a son or daughter who has been greatly afflicted, now responding and saying, "I love You, Lord, even more than before."

It's this kind of love that is referred to in Romans 8:28, "And we know that all things work together for good to those who love God, to those who are the called according to His purpose." This is a powerfully extravagant promise. When calamity strikes, and we just stand there in the midst of the crisis and give ourselves in loving abandonment to God, the Lord promises to work the circumstances of our calamity around for the good. Please note that this promise comes to only one category of believers: those who love.

All the great men of the Bible had opportunity to be offended at Him — Abraham, Job, David, John the Baptist, and many others. Before we qualify for the greatest service and greatest fruitfulness, we must pass the offence test. "If you don't like what I do in your life, will you become offended at Me?"

"I don't know why You're doing this to me," the saint cries. "I don't understand Your purposes in this, I don't know why I'm going through so much pain right now, but I've seen too much of You to stay offended at You. You're too beautiful, too wonderful, too gracious, too loving, too giving, too breathtaking for me to stay mad at You. I can't stay offended at You; I love You too much. So I don't understand anything about what You're doing in my life right now, but I love You, Lord, I really do."

> God can bring into greater fruitfulness only those who have set their love for God above their work for God.

God can bring into greater fruitfulness only those who have set their love for God above their work for God. The Ephesians were faithful workers, but had left their first love, and Jesus told them He would have to remove their place of influence if they didn't get the order reversed. He will use offending circumstances to prove whether our love for Him is foremost in our hearts.

## The Love Test

A few years ago, God was calling many in the body of Christ to learn to rise up in faith and kingdom authority. Many of the books, tapes, and conferences were keynoting on faith and the overcoming life of victory in Christ. We were learning how to believe for healing, for financial provision, for restoration of relationships, and for the salvation of loved ones. The message was powerful, ordained of God, and was trumpeted around the globe. God wanted us to learn the "faith test," and He gave us opportunity to be challenged and to grow in our faith.

It is now my perception, however, that the Spirit is changing directions and is now taking many members in the body of Christ through what I will call a "love test." He uses very similar means as when He applied the faith test, i.e., He introduces the love test through calamity, trial, and pressure. But this time, instead of asking, "Will you believe Me?" He's asking, "Do you love Me?"

One common denominator in the love test is this: When calamity hits, and you pull out the "faith formulas" that always worked a few years ago, you discover that nothing's changing. You're memorizing the word like you did before, you're confessing the promises that were so real to you back then, you're rebuking the devil, you're under the blood, you've got others agreeing with you in prayer — and it all appears to be to no avail. Not only is nothing changing in your circumstances, but you don't even sense the Lord's anointing on what you're doing.

You begin to panic. "If confessing God's word isn't enough," you think, "then what can I possibly do?" You need help to see, dear friend, that you're not in a faith test right now, but a love test. You can study English eight hours a day for an entire week, but it won't help you pass a math test. Similarly, the things that helped you through the faith test won't help you in the love test.

What you learned in the faith test is still valid and wonderful. The Lord doesn't want you to abandon what you learned back then. But He's adding to you, and now He wants you to learn about the love test.

Job wasn't healed because of an exercise of his faith. He was healed at the culmination point of God's dealings in his life. The timing of it was totally up to God. There is a healing that comes as an exercise of faith, and since it's the most common form of healing, we're most familiar with it. But there's another kind of healing, and it comes to those who pass, not the faith test, but the love test. This is the healing of Psalm 91:14, "Because he has set his love upon

> **But there's another kind of healing, and it comes to those who pass, not the faith test, but the love test.**

Me, therefore I will deliver him." The issue for Job was, "Will you love Me, no matter what I do to you?" All Job could do was stay in God's face and just remain loyal to his Friend. Because he was faithful and diligent to keep his face before God, God eventually met him and revealed Himself to him (Job 42:5).

## "Do You Love Me?"

"What is this love test?" someone might ask.

It is the test the Lord allows to come into our lives to determine, "Do you really love Me?" The Lord wants to know if we love Him, or if we love a Jesus of our own mental creation. He's wondering, "If I begin to show you who I really am, will you still love Me?"

He's testing us to see if we're merely "fairweather Christians." He's saying to us, "I know you love Me when I bless you and supply all your needs. But will you still love Me, even if I halt the blessings to your life and allow some troubles to touch you?" The big question in the face of adversity is, will we love Him or will we be offended by Him? If we stay true, our love will be purified and strengthened.

## Peter's Love Test

> Luke 22:31, And the Lord said, "Simon, Simon! Indeed, Satan has asked for you, that he may sift you as wheat. 32 But I have prayed for you, that your faith should not fail; and when you have returned to Me, strengthen your brethren." 33 But he said to Him, "Lord, I am ready to go with You, both to prison and to death." 34 Then He said, "I tell you, Peter, the rooster shall not crow this day before you will deny three times that you know Me."

This is the passage where Jesus announces to Peter that his love test is coming. Peter asserts in verse 33 that his love is so true that he'd even be willing to die for Christ's sake. The Lord knows the true condition of his love, however, and has destined a way for Peter to see it as well.

Suddenly Simon Peter is thrown a curve ball. Jesus is arrested, all the disciples forsake Him, and the chief priests are having their way with Jesus for the first time ever. Peter had always seen Jesus stand up to the Pharisees, but now he sees Him meekly submitting to their abuse. This was not in Peter's plans. Caught off balance, Peter denies three times over that he knows the Lord. When the rooster crowed, Peter was reminded of Jesus' words and suddenly realized he had fulfilled them. When the real crisis hit, and Peter had the opportunity to prove the depth of his love, he crumbled. Despairingly, he realized how small his love really was.

After His resurrection, Jesus wanted Peter to realize the true nature of the test he had just failed. So three times Jesus asks him a very purposeful question. The question was not, "Do you believe in Me?" because it wasn't a faith test. The question was, "Do you love Me?" It was a love test.

Three times the question was asked, corresponding to Peter's three denials. "Simon, son of Jonah, do you love [agape] Me?"

Three times Peter affirmed that he loved [phileo] the Lord, but at the third question he became grieved and so he said, "Lord, You know all things; You know that I love You" (John 21:17). Broken, Peter was saying, "Lord, You know all things. You know how much I love You. But it's not as much as I once thought it was. I used to think that I loved you with *agape* love, but now I feel like my love is more like *phileo* love. I've seen the failure of my love. I don't love You the way I want to, but I really do love You. You see the pain in my heart, Lord, and You know how much I long to love you fully."

The purpose of the test was fulfilled when Peter failed. The Lord wanted to break Peter of his self-reliance so that he would learn to depend on God for everything. He came to realize that he couldn't even love without Christ's help. Our love is perfected, not when we become strong in love, but when we become so weak that we lean on the Lord for His love to empower us.

## He Loves Me!

The Lord Jesus is asking a question of many believers in this hour: "Do you love Me?" And here's how He's asking it. He's allowing them to come into severe crisis, and instead of responding to any of the methodologies they learned in the faith test, He's watching them struggle in the midst of their confusion. They don't have any idea what's happening to them, but He's after something. He's wanting to determine if they'll remain true in their love or if they'll get offended and turn away from Him. He's wondering, "Will you let Me quiet you with My love?" He wants to bring us to the place where nothing else really matters, just as long as we know He loves us.

"But look at you — you're a mess!"

"So what? He loves me!"

## A Longing To Know His Love

Jesus made a most disturbing prediction in Matthew 24:12: "And because lawlessness will abound, the love of many will grow cold." Or to say it another way, He said, "Many will be offended" (Matthew 24:10). This prophecy is being fulfilled right here and right now. We live in a lawless generation, where anything goes, and where men have free license to pursue their

> He longs for our exclusive affections and for a love that matches His.

own private pleasures. Things that tend to distract our love are proliferating more and more and becoming increasingly accessible. Many saints are succumbing and are being drawn away from true devotion to Christ.

As Jesus looks with fiery eyes at His bride, He burns toward us with great jealousy. He longs for our exclusive affections and for a love that matches His. So what does the King do? He sends pressure, affliction, calamity, distress, crisis. Why? Because He understands Psalm 119:67, "Before I was afflicted I went astray, but now I keep Your word." He's looking for a prayer to rise from within the depths of our being: "Oh Lord, save me! Lord, help me to see Your love. I don't understand how You could love me and yet allow this to happen to me. I need a revelation of Your love. Quiet me, Lord, with Your love!"

He smiles because that's a prayer He loves to answer.

Just as the Israelites' afflictions in Egypt caused them to cry out to God for a deliverer, even so our afflictions will put a deep cry within our hearts for our Deliverer, our heavenly Bridegroom, to come for us. Without that affliction, we become accustomed to Egypt, and leave our first love. Therefore, we can expect to see the people of God encountering ever increasing affliction in this hour.

To the one who allows the affliction to kindle a deeper love the promise comes: "Because he has set his love upon Me, therefore I will deliver him" (Psalm 91:14).

# 14

# CONFIDENCE IN HIS WAYS

The previous chapter dealt with how we come to a place of quietness. This chapter will focus on increasing our confidence in God. When our hearts are quieted by God's love, and we find a renewed confidence in God, then we have found the pathway to strength and to overcoming victory. You'll recall our text:

> For thus says the Lord GOD, the Holy One of Israel: "In returning and rest you shall be saved; In quietness and confidence shall be your strength" (Isaiah 30:15).

## Under Seige

Look with me, please, at the verses that follow:

> Isaiah 30:19, For the people shall dwell in Zion at Jerusalem; You shall weep no more. He will be very gracious to you at the sound of your cry; when He hears it, He will answer you. 20 And though the Lord gives you the bread of adversity and the water of affliction, yet your teachers will not be moved into a corner anymore, but your eyes shall see your teachers.

The Lord is speaking comfort to His people. The people are crying, "The Assyrians are coming — we're going to be invaded!" God responds by saying that He hears their cry and He will answer them. Even though the answer may not come in the form that they expect, it's most certainly coming.

Verse 20 describes a seige. The words, "the bread of adversity and the water of affliction," are descriptive of what happens when a city is put under seige. Food commodities and water supplies are cut off, and the inhabitants of the city are slowly starved into surrender. The Lord knew that Jerusalem would not simply come under seige, however. Jerusalem would actually fall; the people of Judah would be taken into captivity and would be carried off to far-away Babylon.

Then the Lord adds, "yet your teachers will not be moved into a corner anymore, but your eyes shall see your teachers." God is saying, "I will give you teachers who will explain what's happening to you. I know you won't understand because you've always thought that it was impossible for Zion to be moved. Your understanding of that truth is wrong. Zion is going to be pillaged, and you're going to be exiled to Babylon. But I'm going to send you teachers who will explain all this. I know that what is happening to you goes against your theology, so I'll send you teachers who will straighten out your theology and give you understanding into my ways and purposes. They will help you understand the purpose of your captivity." The Lord fulfilled that promise by giving them several teachers, including Jeremiah, Ezekiel, and Daniel.

> **"I know that what is happening to you goes against your theology, so I'll send you teachers who will straighten out your theology and give you understanding into my ways and purposes."**

## Restoration

Let's continue with our passage in Isaiah 30:

> Isaiah 30:21, Your ears shall hear a word behind you, saying, "This is the way, walk in it," whenever you turn to the right hand or whenever you turn to the left. 22 You will also defile the covering of your graven images of silver, and the ornament of your molded images of gold. You will throw them away as an unclean thing; you will say to them, "Get away!" 23 Then He will give the rain for your seed with which you sow the ground, and bread of the increase of the earth; it will be fat and plentiful. In that day your cattle will feed in large pastures. 24 Likewise the oxen and the young donkeys that work the ground will eat cured fodder, which has been winnowed with the shovel and fan. 25 There will be on every high mountain and on every high hill rivers and streams of waters, in the day of the great slaughter, when the towers fall. 26 Moreover the light of the moon will be as the light of the sun, and the light of the sun will be sevenfold, as the light of seven days, in the day that the LORD binds up the bruise of His people and heals the stroke of their wound.

In verse 21, the Lord is promising to lead and guide them back to their homeland. They will know the voice of the Lord giving them sovereign direction, as He restores them to their heritage.

In verse 22, the Lord is saying, "When I do this thing, and when I release you from your captivity, never again will you return to idolatry. I will cure you of your wandering lusts. I will purify your affections and give you an exclusive love for Me alone." This is precisely what happened with national Israel. Before their exile to Babylon they struggled constantly with idolatry, but after their return from exile they never again returned to idolatry like they did in the former days. God had done such a severe work in their hearts that they remained true to Jehovah, generally speaking, for many centuries. Six hundred years later, when Jesus comes on the scene, the people of Israel have many faults and shortcomings, but pandering to the false gods of their neighboring nations was not one of them. So we see here the enduring work that the captivity wrought in their hearts.

The "light" of verse 26 is "understanding." The Lord is saying, "When I heal and restore you, you will understand so much more about Me. Your understanding of my heart will be seven times greater than what it was before. You will truly know Me." Applied to our lives today, I believe this is a promise of an increased revelation of Jesus Christ. If we're faithful through the time of captivity, the Lord will restore us to a place of great revelation, and He will show us His love on the cross. He will reveal the greatness of redemption's plan. He will disclose the great truths of the kingdom. He will feed us with insights on the gospel.

## God's Ways

Verse 26 truly is a declaration of God's ways. God is revealing Himself as the Lord who "binds up the bruise of His people and heals the stroke of their wound." When you have been wounded (incarcerated) by God, the thing that will breathe confidence into your spirit is the revelation that God is the one who heals the stroke of your wound. As you grow in your understanding of who God is, your confidence in Him will simultaneously grow.

Confidence happens when we come to understand God and His ways. When we really get to know God, confidence is automatic. If we truly come to know Him, we'll be confident that He will be true to His person.

> **When we really get to know God, confidence is automatic.**

Quietness says, "I know He loves me!"

Confidence says, "I know God is working on my behalf for the good."

## Knowing God

To know God, you must know His ways. This is seen clearly in Exodus 33:13 where Moses prays, "Now therefore, I pray, if I have found grace in Your sight, **show me now Your way, that I may know You** and that I may find grace in Your sight." Moses recognized that if he was to know God, he would have to get to know God's ways. If you get to know God's ways, then you've come to know God. And this is the basis for confidence. Confidence comes in knowing God's ways.

Because of my own captivity (which for me came in the form of a physical infirmity), I have given myself wholeheartedly to discovering the ways of God. I have scoured the Scriptures, digging for any and every tidbit I could find that would help me to understand God's purposes in my season of incarceration. I have come away from my search with the bold conviction that the Scriptures consistently portray the ways of God in keeping with Isaiah 30:26. He is a God who "binds up the bruise of His people and heals the stroke of their wound."

## Hurt, Then Healed

Although I could list many more, the following Scriptures point to the Bible's consistent witness of God's ways. God doesn't imprison in order to leave you rotting in your cell. God imprisons in order to set you free, in His time and way, to the honor and glory of His name. Consider the ways of God in these verses, beloved, and may your confidence in Him rise!

- Isaiah 30:26, "In the day that the LORD binds up the bruise of His people and heals the stroke of their wound."
- Deuteronomy 32:39, "I kill and I make alive; I wound and I heal."
- Hosea 6:1-2, "Come, and let us return to the LORD; for He has torn, but He will heal us; He has stricken, but He will bind us up. After two days He will revive us; on the third day He will raise us up, that we may live in His sight."
- Lamentations 3:31-32, "For the Lord will not cast off forever. Though He causes grief, yet He will show compassion according to the multitude of His mercies."
- Nahum 1:12-13, "Though I have afflicted you, I will afflict you no more; for now I will break off his yoke from you, and burst your bonds apart."
- Psalm 66:10-12, "For You, O God, have tested us; You have refined us as silver is refined. You brought us into the net; You laid affliction on our backs. You have caused men to ride over

our heads; we went through fire and through water; but You brought us out to rich fulfillment."

- Isaiah 54:7-8, "'For a mere moment I have forsaken you, but with great mercies I will gather you. With a little wrath I hid My face from you for a moment; but with everlasting kindness I will have mercy on you,' says the LORD, your Redeemer."
- Psalm 71:20-22, "You, who have shown me great and severe troubles, shall revive me again, and bring me up again from the depths of the earth. You shall increase my greatness, and comfort me on every side. Also with the lute I will praise you — and Your faithfulness, O my God! To You I will sing with the harp, O Holy One of Israel."
- Psalm 30:5, "For His anger is but for a moment, His favor is for life; weeping may endure for a night, but joy comes in the morning."
- Psalm 91:14-16, "Because he has set his love upon Me, therefore I will deliver him; I will set him on high, because he has known My name. He shall call upon Me, and I will answer him; I will be with him in trouble; I will deliver him and honor him. With long life I will satisfy him, and show him My salvation."
- Psalm 68:6, "He brings out those who are bound into prosperity."
- Isaiah 43:1-2, "Fear not, for I have redeemed you; I have called you by your name; you are Mine. When you pass through the waters, I will be with you; and through the rivers, they shall not overflow you. When you walk through the fire, you shall not be burned, nor shall the flame scorch you."

The Lord affirms in the above verses that we will know deep waters; we will experience the fire. "Deep waters" and "fire" are terms to describe trauma, depression, anxiety, pressure, crisis, and overwhelming difficulty. But instead of being destroyed by these things, the assurance comes, we will come out the better for it.

## Jacob

David speaks of these things in Psalm 34:17, "The righteous cry out, and the Lord hears, and delivers them out of all their troubles." What a bold

> **But the verse doesn't say the Lord delivers all believers from all their troubles; it says He delivers the righteous out of their troubles.**

declaration — especially considering that this does not seem to be the experience of many believers!  But the verse doesn't say the Lord delivers all **believers** from all their troubles; it says He delivers the **righteous** out of their troubles.  You see, you must do more than just believe.  You must maintain your purity and integrity before God.  You must stand continually before God in faithfulness and uprightness.  It is to the righteous that this promise comes.

A wonderful illustration of this truth is seen in the life of Jacob.  After his son Joseph becomes the Prime Minister of Egypt, Jacob travels from Canaan to Egypt so that he and his family can be fed during the famine.  When Joseph introduces his father Jacob to Pharaoh for the first time, Jacob says to Pharaoh, "Few and evil have been the days of the years of my life" (Genesis 47:9).  Kind of a morbid thing to say to Pharaoh, don't you think?

I looked at that statement and thought, "You don't really mean that, do you Jacob?  Makes you sound like a sourpuss.  Like a grouchy old bellyacher.  Where's the joy of the Lord that you should be exuding as a witness to Pharaoh right now?"  But then I took a second look at Jacob's life, and guess what I discovered — he really didn't have a very happy life at all!  Even so, the amazing thing is that each of us is named after Jacob.  Israel (for his name was changed by God from Jacob to Israel) was the father of the covenant people, and now all believers in Christ are called "true Israelites" (see Galatians 6:16;  John 1:47).

Consider the distress of Jacob's life.  He flees to Haran because his brother wants to kill him.  His uncle Laban tricks him repeatedly, giving him the wrong daughter for a wife, and changing his wages ten times.  Upon returning to Canaan, Jacob loses his favorite son Joseph in what appears to be an attack by a wild beast.  Then a famine hits that brings his entire household to desperate straits.  When he sends to Egypt to buy grain, they return without Simeon.  And the ruler in Egypt insists that they can't buy any more food without Benjamin being with them.  Everything seemed to be stacked against him, all his life.

Just before he dies, however, Jacob makes a most fascinating statement.  Joseph has brought his two sons, Ephraim and Manasseh, before his father Jacob, for Jacob to pronounce a blessing on his two grandsons before he dies.  This is Jacob's testimony as he blesses Joseph's sons: "The Angel who has redeemed me from all evil, bless the lads" (Genesis 48:16).  As Jacob reviews his life, he's thinking, "God delivered me from my brother Esau;  he delivered me from my uncle Laban;  he delivered me from the famine;  he restored Joseph and Benjamin and Simeon to me.  God has truly delivered me from all evil!"  What a glorious declaration of God's faithfulness! Yes, he had a painful life; but in the end he stood vindicated.

This is why the Scriptures declare, "Happy is he who has the God of Jacob for his help" (Psalm 146:5).

## The Straight Ways Of The Lord

I remember someone saying to me at one point, "Even if God doesn't heal you, what He's done in you through this infirmity is worth it because of what He's done in your heart." Different folks have expressed those kinds of sentiments to me, but on this one occasion I went to the Lord in prayer and asked Him, "Lord, what do You think about what this person just said to me?"

As I prayed, this is what I believe I received from the Lord: "Do not pervert the straight ways of the Lord."  What are the

> **"Do not pervert the straight ways of the Lord."**

straight ways of the Lord?  This is the way of the Lord: He bruises, but He also binds up.  He kills, but He also makes alive.  He imprisons, but He also sets free.  Yes, He afflicts, but He also heals.

I'm praying Psalm 67:1-2, "God be merciful to us and bless us, and cause His face to shine upon us. Selah **That Your way may be known on earth**, Your salvation among all nations."

## Paul's Thorn

Whenever the subject of God's ways and divine healing surfaces, there's always the critic who says, "Well, what about Paul's thorn in the flesh? God didn't heal Paul when he asked Him to." It's true that God didn't deliver Paul of his thorn at the time that Paul asked Him to.  However, there's biblical evidence to suggest that God did eventually deliver Paul from his thorn in the flesh.  Although there's room for differences of opinion here, I'd like to present what I see as convincing evidence that Paul was delivered by God from his thorn in the flesh before he died.

First of all, let's look at the passage where Paul informs us about this thorn:

> And lest I should be exalted above measure by the abundance of the revelations, a thorn in the flesh was given to me, a messenger of Satan to buffet me, lest I be exalted above measure. Concerning this thing I pleaded with the Lord three times that it might depart from me.  And He said to me, "My grace is sufficient for you, for My strength is made perfect in weakness."  Therefore most gladly I will rather boast in my infirmi-

ties, that the power of Christ may rest upon me. Therefore I
take pleasure in infirmities, in reproaches, in needs, in persecu-
tions, in distresses, for Christ's sake. For when I am weak, then
I am strong (2 Corinthians 12:7-10).

Much speculation is made over what this thorn was exactly. Some
say Paul was developing cataracts. Others think it's a reference to perse-
cution. Personally, I'm convinced it was a physical infirmity of some
sort that hindered and limited his full physical strength and functional-
ity. Paul says the thorn was in his "flesh," which gives the image of a
physical pain that didn't totally debilitate or immobilize him, but it hassled
him, distracted him, and slowed him down.

## Strength Perfected In Weakness

Paul was given the thorn in his flesh to learn a very valuable lesson.
The Lord was teaching him first-hand that, "My grace is sufficient for
you, for My strength is made perfect in weakness." Many people quote
that verse as though they really believe it, but they've never really expe-
rienced it in the same way Paul did. God taught Paul that when he was
weak and feeling inadequate for the challenges of the ministry, God's
strength was able to be manifest through him. In fact, when he felt good
and virile and strong, he was probably limiting the effectiveness of the
Spirit through his life. He learned that when he was feeling strong, he
was prone to constrict the flow of God's blessings through his life. On
the other hand, when he was weak, he became a better conduit of God's
grace because he realized how desperately dependent he was upon the
Lord. The Lord was showing him that when he was feeling incapable
and handicapped that he was actually more useful to the Master!

How easily we become full
of ourselves. We think our
strengths are kingdom assets,
and God often views them as
kingdom liabilities. Why? Be-
cause we tend to depend on our
strengths, without even realizing it, instead of on the Holy Spirit.

> **We think our strengths are
> kingdom assets, and God often
> views them as kingdom liabili-
> ties.**

This was highlighted to me recently at a leadership conference I
attended. One of the speakers (whom I won't name) is an elderly man
with a well-recognized ministry. When he took the podium, he spoke of
how good he was feeling that evening, considering his age. He remarked,
"I feel like a 25-year-old man tonight!" He was delighting in the sense
of strength he was receiving by virtue of the anointing of the Spirit upon
him. As the service progressed, he stopped and made a most intriguing

statement. He said, "Please pray for me. I really am feeling so very good tonight. In fact, I'm feeling so good that it's working against me." What he realized was this: When he felt strong, his tendency was to "run with it," get caught up in the momentum of his own strength, and lose that dependence upon the Lord that is so necessary for true fruitfulness. In all my years in Christian circles, this was the first occasion when I saw a man in ministry who really understood the principle, "My strength is made perfect in weakness."

## Was The Thorn Removed?

In 2 Corinthians 12:7-10, we're not told that Paul's thorn was ever removed. Nor are we told that it remained permanently with him. On that passage alone, we have no basis to make either determination.

There is another passage, however, that provides an interesting perspective on Paul's thorn. It is contained in a book of the New Testament that Paul wrote approximately ten years after he wrote Second Corinthians. In fact, it's the last book that Paul ever wrote. I'm referring to the book of Second Timothy.

Second Timothy is a very unique and fascinating book. It is intensely personal and transparent, and it reveals the fatherly heart of Paul just before his decease. Paul realizes that he's about to die, which is seen readily enough in 2 Timothy 4:6-7, "For I am already being poured out as a drink offering, and the time of my departure is at hand. I have fought the good fight, I have finished the race, I have kept the faith." Whereas years earlier in Philippians 3:13 Paul said that he had not yet apprehended the goal, now in Second Timothy he says he has reached the finish line, and he knows his death is at hand.

Now, at death's door, Paul makes a statement that is warmly reminiscent of Jacob's statement that we mentioned above — "The Angel who has redeemed me from all evil" (Genesis 48:16). Paul, too, makes a declaration that God has redeemed him from all evil. Standing at the portal of eternity, Paul makes this awesome declaration of God's goodness: "But you have carefully followed my doctrine, manner of life, purpose, faith, longsuffering, love, perseverance, persecutions, afflictions, which happened to me at Antioch, at Iconium, at Lystra — what persecutions I endured. **And out of them all the Lord delivered me**" (2 Timothy 3:10-11).

- Fact: Paul faced persecutions and afflictions at many more cities than just Antioch, Iconium, and Lystra.
- Fact: Timothy traveled with Paul to many more cities than just Antioch, Iconium, and Lystra.

Therefore, it is my contention that when Paul says "at Antioch, at

Iconium, at Lystra," he is not referring to the persecutions and afflictions he experienced in just those three cities alone. No, in a manner of speaking he is saying, "at Antioch, at Iconium, at Lystra, **and so on.**" Those three cities are but the beginning of his list. They were the first cities he visited with Timothy. But Timothy would know well that Paul was referring to many cities — too many to list. Paul was referring to **all** the persecutions and afflictions he endured throughout his many travels. And as he looks back over all his persecutions and afflictions, he makes this comprehensive statement, "And out of them **all** the Lord delivered me."

Paul could have said, "And out of them all the Lord delivered me — all, that is, except that dreaded thorn." Ten years after talking about the thorn in his flesh, he's now talking about how God has delivered him from all affliction. It seems most conclusive that Paul was saying that God also delivered him from his affliction known as his thorn in the flesh.

Paul even takes it a step further, and looking ahead at the few hours that yet await him, he declares: "And the Lord will deliver me from every evil work and preserve me for His heavenly kingdom. To Him be glory forever and ever. Amen!" (2 Timothy 4:18).

> **Paul is testifying, "God has delivered me, and He will deliver me!"**

Totally awesome! Paul is testifying, "God **has** delivered me, and He **will** deliver me!" Paul is giving glorious affirmation to Psalm 34:19, "Many are the afflictions of the righteous, but the Lord delivers him out of them all."

## Why Do Some Prayers Remain Unanswered?

This brings us squarely to the question that virtually every reader is wanting to ask, "If God wants to deliver us from all trouble, then why are so many saints not delivered from their troubles?"

Guess what? I really don't think I have anything to say right now that could satisfy your heart on that issue. Now, don't get upset with me and toss this book. I'm being very straightforward with you, and I'll give you my best answer (feeble as it is).

To put it simply, I don't think we'll get all the answers in this life. I don't know why our experience in the kingdom of God so often seems to fall short of scriptural patterns. But I have resolved this much: I will not adjust my theology to accommodate my experience. That would be "sub-kingdom theology." I will not adapt my expectations or faith stand or view of God's word because I'm still not healed or because someone else is still not healed. Instead, I'm going after God with everything I've got.

Some leaders preach a gospel that prepares people for the status quo. I want to preach a gospel that calls people higher.

> **I want to preach a gospel that calls people higher.**

It's time to preach God's ways and represent them accurately. I'm going to say it again: Yes, it's God's purpose to refine you in the furnace of affliction, but it's also His purpose to deliver you!

## A Testimony!

I believe with all my heart that God wants to give you a testimony! Let me direct your attention to the "faith chapter," Hebrews 11. One of the foremost concepts in that chapter is wrapped up in the words "witness" and "testimony." Look at it with me:

- "For by it [faith] the elders obtained a good **testimony**" (Hebrews 11:2). Faith opens the door to a testimony.
- "By faith Abel offered to God a more excellent sacrifice than Cain, through which he obtained **witness** that he was righteous, God **testifying** of his gifts; and through it he being dead still speaks" (Hebrews 11:4). Abel's testimony was, "Access to God's heart is found through the shedding of blood." Even though Cain murdered him, Cain couldn't eradicate Abel's testimony.
- "By faith Enoch was taken away so that he did not see death, 'and was not found, because God had taken him'; for before he was taken he had this **testimony**, that he pleased God" (Hebrews 11:5). God gives His godly ones a testimony.
- "And all these, having obtained a good **testimony** through faith, did not receive the promise" (Hebrews 11:39). They did not receive the fullness of God's promise, which is Christ. They simply lived too early to enjoy Christ's incarnation. But even though they didn't enter into God's fullness, they still obtained a testimony!
- "Therefore we also, since we are surrounded by so great a cloud of **witnesses**, let us lay aside every weight, and the sin which so easily ensnares us, and let us run with endurance the race that is set before us" (Hebrews 12:1). The great men and women of the Bible stand as witnesses before us, testifying that they endured great suffering, the answers to their prayers were often delayed, they persevered through the fire until God came through for them, at which time they "obtained promises" (Hebrews 11:33).

Like them, we may not enter into God's fullness in every respect in this life, but there are many scriptural witnesses surrounding us who declare, "God wants to give you a testimony!" I'm after the kind of faith that obtains promises and receives a testimony. I've been responding to Jesus' invitation to ask, seek, and knock in these three ways:

1) Ask: I'm asking Him for a testimony.
2) Seek: I want to know Christ.
3) Knock: I want to know His purposes so that I can walk through the doors that will glorify His name.

## My Parents' Testimony

Very briefly, I want to share one of the testimonies my parents carry, which continues to touch my heart to this day. My parents are very godly people who pastored for over 40 years. In 1970, my mother discovered some lumps in her breasts. The Lord spoke clearly to her that if she went to a doctor, it would be her end. So she never had the problem checked out medically but turned her face to seek the Lord.

My parents went on an all-out search for God. They had no medical confirmation of this, but every symptom pointed to cancer. They devoured every book on divine healing they could find. They read the word constantly, spoke the word, and prayed the word. And Mom's health continued to decline rapidly.

They reached their blackest day on March 17, 1970, which was my brother Sheldon's sixteenth birthday. Dad wept with despondency as he figured he was going to have to prepare himself to raise his two sons alone. Mom was heartbroken because she didn't have the strength to get out of bed and prepare a birthday meal for her boy. Both of them launched their morning crying out to God.

That was the day — their darkest day ever — when God met them. The Spirit suddenly spoke a living word to my mother's heart, "Faith without works is dead!" She had read that verse a multitude of times, but suddenly it came alive to her. Immediately she got up and began to do what she couldn't do, which was to make a birthday dinner. Again the Lord spoke to her, "When Arvin [my father] comes home this evening, he is to curse the cancer, and it will dry up by the roots."

Unbeknownst to my Mom, Dad was at the office getting blitzed by God. The Spirit met him in a powerful way, giving him an incredible revelation into God's plan of redemption. When Dad came home that evening, he was barely touching the ground. The glory of God was all over my parents.

After the birthday dinner, Mom and Dad slipped away to pray. They rejoiced, praised, and gave glory to God. Then Dad cursed the growths.

Suddenly, Mom felt warmth in her abdomen area. After a while, she slipped her hand inside her dress to check her breasts, and lo! the lumps were **completely gone**!

For twenty-six years, as of this time of writing, my parents have given testimony to this miraculous intervention of God in their lives. Between you and me, I think God likes my parents. They will tell you that it wasn't because of their great faith because they struggled constantly with doubt and fear and unbelief. But when God came to them and spoke a living word, faith was instantaneous.

Being just a thirteen-year-old, I would come home every day from school to find my Mom on her knees, in the word, in prayer, seeking God. All my parents seemed to do during those three months of illness was seek God. As an impressionable teenager, here's the truth that impacted my heart the most from my Mom's healing: Seek the Lord with all your heart, and He'll visit you and give you a testimony! I witnessed God do

> **Seek the Lord with all your heart, and He'll visit you and give you a testimony!**

it, and their testimony continues to challenge my heart to this day.

My prayer is, "Lord, give me a testimony too, that I can pass on to my kids!" I'm holding out for a miracle in my life that will change the course of my children's lives.

## Martha Theology

Don't ever say to anybody, "Well, if you're not healed in this life, you'll be healed in the next life." That's Martha theology. David declared, "I would have lost heart, unless I had believed that I would see the goodness of the Lord in the land of the living" (Psalm 27:13). David was saying, "I would have lost my confidence in God, if I had thought that I wouldn't see God's goodness in this life, here on the earth."

If you remove the assurance of deliverance in this life, you remove the incentive for perseverance and diligence. If you tell people, "It may not be God's will to heal you in this life," then you minister despair. It is Jesus' promises to heal that spur us forward into the face of Christ. When I know He wants to heal me, I gain fresh momentum in my search for Him. It is

> **When I know He wants to heal me, I gain fresh momentum in my search for Him.**

the diligent search for God that bears fruit in our lives. If healing wasn't for me, I wouldn't bother seeking Him; I'd just give up. But because His word assures me that healing is His will, I gain the strength to continue to pursue Him with all my heart. God's purpose in delaying the answer is so that we might seek Him more fervently, and that desperate search for God is the thing that produces fruitfulness and maturity within us. All this rests upon the fundamental premise that it's God's will to deliver the righteous.

We see Martha's theology in John 11:23-25, "Jesus said to her, 'Your brother will rise again.' Martha said to Him, 'I know that he will rise again in the resurrection at the last day.' Jesus said to her, 'I am the resurrection and the life.'" Martha's theology was this: If you don't get it down here, well, you'll get it in the next life. Jesus had to correct her theology. By raising Lazarus from the dead, He established His intent to touch people with resurrection power **in this life**.

"'But this is your hour, and the power of darkness'"(Luke 22:53). There comes an hour when God allows the powers of darkness to have the upper hand. But it is only for an "hour," and the time of resurrection life is coming.

Psalm 37:9 declares, "Those who wait on the LORD, they shall inherit the earth." God has an inheritance for His people here on the earth, in this present age. I'm so thankful that our message isn't just, "Hang on till heaven!" God has destined great exploits and conquests for His dearly beloved here in this life, on the earth. Let confidence rise in your hearts, saints, God has a glorious inheritance for you in Christ!

Smith Wigglesworth once said, "If I leave you as I found you, I am not God's channel. I am not here to entertain you but to get you to the place where you can laugh at the impossible, to believe and to see the goodness of the Lord in the land of the living."

By His grace, we will not limit the unlimited God.

# 15

# DON'T CAST AWAY
# YOUR CONFIDENCE!

In conclusion, look at this passage which calls us forward to confidence in God in the midst of delayed answers:

> Hebrews 10:35, Therefore do not cast away your confidence, which has great reward. 36 For you have need of endurance, so that after you have done the will of God, you may receive the promise: 37 "For yet a little while, and He who is coming will come and will not tarry. 38 Now the just shall live by faith; but if anyone draws back, my soul has no pleasure in him." 39 But we are not of those who draw back to perdition, but of those who believe to the saving of the soul.

## After God

According to verse 38, faith is the opposite of drawing back. In other words, faith presses forward into the face of God. This same principle is stated in Hebrews 3:12, "Beware, brethren, lest there be in any of you an evil heart of unbelief in departing from the living God." If unbelief is departing from or drawing back from God, then faith is following hard after Him!

When the Scripture says, "do not cast away your confidence," it means, "do not flag in your hot pursuit of the living God." If you're a man after God's own heart, then do just that — go after His heart. You've progressed this far in your burning search for the glory of God that is in the face of Christ, don't quit now!

> **If you're a man after God's own heart, then do just that — go after His heart.**

"But I've been waiting so long," a weary pilgrim moans, "I don't know if I can wait any more." Follow this progression please: If you've been waiting a long time, that means you've been seeking His face a long time. If you've been seeking His face a long time, that means you've been getting to know Him more and more. If you've been getting to know Him more and more, that means you're being changed into the image of Christ, and the glory of God upon your life is growing ever brighter. If you're being changed into the image of Christ, and the glory of God upon your life is growing ever brighter, then why quit now?? Why cast away your confidence now?? Listen, beloved saint, you're getting closer and closer to the "great reward" promised in verse 35. Yes, you can wait upon Him some more!

The enemy realizes that if you persevere all the way through to the victorious reward of verse 35, you will become an extremely effective warrior in the kingdom of God. Therefore, he is pitting himself again you with two chief temptations: 1) he wants you to relax and quit your fervent pursuit of God, or 2) he wants you to sacrifice everything you've gained at the altar of carnal compromise.

If you pursue the love of God from a pure heart (1 Timothy 1:5), you're unstoppable. Nothing in all of heaven or hell can deny the inheritance of the saint who loves God with clean hands and a pure heart. But if you grow weary in seeking God, or if you compromise your purity, you forfeit everything for which you've been straining. That's why the enemy pushes so vehemently upon the persevering saint at these two pressure points:

| |
|---|
| **Nothing in all of heaven or hell can deny the inheritance of the saint who loves God with clean hands and a pure heart.** |

"Oh, forget all this! Just quit!"

"Indulge your flesh — you deserve it!"

To cave in to either temptation is to cast away your confidence.

## Maintain Your Purity!

"Blessed are the undefiled in the way" (Psalm 119:1). One of the things the Lord has reiterated to me throughout my difficult journey is the absolute necessity of keeping myself pure. If I cave in to self-indulgence in the time of crisis, I will forfeit the purpose for which God fashioned this test. Joseph had to pass the purity test (by resisting Potiphar's wife) in order to become the leader of Egypt.

Psalm 34:19 says, "Many are the afflictions of the righteous, but the Lord delivers him out of them all." Notice that this isn't a blanket promise to "them," but a specific promise to "him." Who is this "him"? He is "the righteous." The promise of God's deliverance comes only to those who maintain their righteousness and purity before Him.

## The Psalm One Man

Psalm 1 is a marvelous study in godliness. Verse 1 says, "Blessed is the man who walks not in the counsel of the ungodly, nor stands in the path of sinners, nor sits in the seat of the scornful." The sequence of "walks," "stands," and "sits" describes progressive entrapment in sin. The temptation of sin is to walk by, then to stand and hang out, and finally to sit down in it.

"The counsel of the ungodly" reflects ungodly **values**. You talk about your marriage to somebody at work, and he says, "If I were you, I'd leave your wife!" The counsel of people in the world will always reflect their ungodly values.

"The path of sinners" refers to ungodly **morals**. It may seem relatively harmless, on the surface, to join the men at work for a "guy's night out," but it's dangerous to stand with others who are sinning, even if you are not sinning directly yourself.

"The seat of the scornful" speaks of ungodly **attitudes**. If we hang out with people of the world, we'll begin to talk like them, and eventually even think like them.

## Marks Of Godliness

The psalmist turns now to describe the godly man who avoids all that stuff: "But his delight is in the law of the LORD, and in His law he meditates day and night. He shall be like a tree planted by the rivers of water, that brings forth its fruit in its season, whose leaf also shall not wither; and whatever he does shall prosper" (Psalm 1:2-3).

The godly man, this Scripture says, is like a tree. When I think of a tree, I think of the following qualities.

A tree is:

1. Fruitful in season.

The man of God goes through seasons. Even as there are four seasons in the natural created order,

> **The man of God goes through seasons.**

so the godly experience the spiritual equivalent of spring, summer, harvest, and winter. Not all of life is characterized by the abundance and joy of harvest. There are also dry seasons, cold seasons, and damp seasons. But the godly man progresses normally through all the seasons of life, and has a consistent history of fruitfulness at the right times.

2. Strong in dry times.

The man of God doesn't always look good. In winter, he may lose his leaves. But mark this: In the drought of summer his leaves never wither. Grass nearby is parched and yellow, but the godly man is green and verdant — because his roots go down into the riverbed. He has tapped into the lifesource of the Holy Spirit, and when others are withering, he is refreshed from a hidden water source.

3. Stands out as a landmark.

Trees are often used as landmarks because they stand tall against their surroundings. Similarly, the godly man rises in stature and stands tall in the society of those who surround him. Among the employees he is exemplary. He is an example to his family. His life is noticeable, compelling, and noteworthy.

4. Unmoved by storms.

Like a tree, the man of God is shaken at times by the winds of life. Difficulty might leave him really rocking. But he's never uprooted and moved. Because he is deeply rooted in the grace of God, he has longevity. Long after others have been moved off by this or that, he continues to stand, strong and stable. He is a pillar in his community because he has not succumbed to the popular temptation to pick up and move to another state in the face of great adversity.

5. Provides shade for others.

Because of the qualities of Jesus that radiate from the godly man, he is a source of refreshment and relief to others. A tree doesn't have to try to provide shade — it just happens. In the same way, the godly effortlessly refresh the hearts of others.

6. "Whatever he does shall prosper."

That is both a promise and an unavoidable reality. When the godly perseveres through tough times, the prosperity of God will inevitably manifest. He is blessed because he has found a place of special affection in the heart of God. And in the final analysis, that is the ultimate reward of the godly: the smile of Jesus.

> **That is the ultimate reward of the godly: the smile of Jesus.**

## Zacharias & Elizabeth

While we're on the subject of maintaining one's purity and godliness, I want to point to a very poignant passage regarding the parents of John the Baptist, Zacharias and Elizabeth:

And they were both righteous before God, walking in all the commandments and ordinances of the Lord **blameless**. But they had no child, because Elizabeth was **barren**, and they were both well advanced in years (Luke 1:6-7).

Luke is setting the stage, in these two verses, for the story of the angel's visit to Zacharias while he was serving in the Temple. The angel appeared to him and promised him a son, and that boy became known as John the Baptist.

There are two telling words that describe Zacharias and Elizabeth: they were "blameless" and "barren."

## Barren

First, we see that Elizabeth was barren. Now, few things were more painful to a woman in that culture than barrenness because children were seen as a blessing from the Lord. Psalm 127:3 puts it this way, "The fruit of the womb is a reward." So if children were a reward from God, the absence of children was seen as punishment or a curse. None of us knows about the years of agony and inner turmoil that Elizabeth most likely experienced as she searched her soul for anything that might be impeding God's blessings. "Have I sinned? What did I do wrong?" We don't know how many tears she shed, how many prayers she offered, or how many times she pled with God to show her what was holding back the blessing. I can envision Elizabeth throwing herself upon her bed, burying her face in her pillow, and wailing before God in profound agony.

> We don't know how many tears she shed, how many prayers she offered, or how many times she pled with God to show her what was holding back the blessing.

I'm sure she must have felt much like Naomi, who centuries earlier expressed her despair in this way, "'Do not call me Naomi; call me Mara, for the Almighty has dealt very bitterly with me. I went out full, and the LORD has brought me home again empty. Why do you call me Naomi, since the LORD has testified against me, and the Almighty has afflicted me?'" (Ruth 1:20-21). "Mara" means "Bitter," and Elizabeth knew this same bitterness of soul.

If you want to get an idea of how she felt, talk to a wife who has been trying unsuccessfully for years to get pregnant or bring a baby to full term, and you will taste of the anguish of soul that barrenness brings. It's impossible to know the pain of barrenness, I'm told, unless you experience it first-hand. Elizabeth would have been no different from any other woman longing for a child. By now, Elizabeth had already moved past her childbearing years because it says, "and they were both well advanced in years." Her heart would have been torn with years and years of trying to get pregnant, only to watch her body getting older and older, and finally moving into those later years when pregnancy was beyond all physical possibility. At that point, all hope of ever having a child totally died.

Elizabeth would have doubtless struggled with depression. She probably worked through it and got past it, but I'm certain she would have had valley seasons, times when she really felt rejected and abandoned by God.

The enemy has never changed his tactics, so I can also assure you that in those times of emotional weakness and despondency, the enemy made a point of coming on extra strong to discourage her. He probably had her thinking, "What's the use of serving God? I do everything He requires, and nothing ever changes. He isn't fulfilling the promises of His word. Here I am, laying everything on the line to serve God, and it's getting me nowhere." (The enemy usually speaks to us in the first person, so we think the thoughts are our own, when in fact they are his.)

This is precisely how the enemy hits us today. He'll reserve his heaviest artillery for the times when we're weakest. And the temptation is always the same. He wants us to get mad at God, get bitter over our circumstances, and quit. He wants us to crawl into a cocoon of self-pity and resentment. And then he interjects these thoughts, "That's it — I'm having a cigarette!" Or, "I've had it — I'm going to a bar, and I'm going to have a night on the town." Or perhaps it's like this, "I give up — I'm going to the city to get a stash."

> **The enemy will reserve his heaviest artillery for the times when we're weakest.**

Listen, my friend: If you give into the impulse and indulge the flesh, you will be casting away your confidence. You will disqualify yourself from God's blessing.

## Blameless

Take a cue from Zacharias and Elizabeth. The Bible says "they were both righteous before God, walking in all the commandments and ordinances of the Lord **blameless**." In the midst of their despair and grief, they faced the temptation to indulge the flesh and said, "No." They maintained their purity before God.

They had come to know too much of the Lord to sacrifice that relationship on the altar of carnal passion. Although they didn't understand why their prayers seemed to hit the roof and bounce back, they were committed to loving and serving God faithfully, even if He never answered their prayers.

It is this kind of blameless love that God visits. And oh, what a visit! God didn't just reward them with a regular boy. He gave them a son who was destined to become, in the words of the Lord Jesus, the most powerful prophet of all time. Although barren, they remained blameless, and entered into the reward of purity — the reward of the righteous!

> They were committed to loving and serving God faithfully, even if He never answered their prayers.

## Pursue God!

The enemy will do anything he can to incite us to relax our pursuit of God. During the delay season, he will badmouth God and tell us that God has failed us. Incredible rewards, however, await the soul that will not relent for a moment from seeking the Lord.

"My soul follows close behind You" (Psalm 63:8). Jesus "said to them all, 'If anyone desires to **come after Me**, let him deny himself, and take up his cross daily, and follow Me'" (Luke 9:23). The invitation to follow hard after Jesus is always there, but to desire to come after Him is in our hands. He is offering us the greatest treasure in the universe (Himself), but we've got to want Him. Jesus must be pursued. You've got to run after Him with all your heart and soul. If you don't deny your flesh, you'll fall behind. If you don't take up your cross, you'll choose the wrong path. The pursuit of Jesus must be so all-consuming that it must involve self-denial, the embracing of the cross, and a fervent following of His every word and prompting. It's a small price to pay, though, for such vast wealth.

The most militant thing you can do against the kingdom of darkness is get to know Jesus. This is seen in Daniel 11:32, "But the people who know their God shall be strong, and carry out great exploits." The greatest victories spring from knowing God. Our focus must not be on doing great exploits but on getting to know God. Those who come to know God will inevitably evidence strength and do great exploits. And there's only one way to get to know God, and that is through abandoned pursuit.

> The most militant thing you can do against the kingdom of darkness is get to know Jesus.

I must gain Christ! Not the Christ that doubters formulate through their disappointments but the Christ of the gospels. O, the sword that comes out of His mouth! O, the joy He knows in the presence of the

Father! O the love in His gaze — and the searching fire of His eyes! O the glorious wisdom and understanding of His infinitely merciful and compassionate heart! O the beauty of His holiness! O the power and authority He has given to His Church! I must gain Christ!

## Mustard Seed Faith

How do we pursue God and gain the confidence that produces change? We have something to learn here from the mustard seed.

> Luke 17:5, And the apostles said to the Lord, "Increase our faith."
> 6 So the Lord said, "If you have faith as a mustard seed, you can say to this mulberry tree, 'Be pulled up by the roots and be planted in the sea,' and it would obey you."

A mustard seed has some interesting distinctives:
1) It is a very tiny seed.
2) It grows very quickly and quite tall.
3) Being an annual herb, it has striking growth — some plants will grow as high as twelve feet in a matter of weeks.

Since Jesus likened faith to a mustard seed, we can make the following applications from these distinctives:
1) Although your faith may be small, it has the potential to become something very large and productive.
2) When planted in the right conditions, your faith will grow quickly into a mighty plant. When the disciples asked, "Increase our faith," Jesus' response was intimating, "Put the little faith you have in the right conditions, and it will grow."

> **Put the little faith you have in the right conditions, and it will grow.**

What are "the right conditions" for faith to grow in our hearts? Well, let's consider it first in the natural and then the spiritual application will be easy to see. We're going to see that the right conditions for faith to grow are found only in the context of a hot pursuit after God.

In the natural, in order for a mustard seed (or any seed) to grow, there must be four elements in place: rich soil, water, light, and heat.

**Rich soil:** we need to have a softened, receptive heart. Our hearts are softened and enriched only as we give ourselves vigorously to the meditation of the word of God and to broken repentance.

**Water:** we need the Holy Spirit to rain upon us frequently. We must fervently seek the constant infilling of the Holy Spirit. When God waters our seed of faith, and it germinates, there comes divine life exploding from within!

**Light:** we need the lamp of God's word illuminating us. Even as a seed will not germinate until the daylight hours are long enough, so too we need multiplied hours in the light of God's word. When the living voice of God comes to that seed of faith, it erupts in germinating life. That erupting life of seed faith cannot be stopped by anything.

**Heat:** in the natural, a seed will not germinate unless there's sufficient heat. You can have good soil, plenty of water, and lots of light, but if the soil isn't warm enough, the seed won't sprout. Believe it or not, we also need the heat of pressures, problems, and adversity to cause our faith to germinate. Without adversity, our faith will never grow. Be reminded again that this present distress you face may very possibly be God's gift to you, to enable that seed within you to die and then spring forth in new life.

The wise gardener, seeking to cultivate a mustard plant of faith, will not only expose the plant to the four necessary elements just mentioned, but he will also seek to protect the garden from "the little foxes" (Song of Solomon 2:15) that would threaten our budding faith. Little foxes will damage a crop with their digging at the roots and foraging for food. Those sweet little foxes don't appear to pose much of a threat to anything, but when their work is done, a crop can be seriously spoiled. There are many little foxes we must be on the constant alert against: apathy, temptation, distractions, entertainment, discouragement, etc. Only as we maintain a proper guard against these things can the seed of faith grow.

Consider the fact that the mustard plant is an annual herb. It comes up in the spring, flourishes that summer, and then falls to the earth and decays as winter approaches. It lasts for one season only. Jesus could have likened faith to an acorn, which grows into a mighty oak tree. But no, he likened it to a mustard seed, which grows up quickly into a mighty herb, but then passes away as the season ends.

When I asked the Lord what that meant, I was reminded how that every new challenge or crisis requires a whole new growth of faith in our hearts. You enter a crisis, you seek the Lord most fervently, He reveals Himself to you, faith rises in your heart, and you gain a mighty victory in God's grace.

> **Every new challenge or crisis requires a whole new growth of faith in our hearts.**

"Praise God," you think, "the Lord has grown my faith, this is great!" And then a few years later, a totally different crisis hits you. When it strikes, you collapse. Then you think, "I know I had faith in that last situation, what's wrong now? Why don't I have faith for this new situation?" The answer is, faith is an annual. You've got to grow a new plant of faith with every fresh season of difficulty. You might feel like you're starting from scratch, but that's okay. Go back to square one, and seek the face of God. He has a pathway for you to grow in faith and confidence in every new challenge.

## "I Believed, Therefore I Spoke"

"I believed, therefore I spoke, 'I am greatly afflicted.' I said in my haste, 'All men are liars'" (Psalm 116:10-11). Psalm 116 celebrates the Lord's deliverance from the pains of death and the pangs of Sheol. The psalmist cried for deliverance, and the Lord heard him. Afflictions, by the definition of this psalm, are circumstances clearly allowed in our lives by the hand and purpose of God to purify us and perfect us in godliness. The only time you can say along with Paul, "Therefore I take pleasure in infirmities... For when I am weak, then I am strong" (2 Corinthians 12:10) is when you know the infirmity has been designed by God for your benefit.

When you are grieviously afflicted, it takes great faith to say together with the psalmist, "I am greatly afflicted of the Lord. He has done this thing. His hand is involved here, and when He is done, I will come out as pure gold." Others look at your life and think, "You're living in a fantasy world, if you think you're just going to snap out of this. You may as well accept it — you're a goner. It's lights out for you." Even though others may not verbalize those words, you can feel them looking at you, and you can imagine what they're thinking.

The psalmist was greatly afflicted, and he believed it was from God and that God would deliver him. He believed, and therefore he spoke. But there were skeptics. So he responded to the skeptics in his haste and said, "All men are liars." He was saying, "You people think God is judging me and taking me down, but you're all a bunch of liars. God has His hand on my life, and He's going to deliver me!"

It's fascinating to see how Paul picks up this cry of the psalmist and quotes him: "And since we have the same spirit of faith, according to what is written, 'I believed and therefore I spoke,' we also believe and therefore speak, knowing that He who raised up the Lord Jesus will also raise us up with Jesus, and will present us with you" (2 Corinthians 4:13-14). If you look at the context of Paul's quote, he has just described his experiences of being hard-pressed, persecuted, struck down, always carrying about in the body the dying of the Lord Jesus, and always being delivered to death for Jesus' sake. In other words, Paul is saying, "All these things we've experienced are afflictions that are purposefully allowed by the Lord to season our souls and fulfill His purposes in us."

Paul is making the same declaration of the psalmist! He's saying, "God's hand is responsible for my great affliction. I believe He has allowed it for a specific purpose, and when He has finished His purpose He will deliver me. Even though you critics laugh at me right now, I believe this is so, and so I will speak it forth."

God has caused me to stand before people in the midst of my affliction and declare that He will deliver me. The enemy says, "If God doesn't deliver you, then you've lost all your credibility." But faith speaks, and I will speak.

## Don't Cast Away Your Confidence

"In returning and rest you shall be saved; in quietness and confidence shall be your strength" (Isaiah 30:15).

Therefore do not cast away your confidence, which has great reward (Hebrews 10:35).

The original Greek word in the New Testament for "confidence" almost always occurs in connection with speech. The

> **When New Testament "confidence" grips us, it changes the way we talk.**

word literally means, "outspoken boldness." It refers to a bold confidence that finds expression in the words we speak. When New Testament "confidence" grips us, it changes the way we talk. The words of our mouth bear witness to that confidence that has been nurtured in us by the Holy Spirit.

So take time at the feet of Jesus. Wait upon Him until He speaks to you. Let His word produce a harvest of confidence in your heart and declare the goodness of God with your mouth. Herein lies your strength during the season of delay.

By the grace of God, you're not going to cast away your confidence. You're going to maintain your integrity, and you will continue to seek God's face. Because you're after the "great reward."

**"Blessed are all those who wait for Him."**

(This book is followed by its sequel, The Fire Of God's Love.)

# Description of Resources on the Facing Page

❖ ENVY: THE ENEMY WITHIN reveals how ambitious motives and carnal comparisons between ministries can hinder the release of God's revival power. Explore how 2-talent saints envy 5-talent saints. Riveting, provocative, and timely.

❖ LOYALTY — The Spirit of God is turning the hearts of fathers to children, and children to fathers. Trans-generational loyalty is one of the great hidden keys to the endtime harvest. Will we share in the disloyalty of Lucifer, or the loyalty of Christ Jesus?

❖ FOLLOWING THE RIVER: A VISION FOR CORPORATE WORSHIP — When you fantasize about the ultimate worship experience, what do you imagine it could be like? Bob answers that question after searching it out for many years. Step into the future. See where God is taking this thing called worship.

❖ SECRETS OF THE SECRET PLACE — Bob shares some of the secrets he's learned in making the secret place energizing and delightful. Gain fresh fuel for your secret devotional life with God!

❖ GLORY: WHEN HEAVEN INVADES EARTH is Bob's most recent book on worship — for worshippers with a passion to see God. May your vision be renewed and clarified for a personal, life-changing encounter with God Himself.

❖ PAIN, PERPLEXITY & PROMOTION looks at the book of Job from a fresh, prophetic vantage. Job's life shows how God promotes His chosen vessels to higher heights than they would have conceived possible. Let Job's example compel you toward God's highest and best!

❖ THE FIRE OF GOD'S LOVE compels us toward the passionate love that God is producing within the bride in this hour for her Bridegroom, the Lord Jesus.

❖ IN HIS FACE propels the reader passionately toward a more personal and intimate relationship with Jesus Christ. Challenging devotional reading.

❖ EXPLORING WORSHIP is a 300-page textbook that covers a full range of subjects related to praise and worship. Translated into several languages, this bestselling book is being used internationally as a text by many Bible colleges, Bible study groups, and worship leading teams. Also available is an accompanying WORKBOOK/DISCUSSION GUIDE.

❖ DEALING WITH THE REJECTION AND PRAISE OF MAN is a booklet that shows how to hold your heart before God in a way that pleases Him in the midst of both rejection and praise from people.

# Order Form

## Books by Bob Sorge

| | Qty. | Price | Total |
|---|---|---|---|
| **BOOKS:** | | | |
| ENVY: THE ENEMY WITHIN | ____ | $12.00 | ____ |
| LOYALTY | ____ | $13.00 | ____ |
| FOLLOWING THE RIVER: A Vision for Corporate Worship | ____ | $ 9.00 | ____ |
| SECRETS OF THE SECRET PLACE | ____ | $13.00 | ____ |
| GLORY: When Heaven Invades Earth | ____ | $ 9.00 | ____ |
| PAIN, PERPLEXITY & PROMOTION | ____ | $13.00 | ____ |
| THE FIRE OF GOD'S LOVE | ____ | $12.00 | ____ |
| THE FIRE OF DELAYED ANSWERS | ____ | $13.00 | ____ |
| IN HIS FACE: A Prophetic Call to Renewed Focus | ____ | $12.00 | ____ |
| EXPLORING WORSHIP: A Practical Guide to Praise and Worship | ____ | $15.00 | ____ |
| Exploring Worship WORKBOOK & DISCUSSION GUIDE | ____ | $ 5.00 | ____ |
| DEALING WITH THE REJECTION AND PRAISE OF MAN | ____ | $ 9.00 | ____ |

**SPECIAL PACKET**

Buy one each of all Bob's books, and save 30%.
Call or visit our website for a current price.

|  | |
|---|---|
| Subtotal | ____ |
| Shipping, Add 10% (Minimum of $2.00) | ____ |
| Missouri Residents Add 7.35% Sales Tax | ____ |
| Total Enclosed | ____ |

**U.S. Funds Only**

Send payment with order to:  Oasis House
P.O. Box 127
Greenwood, MO 64034-0127

Name _____

Address:  Street _____

City _____ State _____

Zip _____

For MasterCard/VISA orders and quantity discounts,
call 816-623-9050

Or order on our fully secure website:
**www.oasishouse.net**